Y0-BUD-133

Offices ▪ Stores ▪ Restaurants ▪ Bars ▪ Hotels ▪ Museums ▪ Health Centers

INTERNATIONAL CONTRACT DESIGN 2

Offices ▪ Stores ▪ Restaurants ▪ Bars ▪ Hotels ▪ Museums ▪ Health Centers

INTERNATIONAL CONTRACT DESIGN

ISSN 1043-4100

Library of Congress Catalog Card Number
88-650633

ISBN 1-55859-013-7

This book was produced by
John Calmann and King Ltd, London.

Designed by Cara Gallardo and Richard Smith, Area, London.
Typeset by Fakenham Photosetting Ltd,
Fakenham, Norfolk, UK.
Printed and bound in Singapore by Toppan Printing Co. Ltd.

First edition

Contents

Introduction 6

1 Workspaces, Offices, & Studios 10

2 Restaurants, Cafes, Bars, Clubs, & Hotels 66

3 Stores, Showrooms, & Retail Centers 126

4 Cultural & Public Amenity Buildings 184

Further Reference & Acknowledgements 243
Designers' biographies 243
Acknowledgements 248
Addresses of suppliers 252
Index of designers & projects 256

The task of selecting the most innovative interiors from all over the world is one fraught with difficulties. Inevitably, there will be many more architects, designers, clients, and critics, whose taste is not flattered by the work included in the following pages than those who do find a mirror to their own sensibilities. But that wealth of subjective opinion is the very condition that makes the case for producing a volume such as this, in which we have attempted to present in pictorial and factual detail, with analysis, some of the most influential commercial interiors produced in the latter part of the 1980s.

By concentrating on contract-designed interiors – from stores to seats of government, workspaces to leisure facilities – the focus of this new edition has been on revealing the most interesting locations around the world where various forms of interaction inspire significant new departures in the places in which we meet.

This is because, unlike domestic spaces, the commercial or public interior is almost invariably designed by one party for another to make a statement to a third party. The self-consciousness of our cultural strivings in all kinds of activities – from literature to fine art, advertising to animation – has its relevance to the interior: we are aware that the associations of an image are part of the function and can be taken seriously or treated ironically. The interior designer does not work in a vacuum and neither does the user experience that environment without relating it, consciously or unconsciously, to many other environments.

At one level, a review of leading interiors can concern itself with celebrating or promoting a particular aesthetic. This book spotlights successful innovation that suggests directions for the future (no projects are included which are simply refurbishment or reproduction). There is no one 'style' argued for, no one ideal of beauty or good taste. The diverse range of stimulating work included suggests to this editor, at least, that the reductive approach of presenting a single coherent aesthetic would run counter to our primary purpose of surveying the key work of the past three years.

The simple linking factor behind all the projects included is the use of strong and original methods by clients and designers to put across a distinct and appropriate message to the users. (By 'message,' I refer to the expression of a whole range of different functions that are involved and must be bonded together in the interior.)

In the case of a store or restaurant, getting that communication strategy right is a crucial part of business success. Increasingly, employers are finding that creating a workspace that is finely tuned to employees' needs beyond basic functions is a great help to ensuring a healthier and happier workforce. Companies, indeed governments, are also realising that their buildings and interiors say a lot about their past and present – and future.

There are few things as expressive of their time as a commercial interior: unlike the domestic interior, the commercial interior exists to be constantly tested by a changing round of users. And if the interior 'fails,' which is likely to happen in some way sooner or later, it will be replaced, should this be deemed cost-effective. It is a harsh world in which the aesthetic concerns of the interior designer's craft must live, yet this very threat of transitoriness, this

Introduction

pressure to achieve, ensures that the leading edge of interior design is among the most innovative areas of commercial creative work, free from many of the conservative pressures affecting architecture, yet not usually subject to the same mass-production pressures as products or furniture. Nor, to perhaps make a provocative association, does the creation of an interior have the purely marketing-led objectives of much graphic design or advertising. And yet the production of a new commercial interior is increasingly bound up with the soft science of marketing as it is with the practice of architecture or the artistic pursuit of an aesthetic aim.

For many designers this increase in marketing awareness is seen as an unwelcome development, but it is an undeniable one. The innovation and commitment of a client such as Esprit does not stem from charitable intentions towards designers, but from a commitment to use innovative design as part of a business strategy. Whether or not it is of significance in the history of interiors is of no primary importance to the client, unlike the profile of the corporate image. Perhaps it was ever so, but the pressure on interiors to give identity has never been greater.

Until recently, the creation of interiors was viewed as being on the margins of other activities: a sub-division of architecture, or a facet of corporate image-making. But a combination of factors – economic, technological, and professional – has ensured that the interior has taken on a much clearer significance. To refurbish, reposition, or restate a place by redoing an interior is seen as not only a viable but often a crucial investment in operating a retail environment such as a store or restaurant. Workspaces and cultural buildings also have a shorter life and greater investment in the interior because of the need to deal with more complex human requirements, often with more sophisticated equipment (ranging from the introduction of more computers to the demands this puts on air-conditioning). And the demands are rising all the time – the notion of 'sick-building syndrome' has been a problem for air-conditioned offices in recent years; now one new fear is that the multitude of magnetic fields within a modern commercial interior can cause illness. And perhaps buildings can help overcome sickness – note the Cedars Sinai Cancer Center in Los Angeles and its sculptural spur to the spirit (page 210).

The last decade of the twentieth century is likely to be a highly significant one for developing greater internationalism in interiors. This selection of key new interiors from around the world, all created in the latter end of the 1980s, shows the coming together of a global design approach – without being as reductive as having an 'international style,' they are often clearly the product of a professional culture that draws inspiration from all over the world. Material science, aesthetics, and even budgeting factors are now brought together, compared, and contrasted: the results are unique, but they come out of a global melting pot.

This is not to say that Philippe Starck does not display some distinctly French approach, or Shiro Kuramata a Japanese character, but their references, their inspiration, and their influence can and often do travel around the globe. And their work may do so also – the prolific Starck is here represented by projects from three continents.

The influence of the client, too, can be global, as with many large corporations or retail chains, such as Benetton, whose approach to retail interiors is not dissimilar to that of Coca-Cola in a different area. Again we are brought back to discussion of marketing as a prime generator in interior design commissioning. For while the concern in making the selection of projects in this book has been to pick out excellence in the innovative design of interiors, based on concern with aesthetic, functional, and technological exploration, the character of shopping streets and malls, business districts, and leisure locations comes from the agglomeration of spaces open to the public (not just public spaces). I have selected one store produced by the Next chain in Britain – Department X by Rasshied Ali-Din – but the hundreds of other stores controlled by that retailer are perhaps of more significance in determining the character of interiors today through their having a sheer mass presence. The selection of 72 projects here is an attempt to define the few leaders, not the drove of followers that flesh out the character of the business of interiors.

One criticism that may be levelled at some of the work included is the cost. Many of the Japanese interiors in particular were produced on budgets which, divided over the often small area, is beyond the wildest dream of the designer struggling to improve the functioning and image of a provincial supermarket. The difference in resources may be by a factor of 100 or more. But there are projects of a much more spartan nature included in the following pages as well. I won't say which here, because the question of budget is ultimately a distraction from appreciating the strength of ideas that should be displayed. Whether those ideas demanded gold leaf (as in the comparatively economic Gold Bar in New York) or punctured plasterboard (as in the artfully crafted and lit Sbaiz shop in Italy), the cost of the project is largely irrelevant in the final analysis of whether or not it works in design terms. The fact that it may take a long time to recoup the outlay is not a primary worry unless you have a stake in the company.

While I have stressed the diversity of design directions revealed in the following pages, certain common concerns can be identified that link apparently vastly different projects. The place of metaphor as a device that gives an extra resonance to the interior is perhaps the most significant development.

From the science fiction fantasy of Iosa Ghini's Bolido bar (page 118) to Starck's Cafe Mystique, from Branson Coates' Noah's Ark restaurant (page 76) to Pawson Silvestrin's minimalist cake store Cannelle (page 154), we find extremes of imagery within the interior that make a statement beyond any simple expression of function. These examples, and many other projects in the book, tempt the viewer to find associations with the forms, provoke lateral thinking, and a sense of ambiguity. In many, the mystery of shapes – the turn of a chair leg, the twist of a light fitting, the detail of a counter edge – takes on organic associations. Starck's furniture at the Royalton Hotel, for example, or Arribas's work on the Velvet club – display an ingenious juxtaposing of soft, elegant forms with hard materials, producing objects that have metaphoric associations while still being defiantly part of the solid world. Meanwhile, work such as the remarkable light sculpture at O'Hare airport, Chicago, (page 192) or the audiovisual equipment at PN Club (page 22) show much more upfront attempts to embrace innovative communications technology in the interior without resorting to suggestive forms. They are much more abrasive as a result. The metaphoric content of some projects can be read as having a direct bearing on the 'human scale' that they contain – put another way, they make contact with the user on more than one level.

In recent months there has been talk of 'the cult of the designer' fading, suggestions that it was a very 1980s movement and that now a less egocentric view of creative processes will be sought. This may be desirable, but there is little indication that the committee system gets a lot done when it comes to making inspiring interiors. There are very few big design firms or large corporate clients represented in the following pages – not for want of our looking at many projects that came under those headings. Those few large design operations that do appear are often distinguished by breaking their operations down into smaller units, or else having a strong design leadership. As with most other creative pursuits, the designing of innovative interiors shows little sympathy for truly collective approaches. For example, Foster Associates may be a fairly large architectural practice, but the master architect's stamp can be read on the Esprit store even if the main thrust may be aimed more at airports and urban regeneration projects elsewhere. Arquitectonica had to rope in local project management help on its bank headquarters in Lima, Peru (page 12), but the results are firmly out of the Miami melting pot.

This last point leads on to the question of the growing force of 'imperialism' in design – a less attractive way of seeing the many dynamic crossovers that can be found in designers working away from home. The proliferation of information about new work and design ideas around the globe (among which this book has to be seen as a prime evidence for the prosecution) invites the pick'n'mix approach to design by the less able. A little of this Japanese bar, a little of that American restaurant, a bit of that theater, and suddenly an ill-conceived shopping mall project has put on a fair bit of pastiche design muscle.

Such a trite attitude will certainly not make for an entry into the next edition of this book, but is all too often attractive to some clients, to judge by the confused forms our international culture can take. So, rather than muse on any further collective meanings for the following projects, let us pass on to view some positive contributions to the global commercial environment.

But, one final caveat: I note that my dictionary puts the meaning of 'interior' as 'existing in mind or soul' before it concerns itself with the subject of 'building:' an approach that all the designers whose work is shown here seem to have taken to heart before putting pen to paper.

Propaganda Film Studios,
Franklin D Israel (see p. 18)

1 Workspaces, Offices, & Studios

1 **Arquitectonica**
Banco de Credito Headquarters, *Lima, Peru* 12

2 **Kenji Komoriya**
Edic Studio, *Tokyo, Japan* 16

3 **Franklin D Israel Design Associates**
Propaganda Films, *Los Angeles, USA* 18

4 **Masanori Umeda**
PN Clubhouse, *Tokyo, Japan* 22

5 **Peter Wilson with Chassay Wright**
Blackburn Office/Gallery/Flat, *London, UK* 24

6 **STUDIOS**
Apple Worldwide Manufacturing & Operations Headquarters, *California, USA* 28

7 **Kisho Kurokawa**
Shibuya Higashi T Building, *Tokyo, Japan* 30

8 **Studio Citterio Dwan**
Esprit Italia, *Milan, Italy* 32

9 **Canal**
Libération, *Paris, France* 36

10 **Coop Himmelblau**
Rooftop Remodelling, *Vienna, Austria* 38

11 **Eva Jiricna Architects**
Fafalios, *London, UK* 42

12 **STUDIOS**
Silicon Graphics, *Mountain View, California, USA* 44

13 **Geyer Design**
Geyer Design, *Melbourne, Australia* 48

14 **James Stirling, Michael Wilford & Associates**
Wissenschaftszentrum, *Berlin, West Germany* 50

15 **Armstrong Associates**
Elementer Headquarters, *Maidenhead, UK* 54

16 **Ecart**
Ebel – Villa Turque, *La Chaux de Fonds, Switzerland* 56

17 **David Davies Associates**
Valentino, *Rome, Italy* 60

In the main elevator lobby, glass brick walls enclose the floors for security while also dramatically refracting and reflecting the natural light from above and behind.

Earthquakes and security needs as well as references to Inca ruins played a significant part in determining the building's basic form.

Arquitectonica

1.1 Banco de Credito Headquarters

Lima, Peru

Where the international language of business meets the local architectural form, either compromise or conflict usually results. The consequence is often a triumph for the bland corporate style that can be seen in cities everywhere around the world, and the need of Peru's largest private bank to centralize its services in a massive new building could have been seen as a platform for just such an outcome.

The Banco de Credito headquarters, however, was successful in cultivating a unique corporate image for a number of reasons. Perhaps one of the most important of these was the commissioning of the Florida-based architectural practice Arquitectonica. In creating the new 530,000 square-foot (49,237 square-metre), $42 million office building on the outskirts of Lima, Arquitectonica were faced with such problems as the very real threat of earthquakes, the preservation of Inca ruins on the site, and the need to meet exacting security standards for the interior circulation and to make provision for future expansion of the building. They were able to resolve all these problems without compromising their design concept, and succeeded in bringing the various issues into balance to produce an architectural form of individuality and quality.

For the interior design, the architects had to fit out spaces that ranged from a 40,000 square-foot (3,716 square-metre) computer center to restaurants, a conference theater, a health club, stores, and an art museum. The external design of the building has a clear influence on the internal scheme: the four-story building is raised on piles around a courtyard, allowing abundant natural light into the offices. Its structure is such that it also allows for large interior spaces. The courtyard, in which the ancient ruins are located, also serves as a form of interior space, and the dramatic colours used on its elevation illustrate the opportunity Arquitectonica had to 'create' the view here, which provides a contrast to the view over the suburbs and the Sierra from outside the block.

It is a large building, and in order that no one might lose awareness of where they were in it, Arquitectonica highlighted several 'orientation' features and made these key elements of the design. Cylindrical elevator lobbies, for example, and zig-zag glass-block walls provide focal points that lead back to the courtyard.

The need for extremely tight security in restricting access to different parts of the building explains the development of the striking elliptical feature that forms the main entrance to the bank's offices from the ground level. The basic cube shape of the building does not in itself present an obvious entrance point. Arquitectonica's design therefore plays a key role in its dramatic invasion of the building's form, over and above all other design features on the ground level.

Much of the furniture, finishes, carpeting and paneling were designed by the architects and heavily influenced by the resources available in local crafts and by the colours used in Inca art.

One of the greatest challenges faced by the management of the project was the integration of the international mix of contributors to the design. The American architects worked with a local firm, as well as with a Spanish programming consultancy and a Dutch lighting consultancy. Materials came from Japan, Germany and the United States, as well as from Peru. A change in import laws, while the work was being carried out, required design developments to take greater advantage of Peruvian manufacturing.

Contrasts of view – onto the atrium, the courtyard or across the plain – also generate varieties of light within the building and break down its scale.

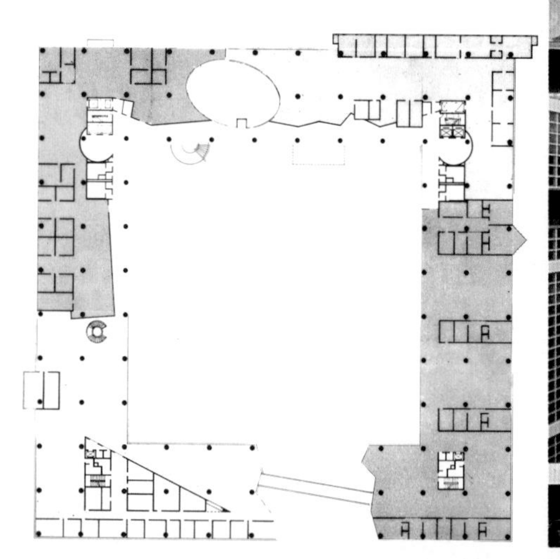

Peruvian crafts and materials were incorporated wherever possible within the bank, giving a distinct character to the corporate grandeur.

Both power and playfulness are expressed by giving the human scale a dominant edge over the monolithic form, breaking the preconceptions of corporate architecture.

1 Banco de Credito Headquarters

Darkness is as important as light in manipulating lighting effects.

Komoriya created a wide range of unusual surfaces and textures to maximize the range of effects of displaying the products.

The shapes formed by tensile structures are transferred to solids, while the actual structures creating the space are disguised.

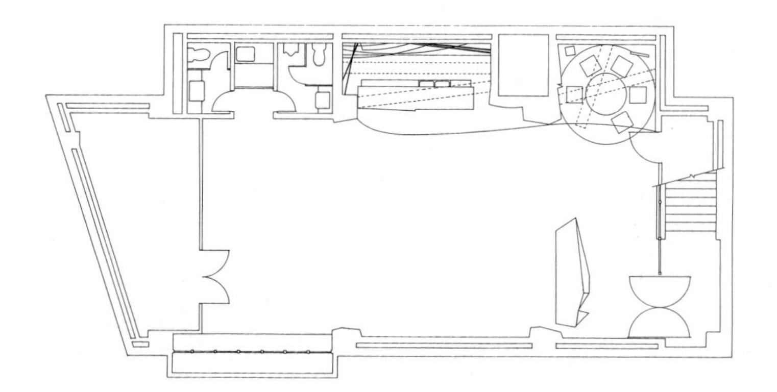

Kenji Komoriya

1.2 Edic Studio

Tokyo, Japan

Edic Studio is a strange space of curiously abstract forms – not quite walls, almost never ceilings – and a sense of the transitory and theatrical. What better way of providing a venue where the product to be tested, explored and sold is, simply, light?

The Lighting Endo Company asked Komoriya to convert a basement area of just 1,764 square feet (164 square metres) into a studio that would test the effects of its lighting products. The client also wanted the space to be suitable for use as a gallery and as a venue for various events, so flexibility was essential.

The result is an interior which makes a virtue of its temporary nature. The walls and ceiling are built on a system that makes it possible to adapt the space to various configurations of solid and void. Sound and lighting programs are run by computer to create a variety of visual effects in three dimensions that might more usually be experienced through film or video. The environment is totally controlled and can change and develop in real time.

The task, according to Komoriya, required not only the complete flexibility of the lighting fixtures, but also a means of altering the way distances were perceived and objects were balanced. 'My idea was to construct a space which followed a rhythm, but not one that followed conventional geometric patterns,' he says. Rather than drawing on any existing architectural forms, Komoriya sought inspiration from trying to realize, in three dimensions, the nature of dynamic forces. Thus, the objects he created to reflect light suggest the shapes produced by tensile structures; in effect, abstractions of all furniture or other interior fittings.

If all this seems extremely purist and remote from demonstrating the lighting products in a realistic mode, then it is worth noting that the client was pleasantly surprised to find *any* objects in the space, having simply requested a plain design. The floor is covered with a vinyl chloride tile; walls are made from steel, plaster board and wood board; the objects are constructed out of steel and steel pipe; the furniture is of steel, stone, wood and cloth. Costs worked out at $655 per square metre.

After such an exercise in abstraction, it is perhaps understandable that Komoriya says his dream projects would also involve him in designing all the furniture . . . and the lighting.

The juxtaposition of different elements suggests the range of activities taking place in different areas of the company.

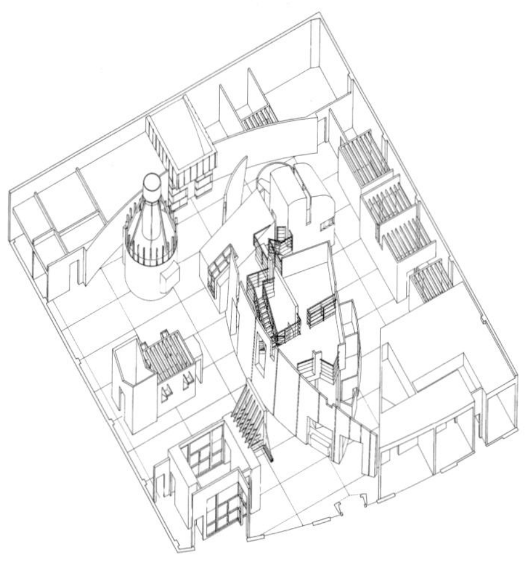

The elements of the interior deliberately float free, enabling the basic building shell to remain visible.

The neutral façade of the warehouse building is kept so that the interior is a welcome contrast to the faded exterior environment.

Franklin D Israel Design Associates

1.3 Propaganda Films

Los Angeles, USA

The combination of a creative client, an atmospheric building shell and an almost suffocatingly tight budget can sometimes result in an adventurous interior. In this project for a film and commercials production company such factors were clearly responsible for the direction taken by the designers in developing a raw, expressive and stylish environment that floats between suggesting the back side of a film set that can be found nearby and the warehouse aesthetic that stems immediately from the building shell.

The classic bow-strung trusses of the warehouse provided a given element for the interior to develop around. When stripped out, the building had heavy, curved trusses, spidery tie-rods and massive brick and concrete walls. The impact of these dynamic forms suggestive of the forces in a building contrasted markedly with the neutral façade of the building, which fits in with a neighbourhood of dusty Hollywood streets just around the corner from Howard Hughes' old film studio. The potential to mix fantasy, power and art is almost in the air: and the designers had the right clients to fulfil this.

The client insisted that the sense of an open warehouse should be kept, even when new offices went in to a density that required two stories in part. Another client pressure, albeit a creative one, was that the cooperative nature of the company meant that many of the staff had a voice in the design and location of different parts of the building program.

An exacting range of different spaces was required. Many areas called for complex technical provisions – sound and film editing facilities, a film vault, and various meeting rooms with projection facilities. Often, the designers needed to observe such details as precise equipment layouts, sound insulation, and static control.

There was also the need to provide a logical flow between the spaces that followed that of the product (film or video) through the various stages of its

creation. There is a firm argument behind the arrangement of private offices, meeting rooms, casting rooms, screening rooms, and so on, that can be defended as solidly as any more familiar formalized scheme of space planning.

The realization of these multilayered demands takes the form of elements dispersed and stacked within the shell; some are freestanding, while others are in a fixed configuration.

At the center of the project is a three-level structure in the shape of a boat, the canted walls around this area giving a recognizable component from which the other parts devolve. With its bulk, vertically and horizontally, it stands out, but it is the central point of this structure in a very real sense, being the location of the company heads. This structure sets up a sense of how the 'pieces,' the room sets, relate to each other.

From this central area, the sense of spaces formed by walls, doors and windows and levels echoes the insubstantiality of the film set. At the same time, the use of a fresh and soothing palette of colours and materials helps ensure this is a pleasant environment to work in as well as being an impressive one to visit. The drywall construction is painted a soft green, with exposed redwood-stained timber frame. Furniture features, such as the refurbished 1940s steel office systems, further develop the film set theme.

Overall, the designers achieve the creation of a 'village' of workspaces that are suited to the compartmentalized nature of the film company's work, that, despite the wide range, still hold together with a unified identity. And this was all produced at a cost of $35 per square foot including all the mechanical systems.

An interplay of curves and flat planes takes place in three dimensions to create the pavilion structures of the offices.

Dramatic tension is heightened by contrasts in dimensions, unexpected cutaways and surprise views – the language of film.

The audio-visual unit dominates the main hall and is deliberately anthropomorphic in appearance: a friendly robot.

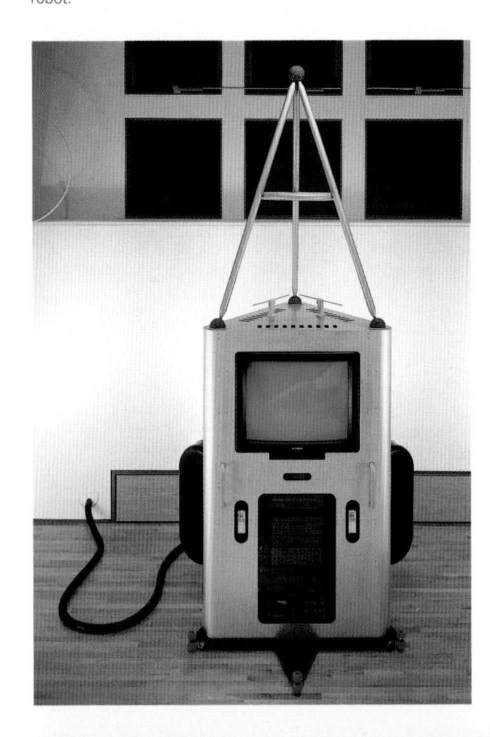

The conference table, with chairs designed by Mario Bellini, is centrally placed in the main hall of the Clubhouse.

The upper lounge features a sofa designed by Umeda and a light feature that depicts 'the cosmos seen from the interior of the womb.'

This mixture of workspace and home is a testament to post-industrial environments. It is a clubhouse in a private dwelling that is used for both leisure and business functions, meeting the demands of business meetings, parties and exhibitions, while simultaneously being an extension of domestic space.

The club is situated in the basement of the three-story residence. The centerpiece of the interior is the main hall which has a ceiling that rises to the first-floor level of the building. In a country where space is at a premium this might seem rather luxurious, but in Japan a room 18 feet (5.5 metres) high is a feature that alone may create a striking effect. Dominating the hall is an audio-visual unit that serves a wide range of functions: it houses a 37-inch (14.5-cm) television monitor, a sound system and speakers, a laser disc player, a satellite broadcast tuner and a radio telephone. This giant robot resembles something from a science-fiction story, and the

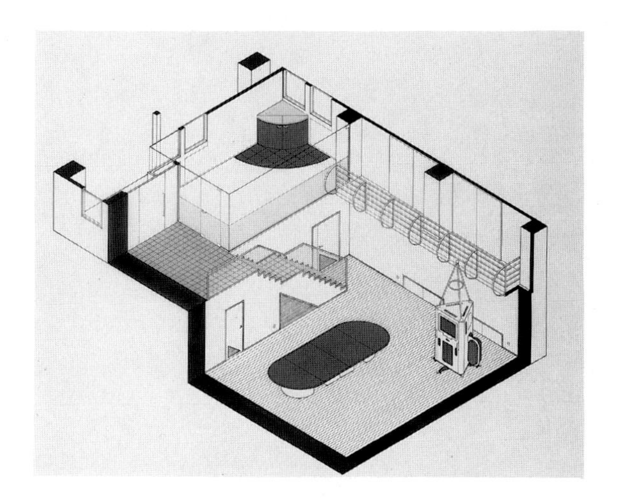

Masanori Umeda

1.4 PN Clubhouse

Tokyo, Japan

effect it produces is enhanced by the programmable lighting unit it incorporates: the robot can be programmed to set and change the moods of the clubhouse. The room also houses a screen for multiple-slide projection.

The abundance of technology could have given the interior the appearance of a badly planned conference center, with suggestion enough of artificial controls to induce tension in any visitor. That it does not do this is a consequence of Umeda's ability to imbue the equipment with a strong message about the interrelationship between people and such tools. For example, on the first floor provision is made, with a refrigerator and drinks cabinet, for more intimate discussion over drinks. Within this standard scenario, however, is a lighting fixture that becomes an object of focus. The curious, fluorescent-painted form is intended to be a feature of which visitors will be conscious, thereby stressing the human element and the designed nature of the environment. For Umeda, this lighting device 'represents the cosmos seen from the interior of the womb.' That visitors might miss the message is immaterial; what is significant is the creation of features that provoke a response.

One of the key purposes of the scheme was to create a 'good impression.' The client, a well-known Japanese management consultancy, wanted a distinctive and dramatic area that would become part of its corporate identity, but this could not easily be provided by a fixed feature: it is found instead in the extensive use of technology.

The club Umeda has created is highly flexible in design, and is intended to cater for up to 40 people. As well as loose furniture, supplementary folding benches are fixed into the walls. Also on the walls are fixed rails from which pictures and other items can be displayed. The main conference table is adjustable by means of combining four separate sections on casters, and can thus cater for a small gathering or for up to 20 people. Mario Bellini's chairs for Vitra are ranged around it. In addition to designing the robot and conference table, Umeda also put her stamp on the furnishings with an original sofa.

The clubhouse is sealed off from the rest of the building to avoid disturbing any neighbours in the quiet residential area in which it is located. This is achieved by means of elaborate soundproofing using Sonex – the material deployed in professional recording studios. This is painted black for the main room, and provides a simple contrast of colour with the white painted walls and ceiling. The main room has an oak floor, with Awaji tiles in the entrance hall and stairs, and carpet in the first-floor drawing room.

As the staircase rises up it disappears into the wall, only to reappear as a dramatic intrusion on the room next to this lobby.

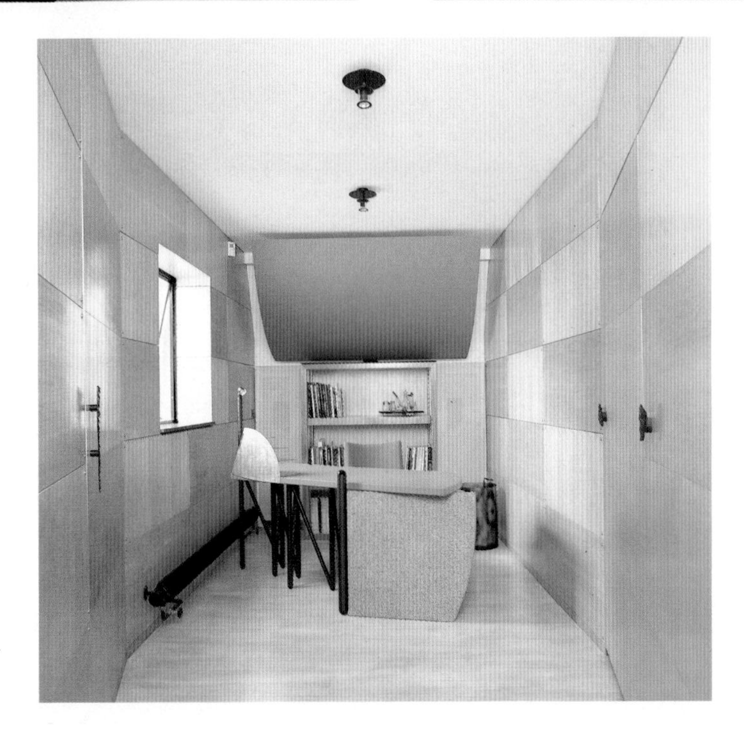

The Floris van den Broecke desk is one of the many specially commissioned pieces of furniture in the building.

Out of five small mews houses the client, an innovative property developer, commissioned the architects to create a space that promotes a new kind of building type. The client lives nearby and wanted this building to exist as an extension to both home and workplace: the ground floor is an office, while the upper floor is the principal gallery space for an entertainment area and exhibition of mostly specially commissioned pieces. Wilson comments: 'This fragmented formula presents a new way of living in the city. As the distinction between home and office becomes indistinct, the complete house becomes the mental assemblage of rooms in separate buildings.'

The architects stripped the existing houses, which form an L-shaped plan, of almost all detail. Windows were closed in, walls were raised to form 'a clear white box, a box of tricks, a toy box,' in Wilson's words – phrases that capture the need of the design to develop a building that took on the 'play' activities of both home and business life. It forms a stark contrast to the development of PN Club in Tokyo

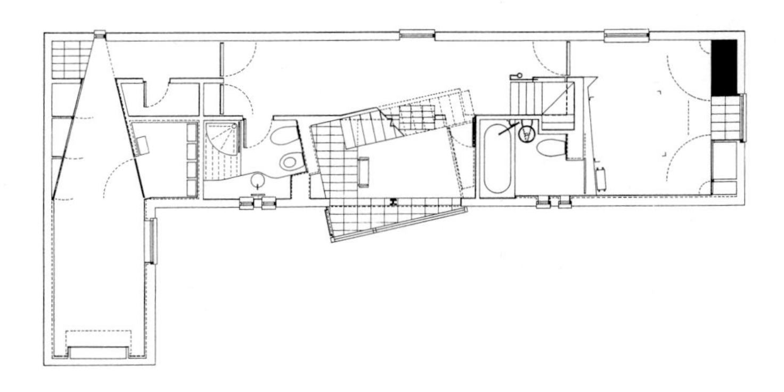

Peter Wilson with Chassay Wright

1.5 Blackburn Office/ Gallery/Flat

London, UK

(see page 22), which shows a 'play' area for business that is still a long way from integrating with the home environment – albeit that the PN Club is actually in the home.

Wilson and his associated architects Tchaik Chassay and Gareth Wright (who ran the main contract) divided the space up within the new building into a series of unexpected and contrasting spaces. The idea of play is boldly taken into the design from the outset, where the arriving visitor is met by two identical doors, neither taking priority, through to the striking sculptural, unique items of furniture that are featured in the main gallery area.

The visitor passes up through the building into a tight long gallery, largely artificially lit and dominated by the curious feature of a stepped underside to a staircase in beech disappearing into the white wall at an angle, suggesting the collision of forms within the interior.

A hole in the wall invites a view through into a neighbouring space, and a nearby door makes entrance possible. Once through, a much more dramatic space is entered, contrasting with the preceding tight area. This is basically a stairwell that is bathed in light from the large window jutting out from the façade of the mews (another feature produced from the collision of the old and new). The curious staircase underside seen previously becomes more easily 'readable' at this point, providing access to the top floor, the gallery and entertainment area.

A skylight runs the length of one side of this main space, giving plentiful natural light, but supplemented also by a series of small windows high up that are like natural spotlights, splashing rays of light on the darker side of the ceiling. In addition, the top portion of the stairwell window breaks into the space, associating it with both the preceding level and the initial approach to the building. It also prevents the gallery from seeming too long and tunnel-like.

But the dominant aspects of this area are the specially commissioned pieces, described by Wilson as, 'the toys in the box.' There is a table by Ron Arad, a sideboard by the artist Bruce McLean, a sofa by Jasper Morrison, and a desk by Floris van den Broecke. Positions were also created for works by artist Andy Warhol and sculptor Barry Flanagan, and others. The hi-fi was adapted and arranged by Wilson, taking on a form that suggests an instrument.

Throughout, there is an emphasis on precise detail: the light is controlled to draw attention to the interior as a performance, and this is carried through from the major movements of the architecture, to the soloist contributions of the furniture, and the exact tuning of finely detailed quality materials. Small 'jokes,' such as figurative touches to handles and a water overflow, support the major trickery of the spaces and forms compacted within this surprising building.

The range of custom-made details and the richness of materials suggest this project was of a high cost, and is clearly not to be assessed against standard yardsticks. It is a statement about the integration of art, design and work for which the patron's innovative contribution should be recognized along with that of the designers.

Industrial steel plating is mixed with highly traditional fittings to produce a functional yet not minimal bathroom.

The conference/dining/gallery area takes over the top floor of the building and features a custom-adapted sound system.

Intriguing views to the outside relate the exterior to the interior. Here the natural environment seen outside is reflected in the timber paneling inside.

A side table designed by the artist Bruce McLean is one of the features of the gallery.

A key requirement was to present a dramatic reception area that would immediately communicate the character of the company to the international range of visitors.

Unplanned discussions are encouraged by a 'break-out' area that aims through design to encourage the relaxation and playfulness hoped for to promote creative ideas in the workers.

Unexpected changes in surfaces and surprise decorative elements seem often to be unnecessary, but fit into the larger plan of creating environments that stimulate rather than soothe.

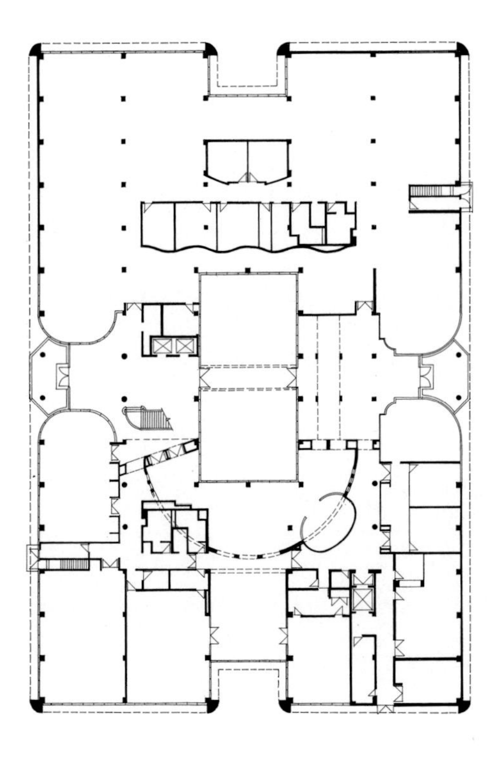

STUDIOS

1.6 Apple Worldwide Manufacturing & Operations Headquarters

California, USA

Apple Computer's distinctive corporate identity and company culture can be seen to underlie not only its 'user-friendly' software, but all its applications of creative expression, from award-winning advertising to architecture. In the interior of the company's headquarters, this is exemplified in an exciting, playful environment that is strikingly at odds with most major corporate statements in headquarters buildings.

Erik Sueberkrop, principal of STUDIOS, has had plenty of opportunity to become immersed in the Apple culture, having previously designed a number of other interiors on Apple's behalf. With this project, he was therefore able to draw on and develop what had gone before. The 105,000 square-foot (9,754 square-metre) space was to be remodeled from the former corporate headquarters, and a key requirement of the brief was the production of a dramatic reception area for international visitors. Also required was a conference hall, three conference rooms, and a 'break-out' area for informal company gatherings (a distinctive Apple requirement). Eating and restroom areas were also included.

The most striking feature of the design is an outdoor garden within the first floor, the informal and changing nature of which permeates into the building around it and is taken up by the fluid plan for the functions taking place in that area.

A distinct loose, almost temporary quality exists in the nature of the spaces formed. Low-cost materials are used imaginatively to create the dynamic playful effect which is so much a part of Apple's corporate expression. The materials are hard, creating a space for activity rather than for rest: polished flake board, tiles and corrugated metal on the walls, a terrazzo bench, and a prefabricated hard-wood floor with ebonized inlay. The budget for the project was $33 per square foot, which may also explain the need for imaginative use of comparatively cheap materials.

The informal nature of the spaces is shown in the ease with which the 'break-out' area for conferences flows into the eating and vending-machine area and lounge. Freestanding pavilions define the space, creating smaller areas in which groups may gather around the vending machine. These pavilions, dispersed around the interior, exist also because the original utility and core elements were awkwardly placed for the development of a spacious and unified plan. Leaving them as freestanding features resolved this problem and had the added advantage of breaking up the space.

A wall that is a sweeping arc links these freestanding elements and defines in a self-conscious way the difference between visitor and employee areas, connecting the two entrances. And the further away from the garden, with its suggestion of informality and change, the more enclosed and restricted becomes the use of space: even at Apple, there is a need for a certain amount of privacy.

By this relatively informal treatment of a corporate headquarters, STUDIOS has been able to provide for the functional requirements in a simple and uncluttered manner, and through this in turn express the dynamic of the company.

The office block is dramatically split open to reveal glimpses of the interior and its interface with the street.

The entrance onto the street shows the exploration of the interrelationship of exterior and interior in the conjunction of materials and forms.

Bold contrasts in colour and scale ensure that the separate components of the entrance take on almost sculptural properties.

Kisho Kurokawa

1.7 Shibuya Higashi T Building

Tokyo, Japan

Kurokawa was faced with a familiar Japanese design problem in this high-quality office building in central Tokyo: how to capture some expression of Japanese tradition within the architectural language of high technology. He also had to deal with the common difficulty of giving some originality to a standard task (the speculative office block) that all too often prompts standard solutions.

Kurokawa's response lies in distinctive forms, and in the relationship he has created between the exterior expression of the building and parts of the interior – a difficult achievement when the planning authorities' requirements differ from the client's wishes.

It is the combination of familiar and unfamiliar that gives distinction to this project. In many office designs, standard luxury materials such as marble and flamed granite are so often used that they do not achieve the 'added value' intended. Kurokawa, however, still makes use of this 'corporate iconography,' in response to demand, but has developed a range of abstract, symbolic associations in his use and form of the materials so that they take on a fresh identity.

The building is a series of contradictions, reflected in the conflicting pressures of external and internal display, historical and contemporary expression. From the outside, it is like a multistory clothes-peg, with a split running up through the 'skin' to reveal the structural 'shelves' of the office floors. This complex yet clear visual aspect is carried through into the entrance lobby in unusual forms and angles and unexpected colour choices. A curving, waved wall is primarily sculptural, but also forms an entrance – it both functions as and symbolizes 'entrance.'

In spite of contradictory elements, Kurokawa's overall design reflects the total corporate identity. While the different elements of the interior – floor, ceiling, external wall, internal wall, public space, private space and so on – have been separated out, they are linked to each other and to the exterior by a grandeur and formality of design that gives way also to a sense of play. A large mirrored area of stainless steel on the back of the curved entrance screen reflects the world outside, as if to draw deliberate attention to the exterior environment that the office worker or visitor leaves behind as they enter the controlled atmosphere within. A large red wall suggests the activity of the elevator bank.

The atmosphere created may be slightly uncomfortable – provoking rather than pleasing – but it counters the lifelessness of many office lobbies. That Kurokawa has achieved the suggestion that this is a location for 'valuable' offices is a result partly of the intelligence of the design, rather than of a mere reliance on the use of luxurious materials. His design aims to do two things. One is to break down the boundary between interior and exterior by having forms cutting through each other, and materials such as the marble entrance floor running from outside to inside. The other is to create what he calls 'an architecture of symbiosis,' merging apparently contradictory elements.

The offices and workshops are linked by walkways over an open courtyard at the heart of the complex.

Honeycomb metal sheeting gives strength with lightness and a decorative quality to this staircase.

Studio Citterio Dwan

1.8 Esprit Italia

Milan, Italy

As former coffee-roasting factories go, the one at the end of Via Forcella in an industrial area of Milan has done well. From being a once-functional shell, this building has been refurbished with all the exacting attention required to make it a fit focus for a company that has had as great an influence as any on retail interiors in the past decade.

This particular Esprit building, however, is not a store. Instead, the former factory still exists as a manufacturing workplace, albeit more glamorous, serving as it does as a design, production and distribution center for Esprit. Here is an interior that shows the client to be as serious about its image in the back room as it is in the storefront.

Architect Antonio Citterio and his associates were faced with an intriguing range of problems in converting the building, despite having the advantage of knowing the area well as it is near their studio. The existing structure was not one large space, but seven separate buildings. For some architects and designers, it might have been tempting to try to combine these elements; for Citterio, however, the existing complex provided an opportunity to create a rich variety of interior and exterior spaces to suit the varied uses proposed.

The seven buildings are linked by walkways and two courtyards, one open and one enclosed, with a skylight (budget restrictions have delayed the glazing of this skylight). The aesthetic is firmly industrial – from the new façades and the entrance ramp to the interior with its exposed surfaces and hard materials. Cement finishes for walls and floors are occasionally offset by less harsh details such as beech flooring, but essentially the only 'soft' elements in the workspace are the people and the objects they use. Citterio's use of perforated, zinc-coated steel for walkways and stairways is one of the strongest statements of aesthetic identity in the scheme – indeed, the use of the material has almost become one of Citterio's trademarks.

The complex only amounts to a total of 18,840 square feet (1,750 square metres) of office, showroom and workshop space, but the variety of forms gained by the overlaying of Citterio's approach onto the already existing industrial architecture produces an interior richer in detail than might be expected with a scheme of similar size but built from scratch.

Citterio's experience in furniture design can be seen in his integration of features such as the reception desk with the prevailing industrial forms surrounding it. Most of the furniture throughout the building was custom designed by the architect. Next to the industrial furniture, exposed pipes and structural parts in turn lose some of their crude functional properties and form an almost decorative effect.

While the designers were concerned to retain the industrial expression of the building, they have also succeeded in integrating it with the corporate identity of the Esprit company. Most importantly, the scheme has proved to be a dramatically light and airy solution to the problems involved in uniting a range of activities in one complex.

Opposite The architecture, interior, furnishings, and graphics all combine in a powerful corporate identity that extends internationally for Esprit.

Outside is a grimy industrial area, but Esprit workers can look in on an environment that allows the weather and nature to interact with the workplace.

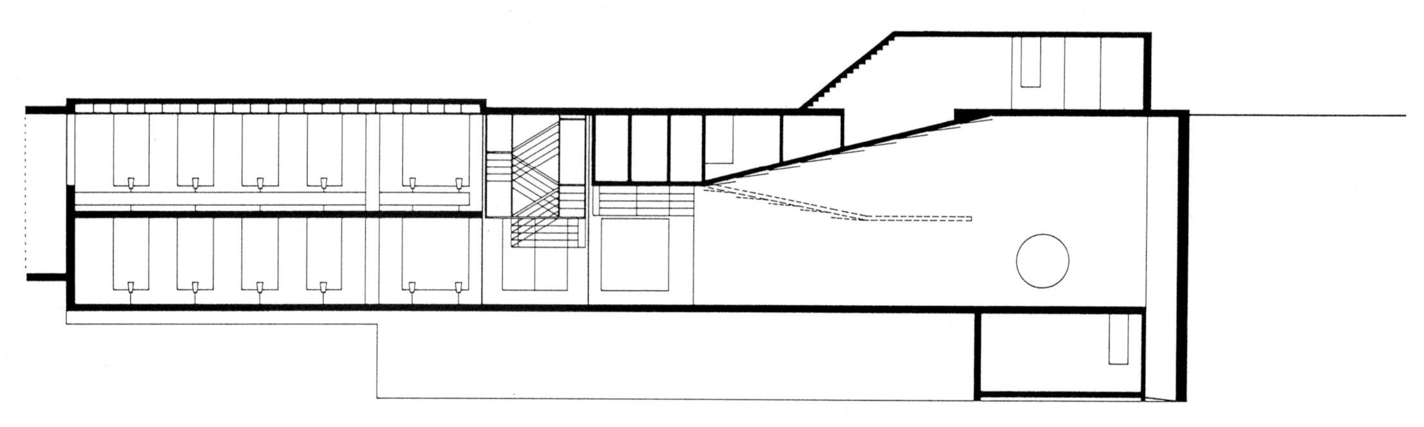

ESPRIT
I T A L I A

Car ramps within the converted car park were retained to provide distinctive spaces that encourage more interaction between office departments.

Natural light is brought in as far as possible by avoiding internal walls, but each department signals itself with bold graphics on glass screens.

The typical clutter of a journalist's desk is not avoided but worked around. Low ceiling heights led to the carrying of services in ducts, rather than raising floors or suspending ceilings.

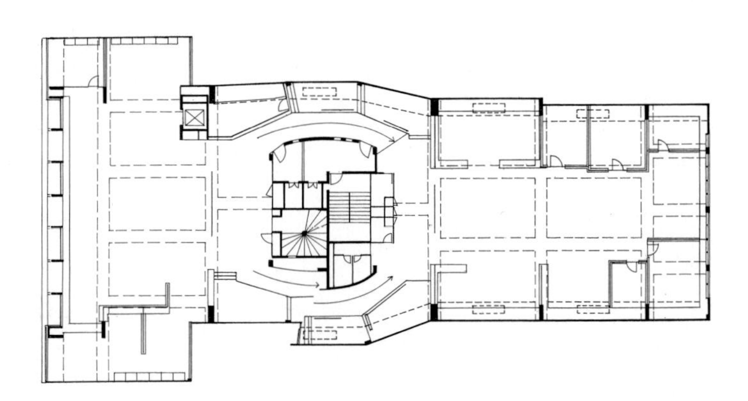

Canal

1.9 Libération

Paris, France

The test as to whether the new offices for the French daily newspaper *Libération* were satisfactory was very immediate: relocation to the new building had to be made in just one day, and the newspaper published and back out onto the streets the following day. It was a success. And from a glance at the offices it would seem that they have always been there. The systems by which the journalists and production staff work give the appearance of having evolved rather than having been designed: an enterprise whose culture has developed within and as a part of its building.

This appearance may have something to do with the choice of a former multistory parking lot for the offices. Despite the obvious problems of low ceiling heights, automobile ramps, and a lack of all the normal servicing found in a speculative office building, Canal have created a hi-tech computerized newspaper office that maintains the character of the business in a way that is lacking in many other new newspaper offices today. Here the office has the additional semi-industrial atmosphere that the newspaper business had traditionally, of journalists working alongside printers.

The nine-story building sits rather like a stranded ship in the city. Its structure enabled a refit that has given rise to intriguing views along and across floors, and to substantial circulation space. The automobile ramp, for example, was retained as a way of enhancing the interaction of employees as they walked from floor to floor (there is an elevator service as well). For 30 years the building housed 400 automobiles a day: now 400 reporters are constantly entering and leaving: Canal have thus used original features to meet common requirements, such as circulation space.

To overcome repetitiveness in the structure, and to define particular workspaces without carving into the building, Canal have used a system of strong graphics to identify floor levels and office functions. Graphics serve also to break up areas of glazing: glass partition walls were introduced in preference to enclosing spaces with solid walls in order to allow as much natural light into the deep-plan interior as possible. A careful balance of bold colours in a harmonious but varied scheme enables different offices to establish individual identities without compromising the fluidity of the whole.

This careful relationship of the orderly with the dynamic is carried through to other design details such as the management of the wiring. Faced with a low slab-to-slab distance that prohibited raised floors or suspended ceilings, Canal have boxed in service ducts on the ceiling; these connect with tree-like structures on the desks, a coil carrying the power supplies down to a plug unit. While the distribution of terminals and task lighting may have the inevitable 'untidy' feel associated with reporters at work, the equipment has been carefully chosen to blend with the planning and decorative scheme.

In their design for *Libération's* new offices, Canal have established an ingenious balance between order and disorder in what could have been an extremely restrictive building structure. The cost amounted to FF2,700 per square metre, including the fitting, the services and some of the furniture.

From within the interior, the contrast between the decorative qualities of the highly functional structure and the ornate façades of surrounding buildings is apparent.

Coop Himmelblau's work is a startling late-twentieth-century intrusion into the nineteenth-century Viennese skyline.

Coop Himmelblau

1.10 Rooftop Remodelling

Vienna, Austria

Each office has a unique form and relationship to the structure as a whole. Interior details are restrained in contrast to the dynamic quality set by the engineering.

'Is it a bird? Is it a plane? No . . .' It's an office for a group of lawyers. The catchphrase that introduces Superman may seem slightly out of place here, but it rightly suggests the fantastic, physics-defying and showman-like qualities of the architecture of Coop Himmelblau above a nineteenth-century Viennese building at a corner site.

The project involved locating 4,000 square feet (372 square metres) of offices on the rooftop. The key space requirement was for an impressive meeting room, with a reception area and smaller offices leading off it.

Coop Himmelblau, headed by architects Wolf Prix and Helmut Swiczinsky, with project architect Franz Sam, sought to create a landmark of a contemporary 'corner solution.' They claim that 'context is no longer a matter of proportion, colours or material of the existing building; to us it is far more the energy line of the visual connection between street and roof.'

In their approach to construction they also attempted to break with attitudes of the past: behind the dramatic steel and glass realization of this scheme is the understanding and inspiration of bridge structure and aircraft technology. There is a desire to express the structural technology of today, and the chaotic forces at work in modern cities, as the character of the architecture and the spaces created. But in order to get these ideas over in the real world of existing buildings, planning regulations and budgets, Coop Himmelblau had to overcome a number of challenges with the offices on Falkenstrasse.

For a start their own ideas had to be pushed to the point at which they might work. It is all very well to aim for a dramatic range of light, open spaces, but how is it possible to fix all that glazing to the structure and the existing building? And, when you have devised a structure that will do the job, how does it become protected from fire and corrosion risks? And, throughout construction, there was a need to maintain the residential use of the building below.

The design develops around the 'taut bow' at the center of the roof structure, a steel spine which cuts through the perception of where the roof line is expected to be, extends awareness of the new intruder into the street below with its overhang and forms the point from which the rest of the structure devolves. It is a steel spine to the curious insect-like creature that seems almost to be the inspiration for the project.

The spaces created within this structure are not only unique as a whole, but are a range of environments that carry many contrasts and opportunity for change. Clearly, the weather can have a dramatic effect on the atmosphere within. But while this drama of the relationship between inside and outside is boldly played out in the conference rooms, the individual offices are less dramatic: they are more livable-in, as is appropriate for a space that may be occupied by the same person day in and day out.

Original treatments for the structure and for achieving the plaster finishes had to be developed, along with installing elevators and heat/energy systems. Despite these high technology requirements, Coop Himmelblau says the budget for the project was 'average' for 'unique architecture.'

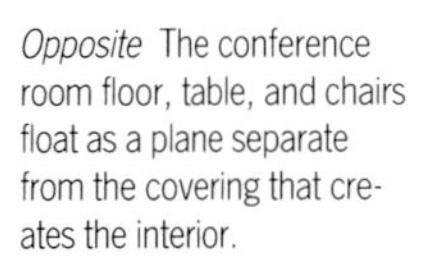

Opposite The conference room floor, table, and chairs float as a plane separate from the covering that creates the interior.

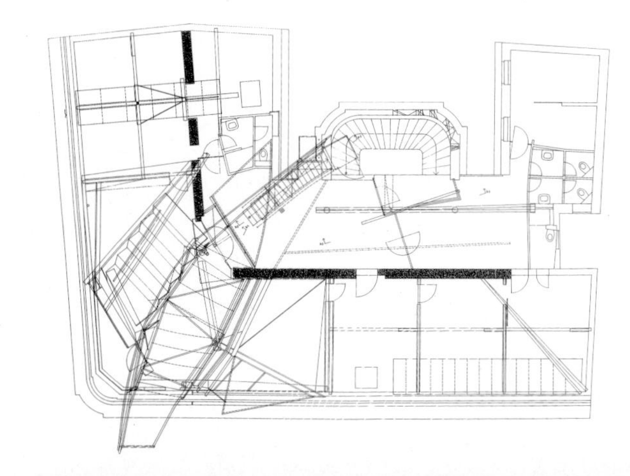

White plaster walls, timber-strip flooring and glazing set the modest backdrop for the structural dynamics.

Approaching the rooftop level, the visitor may see in the staircase the play on loadings that erupt into strange forms above.

Opal-laminated glass screens give privacy to the directors' offices while allowing light to penetrate the building.

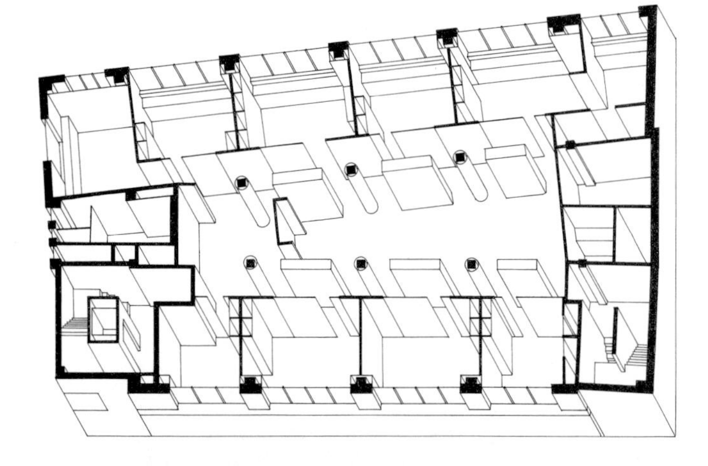

The hi-tech aesthetic is polished in the reception area to a refinement that echoes the ocean-liner Art Deco style.

Ship imagery gives a welcome humour to the office environment, while adding weight to the identity of the clients.

Polished granite flooring and profiled aluminum screens develop the 1930s style without resorting to reproduction.

Eva Jiricna Architects

1.11 Fafalios

London, UK

Standard office space can be the curse of a city attempting to retain a unique expression: business quarters can look similar from one side of the globe to the other. And even if the exterior of a building provides a distinctive feature, all too often anonymous office floors are stacked up behind the façade.

Eva Jiricna's work on key interiors within the Lloyds of London building challenged such common blandness with an original (if controversial) contribution to innovative interior design in the City of London.

Her practice's work for ship brokers Fafalios continues this development of restrained but characterful office space design. Although the client may be a part of a conservative financial market, with no unique physical feature with which to express the nature of the business, Jiricna has developed a distinctive style appropriate to Fafalios and not automatically interchangeable with any other of the floors in the 1930s building in which these offices are located.

The brief included the general refurbishment of the whole building, including the external shell, and a redesign of the common parts to enable the letting of three floors. The principal opportunity for innovative design, however, lay in the space set aside for Fafalios across the whole of the first floor.

A key factor guiding the design was the need to allow as much natural light as possible to penetrate into the deep floor plan. At the same time, there was a need to provide for privacy in some offices and for the separation of various work activities. The final design, therefore, encloses the directors in cellular offices ranged around the perimeter of the plan. Some internal walls are full-height, opal-laminated glass screens with sliding doors which allow maximum light penetration. Fluorescent luminaires and low-voltage spotlights provide contrasting light sources that supplement the natural light.

Furniture and filing storage units were specially designed for the project. Six large cabinets house models of the company's ships, while also ingeniously providing extra storage space for stationery. The boardroom table in maple veneer was also custom designed by the architects, giving them the opportunity to integrate this symbol of corporate power with their design for the interior. The skirting is also maple, but stained gray and lacquered, and doors are maple veneer.

Job architect Tim Bushe, assisted by Carolina Aivars, was faced with a range of problems in the modern refurbishment of an aging office shell. His neat solution to such problems, however, is shown in his treatment of the six columns that puncture the space; these are simply clad in profiled stainless steel, a form and material picked up in other features in the interior. In the reception area, the polished granite flooring and the curved screen of circular-profile, silver-anodized aluminum echo the Art Deco form of a prestigious 1930s office interior without any sense of reproduction.

The clear reference throughout the interior is, of course, to the architecture of the sea – to ship design. This is exemplified particularly in the proprietary ship's portholes (adapted for fire regulations), but the imagery is also apparent in the steel cladding, in the blinds designed to resemble sails, and in the general use of tough materials of quality throughout.

Stage-set associations result from the isolation of the elements within that give the building shell expression to the different areas of activity in a basic shed-structure.

STUDIOS

1.12 Silicon Graphics

California, USA

Several apparently bizarre design decisions were made in the planning of Silicon Graphics' operations. Why are the noisy manufacturing processes intermingled with the engineering offices where peace and quiet would seem to be more desirable? Why is the manufacturing divided between two floors when traditional approaches insist on the efficiency and flexibility of keeping the production on one floor? And why, when the building receives regular visitors, have the manufacturing areas been placed at the front so that every visitor must walk through them?

The reasoning behind such design decisions can only be explained by considering the nature of the client's business. Silicon Graphics Computer Systems is a fast-growing firm manufacturing high-performance computers capable of 3-D modeling. The firm acquired 340,000 square feet (31,586 square metres) of speculative buildings to fit out for all its corporate facilities. At this point in their growth, many companies have made the mistake of dividing up the dynamic mix of elements that has made them successful; being aware of this, Silicon Graphics set out to avoid it. A priority laid down in the design brief for this first building, an area of 90,000 square feet (8,360 square metres) on two stories, was that there should be 'little or no discernible difference between the quality of the two separate environments,' that is, between manufacturing and engineering.

However, while maintaining and encouraging as much interaction as possible between the personnel working in these two areas, and readily offering this culture to visitors, there was also the practical problem of enabling the two functional groups to work efficiently. STUDIOS' solution has been to create a circulation 'spine' that allows the two elements to interrelate, yet also serves as an acoustic barrier.

Flexibility within the interior was an important consideration as the siting of functions had to allow for contraction or expansion of the different parts. The location of each on both floors, therefore, separated only by the 'spine,' facilitates the

Dramatic expression of circulation areas such as staircases gives a form to the factory-like openness of the interior.

An enlivened industrial aesthetic is the result of a brief that demanded no discernible difference in the various kinds of workspaces.

expansion of the differing functions at various points.

The most dramatic feature of the interior is the rotunda which lies at the end of an angled route cut into the building, from which there is entry into both manufacturing and engineering areas, and down which visitors pass. The galleried, double-height space contains the stairs to the upper floor, and provides a natural meeting place for staff, and a dramatic point of arrival for visitors who can watch the manufacturing from an observation and conference area.

The effect of the unusual plan is to celebrate the manufacturing process as a focal point of the company's activity, which, of course, it is. The layout – mixing functions across the two floors and splitting the building into two oddly shaped, two-story units which meet at the rotunda – gives expression enough to the building without the need for the decorative effects of stylish materials or showpiece areas. Instead, low-cost materials, such as painted walls, basic carpeting and ceiling tiles, are seen as entirely appropriate to the functional purpose of the building (the project budget was just $28 per square foot). The key to the success of the design is that the functional purpose is celebrated, rather than suppressed, and that the design offers the possibility for innovative developments between the creative and manufacturing parts of the company. The result is a simplicity that retains a strong sense of the human dimension.

Silicon Graphics is continuing to employ STUDIOS for the design and fitting out of the rest of the complex.

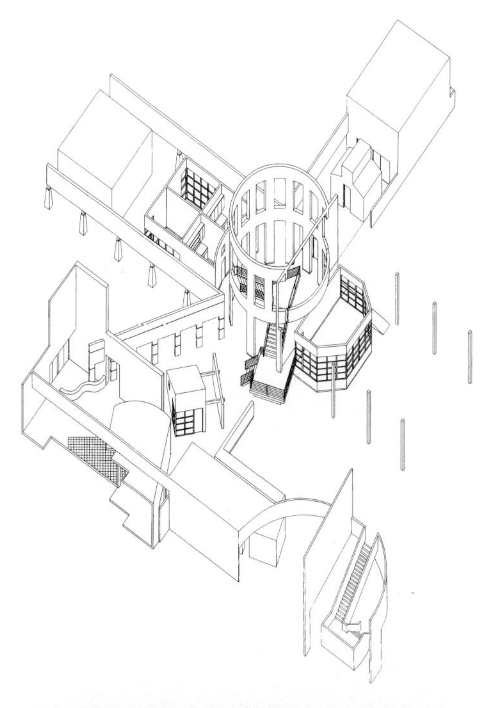

Walls, doors, and floor finishes produce softer and more tactile surfaces to contrast with the harsh industrial space.

The complex interlinking of circulation routes and the two floors is easily recognizable by the exaggerated expression of elements.

The reception area marks out the space as one where both design and designers are at work.

Designers sit at work stations that give the suggestion of privacy while retaining an open studio environment.

Visitors step out of the lift onto a floor covered in rolled steel: a slightly uncomfortable area that is clearly intended to be passed over quickly.

The offices of architects and designers are sometimes dismissed as a bit of an easy brief: function can be sacrificed to image at times, budgets can be massaged by pulling in a few favours, and there are no problems of a client intruding and wanting to change the purity of the idea, or clutter things up with his business.

That said, it is in the offices of studios of the creative originators that the first sitings of ideas about form, space, texture and so on may be first tried out. It is also a shop window for a designer's wares, and can on occasion be seen as the prototype for a range of environments that may follow on.

Geyer Design's own offices manage to combine these factors without creating a too obvious 'designer environment.' Yet they could be taken as a neat catalogue of the ideas of the late 1980s. The environment does not preach one way of designing, but shows Geyer Design looking around with a fair degree of taste at a range of fashionable ideas. The

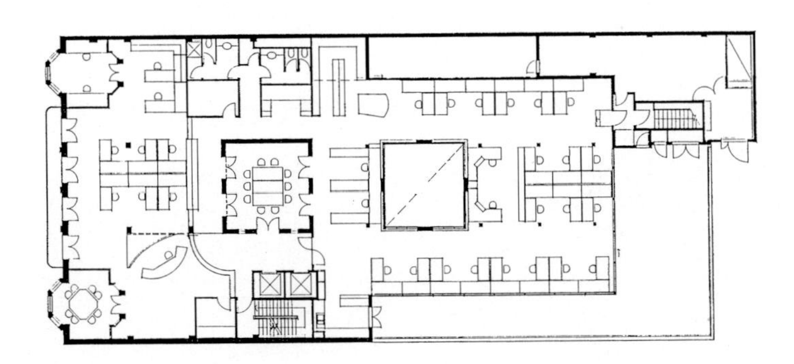

Geyer Design

1.13 Geyer Design

Melbourne, Australia

result is an interior that would fit admirably as a period example in, say, a design history book of the year 2050.

The offices are situated six floors above the busy Collins Street, Melbourne's central shopping and business area, on the top floor of an extensively refurbished 1920s building. The 7,000 square feet (650 square metres) of space (including 1,000 square feet/93 square metres of external courtyards and decks) is located around two central points: one is a transparent light well, the other is an identical size bunker, which houses the conference room.

The plan evolved from a desire to separate out the various workspaces and present them in a manner that allows easy access to different people and facilities without intruding on others. At the same time, the traditional corridor structure was avoided by bringing in the notion of items on show in a gallery or department store; only here the artworks or the products are the people and experiences on offer around the office.

This space planning allows for an efficient use of the area, while creating the potential for expressing the areas in dramatic ways. A hierarchy of spaces is quite clearly established: the main conference room with its 30-foot (9-metre) ceiling being perhaps the most grand, the walkways being the most public, the areas next to outside space needing to respond and celebrate the light rather than look inwards, and so on.

The sense of space and of changing character is often expressed through unexpected changes in surface or colour. For example, visitors are immediately aware of the difference of this environment when they step out of the lift onto a rolled steel sheet that has an indefinite oily colouring. In front of them a translucent glass screen is carried on rollers, suspended from a plum-coloured beam. The reception desk has a slab of fine black marble on a base that looks as though it has been knocked together from leftover pieces of plain timber and steel.

The designers' work stations display an industrial aesthetic that has been refined fully to the standards expected of office detailing. Perforated steel mixes with wood painted and punched to look like metal, a demonstration of the designers' rejection of any predictable design purity: instead the work responds to how materials can function together and how play with the appearance of things can be part of the fun of the environment. A view across the soothing main studio area is brought to a deliberately jarring halt by a bright yellow wall. These references to the crudeness of industrial architecture can also be seen as a response to the neighbouring buildings.

Overall, the offices balance functional requirements, such as access to facilities, and so on, with an awareness of the need to express the function. The complex, lively, but slightly indeterminate style of the result seems an appropriate presentation of the business of offering interior design skills.

Quirky details such as this tightly enclosed internal stair tower break up the repetitiveness of a large office building.

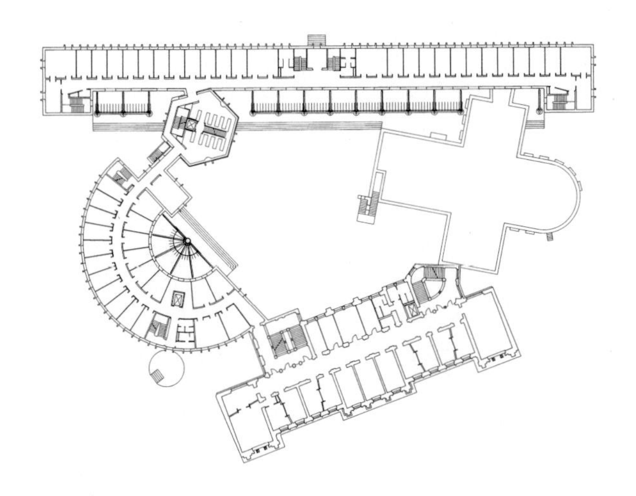

James Stirling, Michael Wilford & Associates

1.14 Wissenschaftszentrum

Berlin, West Germany

'Perhaps too many architects delight in expressing the appearance of simple repetitiveness,' says James Stirling, as a side comment on his search for a unique form for the mass of cellular offices that make up this science-center office building.

The project was won in international competition by his office in 1979, but took nearly a decade to reach an opening date. Parts of the complex are still to be built. Despite the difficulties implied by these delays, the building has a bold, individual and innovative exterior and interior that develop Stirling's work and add a worthy newcomer to the 'cultural forum' of buildings around this site.

Stirling partly explains his approach in his rejection of the rundown modernism of the office environment: 'The WZB does not look like the ubiquitous shoebox post-war office block we are all too familiar with. Here we tried to create a rich social and architectural environment in contrast to the repetitiveness of 300 or so individual office rooms which is the basis of the building programme.'

This approach is signalled on the outside by the bands of different-coloured stucco that pick out the floors of the building. It is also marked by the decision to split up the various departments within this government science center into five linked new buildings around an existing building on the site. Offices are divided into areas for environment, sociology and management, plus the library/archive tower building, and with a fifth unit for future expansion. All connect on every floor and thus the 'architectural ensemble' functions as one institution but expresses the functions and encourages the character of the individual parts within.

The arrangement around a garden, with entrances to all the buildings off it, should be seen as more than a formal architectural statement relating only to the exterior: it also generates views from offices of the other departments, views remarkable for not being of dreary gray buildings but of warm colourful bands of pink and blue above a stone base. The most regular elements are the windows: each is central to a room and is framed by a thick stone architrave. This framing not only develops an exterior expression, but again has a significance for the interior in creating a sense of the walls being wider than they actually are, reinforcing a sense of comfort and security.

This warmth is a quality enhanced by the use of light timber surfaces, as well as the familiar hot colours that Stirling splashes on his interiors. The play with architectural forms (oversized columns and capitals, for example) is more than an academic exercise: it helps articulate the space, ensuring that the building is not a visually neutral backcloth to visually neutral office activities – the oft-seen response that leads to a sterile office environment.

The structure and the plan of the buildings are used to develop a range of curved surfaces that contrast and relieve the basic grid of cellular office design. Workers within the complex can opt for different routes when passing between points

Exterior frames to the windows produce the illusion of extremely thick walls and create higher contrasts of lighting from the blinkered windows, while the oversized column gives a muscular expression to the structural requirements.

around the semi-circle of offices: along principal arterial routes of the central corridors within the office units, or across the courtyard in fine weather. Staff have reacted to the creation of an open space within the building by sometimes moving outside to work in fine weather. It provides a dramatic break away from the fairly enclosed nature of spaces provided by the cell-like offices and the units within the library tower.

The severity of the basis of office life is also challenged by the provocative colours Stirling uses on the interior, such as the burnt orange linoleum that gives such a strong character to corridor areas. Such colouring is never neutral, or even predictable, but seems intended to provide an interior palette of colours that matches the monumental qualities evident in the form.

Details – such as the railings around a stairway – pick up elements of Berlin's heavy but flamboyant style, while motifs from classical and modern architecture can be read almost as 'quotations' within the buildings.

Critics have questioned the logic for the different office blocks (the original structure of the center is likely to change from five to fifteen institutes) and have also suggested a lack of sufficient communal space. Whatever justification there is for such remarks, Stirling & Wilford have always the positive achievement of a building with a distinctive character that meets the brief. If would be difficult to find as expressive a building from the many similar commissions given out each year for repetitive office units.

Instead of one monolith of a building, the WZB is split into units around a courtyard, creating a circulation pattern that demands integration of interior and exterior routes.

Interior fitments opt for a simple strength and warmth of textures and colours to contrast with a colder exterior.

Art Nouveau ironwork draws from the turn-of-the-century style of nearby buildings in Berlin, although the colouring of the interior is defiantly Stirling & Wilford.

The colour palette is kept cool, with the bold use of blue giving drama and contrast, yet retaining a soothing interior.

With an architectural ironmonger as the client, the precise detailing of the staircase elements has a special relevance.

Resources were concentrated in the reception space to create a waiting area that is simple but full of visual and textural interest.

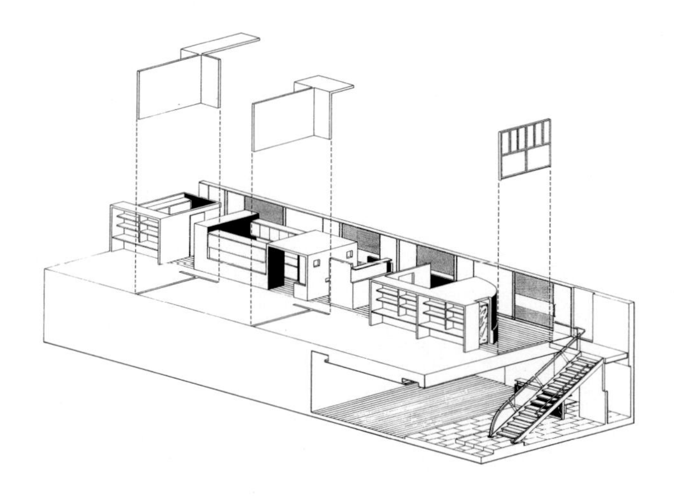

Armstrong Associates

1.15 Elementer Headquarters

Maidenhead, UK

The role of the staircase as a heroic and dynamic part of an interior is rarely more clearly seen than in this project designed by Ken Armstrong and Jennifer Smith. Despite working to a tight budget, the designers were determined to create a focal point that would make a statement about the client, exemplifying the client's quality of manufacture and manner of working.

The client is a company producing high-quality stainless steel architectural ironmongery. It required the architects to convert a two-story space of 6,200 square feet (576 square metres), in an unremarkable light-industrial building, into headquarters that would be a living showroom, providing offices and conference space next to the warehouse.

The design has a refined simplicity expressed in a variety of natural materials. The main focus rests essentially on the staircase, which was designed by Armstrong Associates but manufactured at Elementer's workshops in Denmark; it was shipped back to England for assembly. The parts of the staircase are bolted together; there is no welding. It is constructed from stainless steel and glass, and the open treads are of oak. At the top the mild steel and pyran glass steel meet the half-hour fire-retardant requirements.

The appearance of simplicity is deceptive. Because of the limited budget, Armstrong Associates often had to work with relatively cheap materials for the basic shell of the offices; this required careful control of detail to ensure that the effect of quality was maintained. The creation of a central series of boxes to carry coats, office machinery and stores – almost a series of small pavilions – lessens distractions and frees more space for other use.

Plastered and painted partitions divide the interior into livable spaces, as well as form the required units for the offices. Directors' and secretaries' offices are not closed off completely, but are screened by clear and etched glass. The doors are of oak in steel frames, the materials matching those used on the staircase. Jacobsen and Kjaerholm chairs maintain the Danish influence, while a further focal point is provided by a textile wall-hanging created by Sally Greaves-Lord.

The total budget was £250,000 ($400,000). Armstrong Associates' design demonstrates how, by paring a space to its basic shell and using this from which to build, quality can be found in the careful use of simple, comparatively common materials. This quality is further enhanced by an architectural focal point which draws together all other elements of design into a coherent whole.

Le Corbusier's early development of the family house can be seen to be the precursor of his major work and – by derivation – Putman's approach to design.

Ecart

1.16 Ebel – Villa Turque

La Chaux de Fonds, Switzerland

To restore and adapt a building by Le Corbusier could be seen as a dream job for a designer. The task would combine the opportunity to pay respect to a pioneer of architectural form and theory with a certain opportunity to get one's work in the spotlight. On the other hand, anything less than meticulous dedication to reproducing every detail of the master's original invites criticism. Any departure from the original use of the building is likely to prompt comments questioning its appropriateness.

The effect of the work of Ecart designers, Andrée Putman and Thierry Conquet, assisted by Laurent Buttazoni, in restoring and adapting Le Corbusier's early work, Villa Turque (originally Villa Schwob), could provoke all the above responses. But the justification for its inclusion here is that it is an impressive interior that could only have been produced today.

Le Corbusier's client in 1916 was a successful watchmaker who wanted a substantial but not showy house. When the watch company Ebel bought Villa Turque in 1986 they wanted to restore the architect's early masterpiece, a corporate gesture that fitted well with the company's slogan 'the architects of time.' But Ebel did not want a house: instead, the Villa Turque has been converted into a public relations center, where business meetings may be carried out and guests may be accommodated overnight. Facilities for holding conferences and staging presentations had to be provided. The brief also required the building to be adaptable to holding events such as concerts and exhibitions.

The interior scheme developed by Ecart preserves as far as possible the original functions of the different rooms. The renovation architects Roland and Pierre Studer sought to restore many elements of the original that had been lost by alterations and earlier 'restorations.' Putman and Conquet built on this to try and restore to the design the original logic of its expression of the uses of space within. Thus the ground floor, comprising entrance area, living room, dining room, and games room, provides the more public areas, while the upstairs floor of two bedrooms and bathrooms is kept for the guest suites.

The original symmetries of the building have been restored and are the basis for more recent additions, such as furniture and lighting.

By keeping the upstairs for guest suites, the original domestic character of the building is maintained and the integration of the restored and new elements is easier.

At the heart of the house is the main living room – now a meeting room – where Putman's cool palette allows the play of natural light to be a dominant element.

Ecart created new furniture for each room to draw on the original design pedigree, while satisfying the client's requirements.

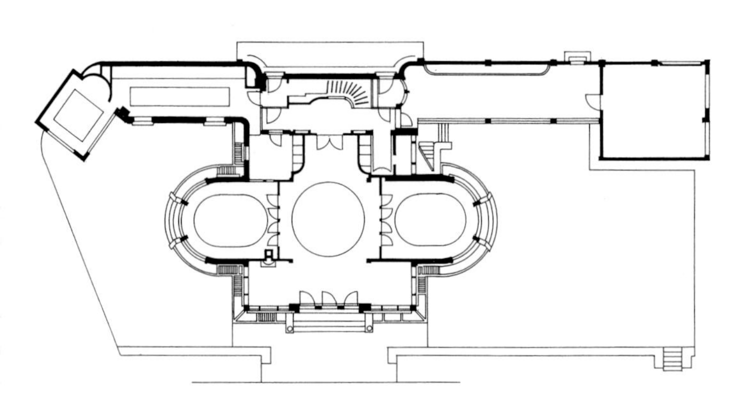

In this neat marriage of the original forms of the home with the new concept of the public relations center, the designers created the basis for the impressive, almost timeless, combination of modern furnishings with Modernist pieces. And although all this post-dates 1916, it finds a place as the historically appropriate descendant of the aesthetic Corbusier was working for in 1916.

Ecart created what it describes as 'specific furniture' for each room. Always sober in form, never built-in, but freestanding, and always sympathetic to the form of the rooms, the furniture arrangements take on the character associated with the gradual accrual of favoured pieces of furniture in a home. A minimal palette is used throughout: oak is used for desks, consoles, tables, vanity tables and headboards in gray and blond treatments, while stained oak provides a parquet floor. Ivory paint is matched with off-white cottons, and the tone is echoed in brown and black horsehair.

Corbusier purists might well be appalled at this palette: the original colour scheme devised by the architect involved ultramarines, ochres and siennas. But he never chose the furniture (the Schwob family did this), and a strong argument could be made for saying Ecart's work picks up on the ideas presented in Corbusier's more fully formed ideas on interiors of a decade later. Besides Putman's own furniture designs, works by Eileen Gray and Mariano Fortuny add to the presentation of a dedicated response to the ideas of Le Corbusier.

The intricate Putman-designed lights of the living room contain suggestions of the art and craft of watchmaking, appropriate to the fortune that originally built the house and that which restored it. At the same time as having a fitness to the particular building, many of the elements – including the colour scheme – have a strong connection with the corporate design tradition that Putman has carried through into Ebel's boutiques.

A development that may seem rather wilfully errant from the original design is the styling of the bathrooms, where mosaic tiles from Venice in gold, black and silver add a new richness, as do plumbing fittings that copy those of the Orient Express. But historical justification of a sort can be presented in that the underlying plan of the whole house takes as inspiration the Byzantine cross: why not suggest this with reference to the route to the east?

The finished interior provides three guest suites around the focus of the conference facilities in a total area of 5,000 square feet (464 square metres). It certainly avoids being a museum, but manages to meet its requirements for a workable modern space at the same time as providing an essay on the tradition of Modernist ideas in interior design that Le Corbusier helped inspire. And, in its breaking of traditional work environments, its integration of activities, it contributes to the development of a new building type (see also Blackburn Office, page 24 and PN Club, page 22) that Corbusier's radical visions also anticipated.

The ingenious use of mirrors as a decorative feature in their own right also helps to lend grandeur to the staircase.

Modern studio spaces within the palazzo are uncompromising in their contemporary character while retaining the elegance of the older rooms.

David Davies Associates

1.17 Valentino

Rome, Italy

It might be difficult to imagine a more attractive brief for a designer than the refurbishment of the studio and office headquarters for the *haute couture* fashion house Valentino, particularly as the location is a sixteenth-century palazzo in Rome.

The choice of the London-based David Davies Associates (DDA) was therefore an intriguing one, not only because they are not Italian, but also because they are not generally associated with those architects and designers who specialize in the restoration of period interiors. DDA's experience in retail design, however, seems to have served the designers well in their aim to restore the Valentino building, and to portray its image and function.

Designers Peter Kent and Peter Moore have achieved an appropriate adaptation of the palazzo in order to incorporate and express the function of their client. It is stylish, but classic. The grandeur of the existing fabric is always acknowledged, but never to the point where there might be a loss of confidence in adding a modern expression.

The planning of the whole complex has taken advantage of the fact that the studio and the offices are situated around a courtyard; the space available for use is therefore 'strung out' in a linear fashion. In a key corner location is Valentino's own studio: on one side it is next to the main design studio, off which are the collection room and a buyers' office; on the other side lies Valentino's office, then his secretary's office and his business partner's office, their dining room and private bathroom, and finally the conference room.

Features introduced in the studio and buyers' rooms show the benefits of drawing on the retail design revolution of the late 1980s: neat and economical storage systems, and furniture and lighting that present a simple and encouraging setting for work. Around, above and adjacent to such efficient workspaces, however, are the original rich, dramatic and decorative parts of the building, such as elaborate frescoed ceilings (restored by the Rome Academy of Arts). The clutter of a fashion house at work – designing, marketing, buying and selling – adds flesh and colour to the almost skeletal frame of some of DDA's architectural elements.

In spite of the simplicity of some of their work here, the designers are not strict functionalists. They demonstrate their flair in bringing together the newer, working parts of the interior with the older, more ornate features of the building. A maple strip floor with a green slate border is both simple yet rich; doors with verdigris frames, brass handles and fluted glass panels are modern yet echo an older craftsmanship. Although *marmorino* (marble-dust plaster) walls are used perhaps excessively in many fashionable retail interiors, here they are entirely in keeping.

From the staircase to the principals' offices, through to the conference room, there is a complex blending of elements, old and new, that will signal to any visitor (should they need it) that this is a most elegant use of a *piano nobile*.

The elaborate sixteenth-century ceiling and period furnishings are the context for modern paneling and light fixtures.

The banister detail shows the possibilities of a delicate decoration in a modern aesthetic.

An eclectic mix of sources can be observed in this bathroom, which avoids looking modern yet is neither of a specific period.

Provocative contrasts of character are made here with ribbed glass doors opening onto a frescoed ceiling.

The requirements of the studio's work practices generated attractive new fitments such as these storage/display cabinets.

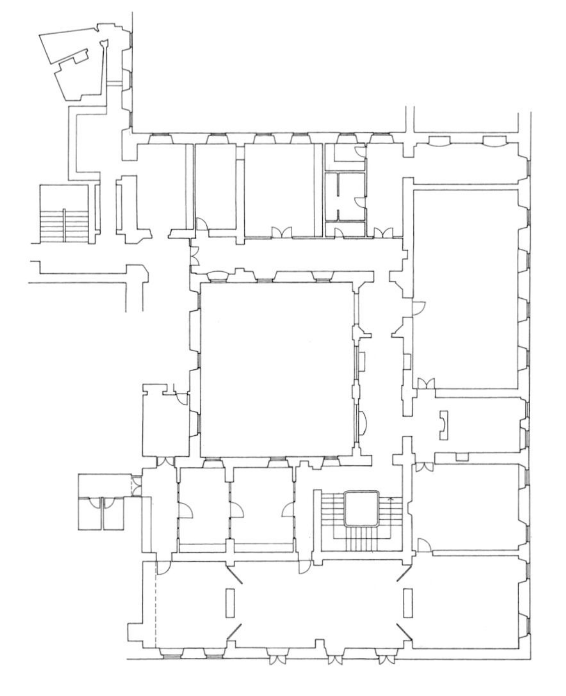

Not only did David Davies Associates design the overall interior and fitments but they also produced furniture such as these chairs.

Bolido, Massimo Iosa Ghini
(see p. 118)

2 Restaurants, Cafes, Bars, Clubs, & Hotels

1 **Philippe Starck**
Cafe Mystique, *Tokyo, Japan* 68

2 **Building**
Trattoria Angeli, *Los Angeles, USA* 72

3 **Conran Design Group**
Review, *London, UK* 74

4 **Branson Coates Architecture**
Noah's Ark, *Sapporo, Japan* 76

5 **Fitch RS**
Mitchell & O'Brien, *London, UK* 80

6 **Shin Takamatsu**
Kirin Plaza Osaka, *Osaka, Japan* 82

7 **Philippe Starck**
Royalton Hotel, *New York, USA* 84

8 **Takashi Sugimoto & Koji Okamoto**
Libre Space, *Tokyo, Japan* 90

9 **Thomas Leeser**
The Gold Bar, *New York, USA* 92

10 **David Chipperfield & Partners**
Bingo, Bango, Bongo, *Tokyo, Japan* 94

11 **Chassay Wright Associates**
Fred's, *London, UK* 98

12 **Satsuo Kitaoka**
Bar Akasaka, *Fukuoka, Japan* 100

13 **Charles Arnoldi with Solberg & Lowe**
DC3, *Santa Monica, USA* 102

14 **Shiro Kuramata**
Comblé, *Shizuoka-shi, Japan* 106

15 **Shiro Kuramata**
Kiyotomo Sushi Restaurant, *Tokyo, Japan* 110

16 **Jeffrey G Beers Architects**
China Grill, *New York, USA* 112

17 **Shigeru Uchida/Studio 80**
Itchoh, *Aoyoma, Tokyo, Japan* 114

18 **Shigeru Uchida/Studio 80**
Itchoh, *Roppongi, Tokyo, Japan* 116

19 **Massimo Iosa Ghini**
Bolido, *New York, USA* 118

20 **Alfredo Arribas Arquitectos Asociados**
Velvet Bar, *Barcelona, Spain* 122

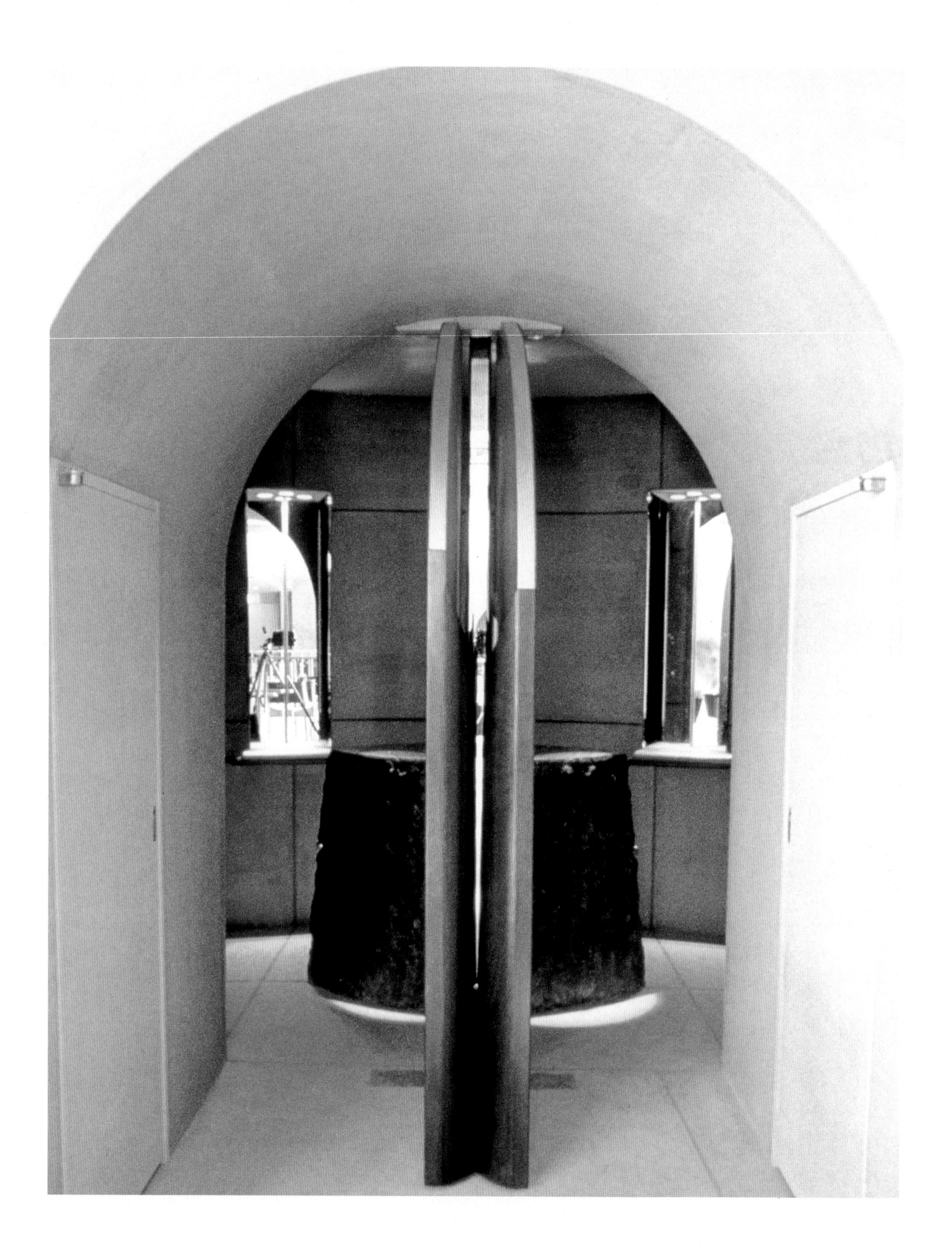

Spatial characteristics change on each of the three floors, the basement here having a much more intimate nature than the open display and noise of the floors above.

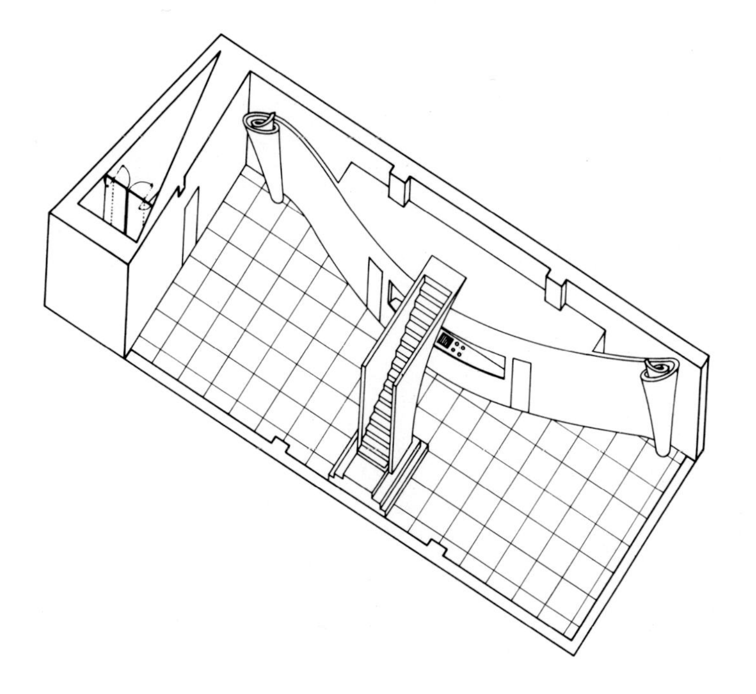

Philippe Starck

2.1 Cafe Mystique

Tokyo, Japan

From this project, the client, fashion company Belle Tricot, wanted 'a French-style, big popular cafe,' according to designer Philippe Starck. And indeed, once visited, Cafe Mystique should be easy to remember as a place to which to return. The main reason for some customers' visit may even be just to try and discover what it is that Starck is attempting to do in his design, and where he might have acquired the staircase.

The brief from the client was substantially to remodel a building (including considerable structural work), and to carve out a cafe and restaurant on three floors in the fashionable center of Tokyo. The basic plan has the restaurant in the lower ground/ basement area, with the activity of the cafe on ground and first-floor levels. This arrangement not only separates the bustling, noisy cafe from the quieter restaurant, it also enables the more dynamic activities to be seen through the large window area from the street. The identity of the interior serves as an effective advertisement. When the cafe is closed, however, two double-height metal doors roll in front of the windows and shield the interior completely from view. The façade then becomes two-dimensional, a huge purple screen with just one distinctive motif, and no name.

The doors may be dramatic, but they serve merely as a form of 'fanfare' for the centerpiece of the interior, the staircase. This monumental feature rises in the middle of the restaurant, directly in front of the entrance. Starck describes it as 'frog-shaped,' and it does indeed have both the ugliness and the elegance of that creature. The mass of the staircase contrasts sharply with the lightweight, florid curves of the hand rails, and the point at which it joins the first floor is intriguing: Starck has stepped the edge of the entire floor slab so that it comes down to meet the rising staircase. The effect is to draw as much attention as possible to the intrusive, growth-like nature of this staircase: its soft forms also contrast with the hard, squared-off concrete finishes of the basic building shell.

For some designers, this might be statement enough, but Starck carries the original detail through into the services, decoration and fitting out of the interior. All the furniture is original, and the chair, with legs 45 degrees out of their usual position, depicts yet another intriguing idiosyncratic Starck design. Decorative motifs make up a frieze in gold leaf above the diners that features, according to Starck, 'various symbols and signs Man has used for years.' These images range from primitive depictions of the human form to the hammer and sickle and the Shell petroleum company logo.

The interior cost Y340 million (approximately $2.4 million), which worked out at a substantial Y550,000 ($3,900) per square metre, but this included considerable structural renewal. Starck took full advantage of rebuilding work to produce a unique form, despite having to design to a substantially reduced budget during the course of work.

Images from primitive art to popular logos are incorporated as motifs in the gold-leaf-covered frieze that runs around the restaurant.

Massive steel doors close across the façade of the restaurant when shut, creating a memorable identity that is part of the 'mystique.'

Large structural elements are more than matched by Starck's great mound of a staircase that rises from the ground-floor entrance area.

When open, the steel doors roll back to reveal a glass façade that shows off the restaurant while giving diners a view out.

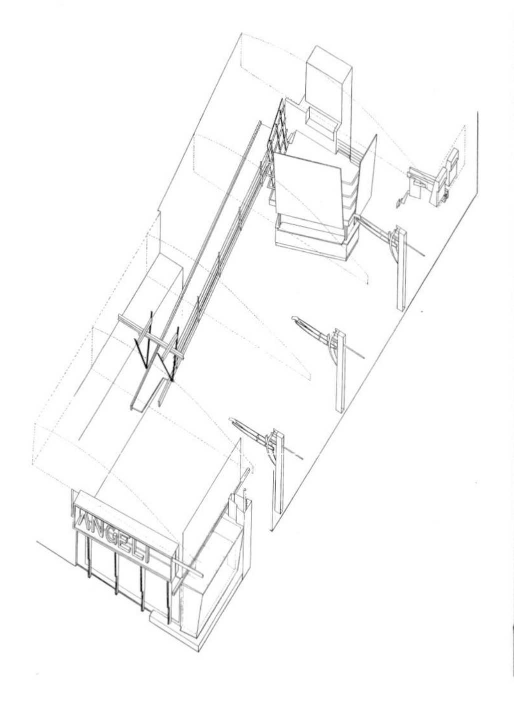

Cor-ten steel elements combine decorative properties with a reference to the industrial origins of the building.

Exposed roof trusses, white plaster walls and ceiling open out a simple, yet grand space, with the tables as the main feature.

Angeli's character and function are clearly seen through the windows, as a living advertisement to passers-by.

Building

2.2 Trattoria Angeli

Los Angeles, USA

People do not walk to Angeli. This is not the trattoria of a medieval Tuscan hill-town or the back streets of Naples: this is Los Angeles, where the environment reflects the scale and the pace of the car.

From the outset, therefore, the client and designers of Angeli sought to develop an Italian restaurant that would be genuine in character to complement the food, yet fitting for the location. Their fresh approach can be seen initially in the main street façade which is a wall of cor-ten steel – in effect, an eye-catching advertisement which promises that Angeli will be a different kind of restaurant. The actual entrance is round the corner, the approach from the parked car.

Inside, there is the suggestion of the openness and liveliness of a Mediterranean restaurant, but this is not achieved by imitation. Designers Michele Saee, Richard Lundquist, Max Massie and David Lindberg worked towards understanding an aesthetic, rather than mimicking detail, and in so doing have helped to spawn a new form: the Californian Italian restaurant. (Iranian-born Saee had already had the advantage of working on a previous Angeli restaurant from his days at Morphosis, as well as having trained and worked in Italy.)

The 4,000 square-foot (372 square-metre) restaurant is on two floors: a 3,000 square-foot main floor (280 square metres) that seats 100 diners, with an additional 1,000 square-foot (93 square-metre) storage and private dining area on a mezzanine level. The main dining area is a large open space that does nothing to hide the semi-industrial nature of the building (it had previously been a carpet warehouse). Simple chairs and tables designed by Building tend towards the rustic Italian but without being fake, and are appropriate in scale and shape to the trattoria image. Beyond the main dining area, towards the back of the restaurant, is the pizza-making area. The kitchen is adjoining, and, while separated from the dining area, is connected to it by views through the glass wall, further contributing to the sense of informality and activity. The bar is at the front and to one side of this service area.

By exposing the timber bow trusses of the roof, the designers have put a strong aesthetic stamp on the interior, which they have then taken further. A steel catwalk has been introduced along one wall, creating greater awareness of activity as people moving to the back of the restaurant, and to the facilities on the mezzanine floor, parade past the main area of diners. The elaborate brackets for the lighting echo further the industrial building structure. The natural cement-finish walls and cement floor are a move away from the soft restaurant traditions, but are honest to this interior and functional also, creating hard surfaces that reflect sound in the same way as the tile and stone of the traditional trattoria. Panels of douglas fir for the wainscoting and screen add warmth and relate to the wooden beams.

During the day, natural light enters at a high level, reflecting off the beams to bring out the colour of the wood and break down any direct light. The artificial sources reinforce this effect with uplighting.

Although the design has a distinct character and uses good quality materials, the development of the industrial aesthetic appears to have helped to keep the budget down – the cost was $250,000.

Streamlined style and light colourings integrate the new bar with the curve of the building and the palette of the original design.

Both the matt-white painted plaster and the carpet pattern faithfully reproduce the original designs, while new lighting and chairs match the mood.

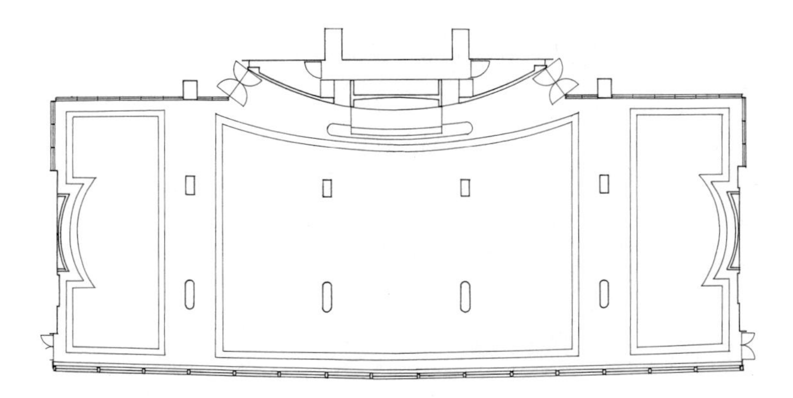

Conran Design Group

2.3 Review

London, UK

The South Bank Centre lies in the heart of London. Since its origins in the 1950s, however, the buildings on the banks of the River Thames have often been criticized for having a desolate air, lacking the sense of life that might be expected from an entertainment complex.

The Royal Festival Hall is usually exempt from the full severity of such criticism, but only as the result of the introduction of catering and retail facilities that attract regular activity to its concourse areas.

All this acts as a backdrop for Review, a successful new 120-seat restaurant facility located in an advantageous position on the river frontage of the Royal Festival Hall building. It utilizes the large, double-height windows to provide a spectacular view for diners, and looks entirely in keeping with the 1950s aesthetic of the building, yet is far from being straight reproduction.

Before work could start, the space had to be stripped back to remove asbestos. The designers also had to work within the restrictions imposed by the fact that the Royal Festival Hall is a protected building. The functional requirement was for a restaurant that could cater for public and private functions simultaneously, with a serving area large enough to be used for a substantial amount of the food preparation.

The designers responded by studying the qualities that distinguished the 1950s combination of modernism and the certain flamboyance that typified 'The Festival of Britain,' for which the Royal Festival Hall had originally been built. This can be seen in the use of high-quality, classic finishes and the simple, uncluttered layout, which are enhanced by discreet flourishes such as the gentle curve of a chair leg or the shaping of the movable oak screens that serve to separate private dining parties from other dining areas. The natural wood finishes, the matt-white, painted plaster, and the carpet are details taken fairly faithfully from the original design of the Royal Festival Hall. Canopies have been hung from some areas to alleviate the 'coldness' of the high ceilings.

The design of Review reflects the riverside position, echoing it in soft wave forms, and in the simple colour palette which takes its tones from the changing light visible on the water outside.

Sprayed concrete is the dominant material in moulding the image of an 'ark' as a classical temple resting on a rock.

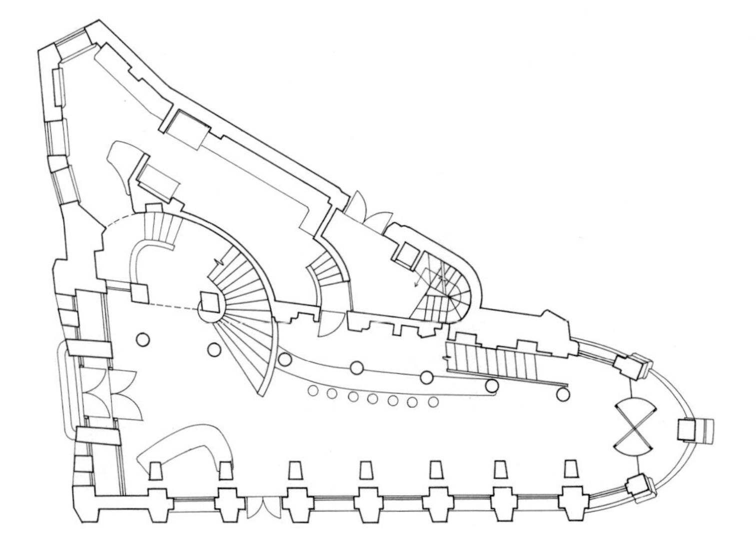

Branson Coates Architecture

2.4 Noah's Ark

Sapporo, Japan

Branson Coates' first complete building in Japan, coming after a number of projects for interiors in Tokyo and elsewhere in the country, produces a sophisticated collage of cultural references and forms as a design statement about the complex nature of the present age. Nigel Coates sees the task of the designer as being to present problems rather than solutions, and thus his assembly of imagery for Noah's Ark does not create one easily definable meaning but rather 'territories of meaning.'

The client wanted the restaurant to become a major landmark in Sapporo, the capital of Hokkaido and the fourth largest city in Japan. The building is part of a larger development project including shops and a hotel complex. Its form as a two-story building with classical overtones was intended to provide a strong architectural presence to help draw visitors to the area. Sapporo has grown out of nothing in less than a century, and the desire to imbue the area with a sense of culture and enhance its value was a strong consideration.

The triangular site is situated by a small river. It was a challenge to conceive of any conventional form that fitted the site, and the idea of a ship – Noah's Ark – washed up on the side of the mountain following the deluge, presented itself early on.

On the outside, the project takes the form of a classical temple-styled ship resting on, and almost carved into, a rock (achieved with copious use of sprayed concrete); in the complex interior spaces, there is a rich range of Etruscan cultural references, although here their form is diffused and given a contemporary application.

Sandblasted wood used in the construction of furniture, windows, and other fittings accentuates the impression of age, perhaps evoking the 'fossilized wood' that might be found in a rediscovered ark. Sprayed concrete walls with aggregate and coloured terracotta tiles refer in part to Etruscan houses carved in sandstone, and help to give the interior the quality of a rustic temple.

An impressive budget of £2,940 ($4,704) per square metre enabled the designers to commission a number of young English artists and designers they had worked with on other projects to create many of the interior details, objects and wall paintings. These contributors were given a relatively free rein on the imagery they employed, and their work further enriches the design, providing a sense of accumulation, and, as Branson Coates see it, a layering of past and future which can often accentuate the present.

The wall paintings of Stuart Holm and Adam Lowe are partly inspired by Etruscan art, and feature many animal and plant forms. Other artists and designers involved include Tom Dixon (chandeliers), Jasper Morrison (rug), Annabelle Grey (fabrics), and artworks by Oriel Harwood and Mark Quinn.

The design of the staircases, however, is perhaps the most expressive part in helping customers interpret the interior. There are two staircases: one is linear, and like a ship's boarding ramp, while the other curves up more elegantly around the columns to meet it, with a procession of painted animals ascending its walls. Building regulations prevented the designers from placing the ramp on the outside of the building, so they internalized it, to good effect. Together the staircases provide a sense of the movement and space created, of the kaleidoscopic cultural references within the interior design – they are perhaps the question marks on Branson Coates' series of tantalizing questions.

Sandblasted wood gives many fittings the 'fossilized' associations aimed for by the architects, here seen on the ship-style, boarding-ramp staircase.

Aggregate and colouring added to the sprayed concrete produce varied forms and textures and allude to the Etruscan decoration of houses.

Many young artists were involved in the project, giving a variety to the design.

Original furniture, such as the stools, is integrated with details that are closely derived from the style of New York diners, while being taken to a more sophisticated level.

Revolving doors and a glass screen separate the bar area from the dining room and delicatessen.

Banquette seating, ribbed glass screens, and patterned mosaic flooring are all new, yet true to the spirit of the restaurant's role models.

The dividing line between reference and reproduction is a narrow one: the more of the former there is in an interior, the more meaning can exist beyond the mere functioning of an environment; the more of the latter, the more superficial can seem the whole strategy once the fashion for that style has passed on.

Mitchell & O'Brien sits happily between reference and reproduction. Designers Carlos Virgile and Nigel Stone, who head up Fitch's Special Projects Unit, started from a brief to create 'the best New York Jewish deli' – only the location was in Soho, London. The response to this was to create a three-dimensional collage of what 'New York deli' connotes – putting together elements taken straight from New York precedents, from Edward Hopper paintings, and from the Art Deco period that provides the imagery for much of the best New York architecture.

At the same time, the project clearly has to suit a perceived local need. The 1,940 square feet (180 square metres) of space had previously been an unsuccessful restaurant, but the new owners had a strong idea of dividing the area into a delicatessen, a restaurant, and a bar, thereby developing a character that reflected the various social activities of the Soho streets. The target audience ranged from the trendsetting types frequenting Soho, to the traditional consumers of the food who would have to be attracted in by the quality of the Jewish delicacies.

The designers realized the tension involved in using the 'retro' elements, commenting that, 'There is a fine dividing line between nostalgia and re-using Art Deco . . . the main obstacle was to control this aspect, creating an environment that works as a contemporary design as much as an evocative one.' Such an image-led brief could have led to a highly over-designed response: Virgile and Stone were aware of this and actively sought understatement. The character had to emerge partly through how people used the space, and how good the food and drink proved to be.

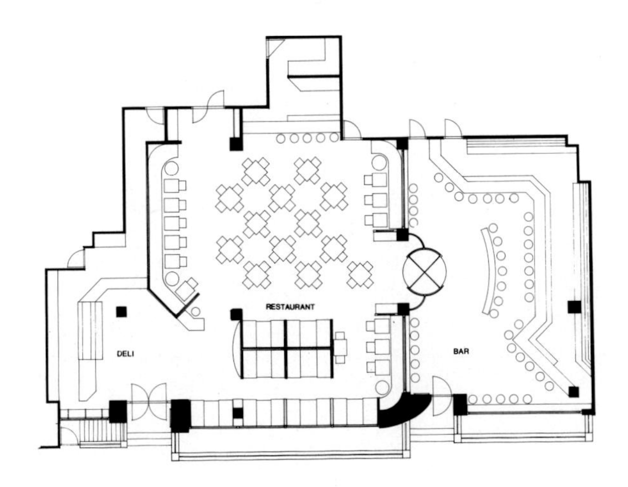

Fitch RS

2.5 Mitchell & O'Brien

London, UK

In order to create the framework for this organic development, the designers studied New York bars but also saw the demand for the European cafe atmosphere. From this came a scheme that actively avoids reproduction elements – it either lifts original period pieces, or creates neutral elements. (This displays their debt to the atmosphere of Hopper's paintings: light and space, rather than specific objects, creating the strong character.)

The key planning element that presents the image of Mitchell & O'Brien is, perhaps, the half-glass screen that divides the middle of the space, separating the bar from the restaurant and delicatessen. A revolving door (bought from an architectural salvage company) provides access within the building, but both areas are accessible from outside, enabling the two areas to work without interrupting each other, yet contributing to the sense of activity within. The strong gilded metal façade unites the two doorways outside and sets a clear identity for the whole.

Virgile and Stone were not seeking to transplant New York to London, but they did acquire original features from the United States: nearly 2,000 feet (600 metres) of mouldings were picked up, as were the 1930s restaurant chairs (originally used in a chain of family diners). These acquisitions not only helped achieve the identity, but contributed to a standard of craftsmanship in details that would not normally be possible on a budget of £250,000 ($400,000) for such a project today.

Where original features were not available or desirable, there was no attempt at faking: for example, the lighting is not a reproduction, but involves some original parts taken from the Adelphi Theatre with some new elements. Interestingly, there are no low-voltage halogen lights, so popular with similar developments. The banquette seating is not original either, but it is timeless – as much of now as of the 1930s.

The flooring is all new, but augments the aesthetic by using either mosaic ceramic tiles imported from the United States or industrial linoleum (in the bar). Both of these materials would have been available to the designers of the original delis, and are also popular in the less sophisticated bars and restaurants of today.

The idea of presenting an image that underplays the quality (and pricing) of the goods within is an important one with Mitchell & O'Brien: customers know it is not original 1930s, but appreciate that the image is not false but evokes the ambience of such a venue as those presented in Hopper paintings and black-and-white films. The quality of the design details – as the quality of the food and drink – is confirmed by repeated custom, rather than exposed as two-dimensional, the usual fate of projects that fail to achieve such a happy marriage of the old and new.

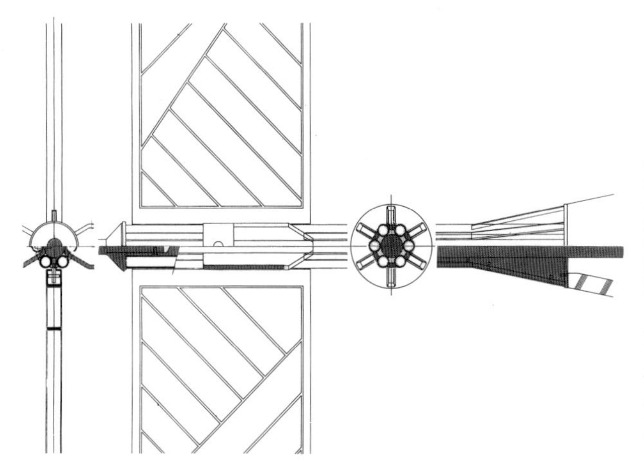

This is power architecture: the lavishness and dynamic character of the building's aesthetic is intended to embody the qualities of the sponsoring company.

The activity of the busy district outside is deliberately reflected in the highly polished surfaces of the dark lobby, where they become a subject for meditation.

Forms taken from nature underlie the design of lighting and surface treatments throughout the building.

Shin Takamatsu

2.6 Kirin Plaza Osaka

Osaka, Japan

During its brief period of existence, the Kirin Plaza Osaka building has become a major landmark in a part of the city in which it can be difficult for a landmark to stand out. The Shinsaibashi area is famous for its hectic shopping crowds, packed bars and restaurants, music halls and theaters. At a major crossing point in this area, the hotel and insurance branch of the giant brewing corporation Kirin commissioned Takamatsu to create a multipurpose entertainment building.

It is a lavish building which expresses the corporation's culture in an attractive manner through the provision of two restaurants, a bar, a cafe, a recording studio and a small gallery. It contains no offices relating to the company's functions.

The building is surrounded by a multitude of bright signs advertising its presence. Takamatsu placed four enormous white beacons on the top of the black column of the building, making a powerful abstract statement amidst the commercial 'hard sell.' Inside, he sought to reflect the activity of the exterior by creating a lobby that uses a range of shining polished surfaces in steel, brass, aluminum and stone to capture, in a restful manner, the vibrant life of the city.

Takamatsu sought to keep his use of the space as flexible as possible, as the building is comparatively small to accommodate all the functions for which it may be used. The entrance lobby on the first floor, for example, includes a cafe, a flower shop, and a ticket counter: both an economical and an exciting use of space. The space on the fifth floor can be used as a hall for parties, as a cinema or as a recording studio.

This range of uses arose from protracted discussions in which the architect and client sought 'to discover a meaning for this building.' That meaning is now expressed in what appears to be a neat contradiction: a multipurpose entertainment building that is intended as a point of rest. This in turn explains the cool and indeterminate qualities of Takamatsu's design that take on a monumental expression (appropriate to a building commissioned to mark the 100th anniversary of the Kirin company).

A substantial budget enabled materials of the highest quality to be used. Takamatsu devised an original artificial stone mix, containing aluminum chips, which is used for the floor, and a different original artificial stone was created for use as a stucco wall treatment. The black artificial stone is used again, mixed with brass chips, for a large table, supported on a metal structure.

This inventive play with materials is seen again in the bench that serves partly to screen the elevator hall from the salon. Pieces of plywood are painted with metallic colours, giving quite the reverse effect of pieces of metal appearing as stone, where they become more permanent – here they appear merely skin deep and temporary.

The lighting fixtures draw on a range of imagery – floral for the wall and column fixtures, and cloud and sky for the pendant structures. The design of the carpet also reflects the external environment, with an elliptical form echoing the ellipse of darkness represented in imagery of the night sky. The ceiling in turn is patterned with imagery of forests, clouds and, Takamatsu suggests, 'foams of beer.'

Starck's approach to hotel design is to treat it almost as theater, and this is signalled from the outside by the lighting, the curtains, and the impression of a proscenium arch.

Philippe Starck

2.7 Royalton Hotel

New York, USA

In this once seedy Manhattan hotel, French designer Philippe Starck has fashioned a startling essay in pastiche on the hotel architectural style. Credit must also be given to his clients, Ian Schrager and the late Steve Rubell, however, whose previous contributions to pop culture include Studio 54 and the Palladium nightclubs. They worked with Starck, often over the fax, to create an interior that is comfortable and yet provocative.

Starck described the task as the creation of a new form of elegance at a reasonable cost. It is understood that this cost was finally in the region of $10 million, a reasonable sum perhaps, considering the number of custom-made details and the value of encouraging return visits of the hotel's guests. For certain the elegance promised has been achieved.

A series of domestically scaled public rooms gives the hotel the flavour of 'home.' In contrast, however, mahogany, gray stucco and upholstered walls reflect the more public image normally associated with a hotel. Deep blue carpeting, green marble bars, and strange organic forms to the cast aluminum furniture further extend this self-conscious handling of the luxury hotel form. Handled badly, the effect could have been one of bad taste, or at least somewhat gimmick-ridden, but it is held together by Starck's delicate line which is carried through from chair leg to lighting. The natural imagery of many elements is emphasized in the repeated horn image that can be found in lights and door handles.

In the bedrooms the Royalton combines again a genuine elegance (associations have been made with the style of an ocean liner) with the excess of having, for example, a working fireplace in some rooms. The velvet-covered armchairs have a back that is raked at a slightly wider angle than might be expected. Indeed, throughout his design of the furniture, Starck stretches the elements of tradition until chairs and tables are seen to do more than just function as items of furniture. They also comment, through their forms and the textures of the materials, on the culture of comfort and elegance.

Linearity is defined by many of the details: legs of tables, chairs, stools, and other furniture rework curving, natural forms.

Deep-blue, studded-leather padding under the bar cushions knees while stool cross-peg provides a footrest and rejection of any suggestion that Starck's decorativeness is not also functional.

The bathrooms seem almost spartan, with Vola taps and slate tiling, when contrasted to the public areas of the hotel.

Slate, steel, and leather break with the traditional soft elements of a guest suite, yet work to create a style-conscious mode of comfort.

Curving, natural forms are repeated in the horn lamps and chair legs, while the deep blues of the carpet contrast with the warm colour of the door.

Exaggeration can be found in almost every element – from the padding to the chair seat and the light dish – yet the overall effect is elegant.

A sculptural wall separates the bar from the dining area with a structure made from used steel and timber components.

Solids and voids, curves and straight lines, timber and stone, light and shade; Libre Space is a place of contrasts.

Highly polished black marble on the floor and raw concrete on the ceiling illustrate the juxtaposition of hard elements.

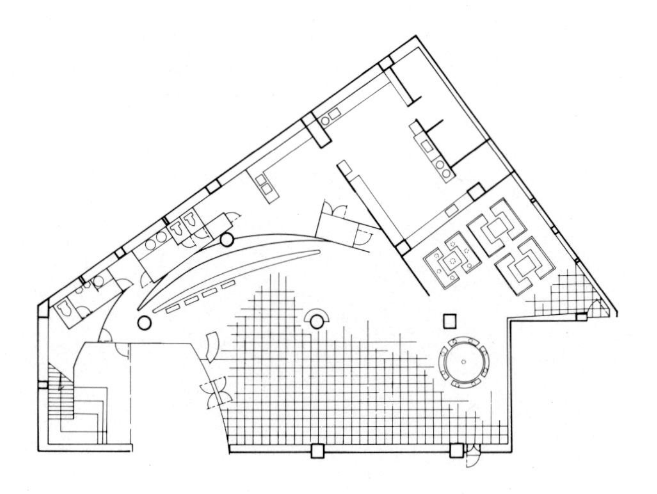

Takashi Sugimoto & Koji Okamoto

2.8 Libre Space

Tokyo, Japan

The Asahi Beer Company approached the designers of this project with an attractive proposition: to produce a pilot 'store' for the company which would enhance its image. Beyond that initial brief, it was up to the designers to produce what they thought would best reflect it. Libre Space might therefore be seen as the realization of an architect's and a designer's 'dream bar.' A budget of Y350,000 ($2,500) per square metre might also serve to strengthen this impression.

The restaurant/beer bar is in the basement of the Japan Quest Building. It makes full use of the opportunity to control the lighting completely, and of the heavy structure of beams and columns, to give the place form and character. The atmosphere of the bar is created initially by this primary resource: an enclosed space, offering the opportunity for intimacy and privacy.

The design is developed from this, with a sensitivity to the need for quality, and a sense of history. Certain features are used also, however, to strike a pragmatic balance and to guard against a sense of the fragile. For example, the use of black marble on the floor and columns provides a durable and high-quality addition to the frame of activity.

Tables and benches are of solid walnut with an oil-stained finish. The shaping of the benches as sections from the circle of table is a detail that is both functional in the use of space and ingenious in providing a framework within which customers can disperse themselves in that space. Low-voltage halogen spotlights pick out the tables as centers of activity.

While these features provide the essential fabric of Libre Space, the originality of the design comes into its own with the sculptural wall which separates the bar from the dining room. It is constructed from used steel and timber, with parts of new steel and walnut that relate it to the materials used elsewhere in the bar. This work by the artist Aijiro Wakita exists as an integral part of the architecture and not as a decorative afterthought.

The effect of Libre Space comes from its juxtaposition of features: high-quality materials juxtaposed with 'junk' elements; hard steel and marble with the softer, warmer effect of wood; a bare grid ceiling of rough concrete with the polished smoothness of the floor; light with dark. Within this spectrum, it has the capacity to reflect the range of moods – from happy to sad – that its occupants may feel.

Customers at the bar sit before a hole in the floor that drops through to the basement, with their drinks on a seemingly sloping counter.

Behind an unprepossessing lock-up façade the interior is a striking and almost magical environment.

In a small store unit in the East Village is 'the tallest bar in the world.' So claims the architect and co-owner Thomas Leeser, and perhaps he is right: it might be difficult to find another bar with a counter that is 12 feet (3.6 metres) high.

You do not need to be a basketball player on stilts, however, to be served here. The gold-leaf covered, concrete monolith of a bar unit begins on the basement level and actually only rises to a relatively normal height on the ground floor, but customers can appreciate its depth by looking down the hole in the floor that lies between them and the bar top.

The design of The Gold Bar aims to give a 'dislocating' experience. The bar top appears to slope so severely that it is difficult to envisage a glass remaining upright. Tipping glasses are, however, not actually a problem as the floor too is on a slight slope – though this in fact accentuates the dislocating experience. Further 'uncertainty' is provided by a floor made from thin steel plates, and by the fact that

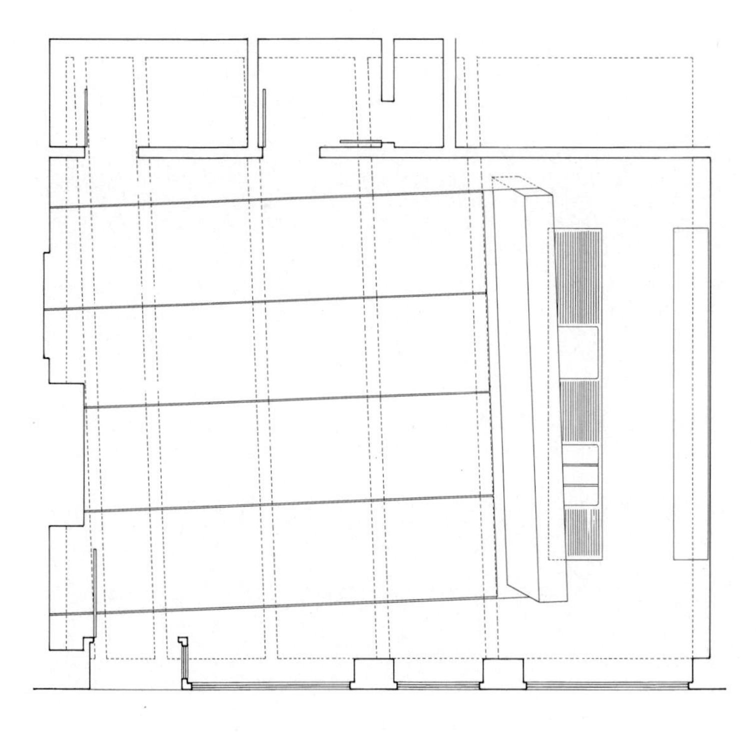

Thomas Leeser

2.9 The Gold Bar

New York, USA

the only lighting comes through the slits between these floor plates and the hole before the bar.

These bizarre tricks are aspects of an approach that has led Leeser to be dubbed with the dubious description of 'deconstructionist.' But while clever theories may be formulated about what these building jokes mean, it is clear that the bar works simply as a fashionable spot at which to drink.

The project began as an opportunity to take over a very small former liquor store in the heart of an area populated by artists, actors and students. The brief was to design a minimal bar that would serve the local clientele and also attract people from further afield. Leeser says that he wanted a 'high image with an atmosphere of a private cocktail party. The design was to serve a highly promotional purpose, in order to attract an international crowd.'

The promotional and international intentions succeeded. In spite of the fact that only drinks are served, and that all drinks come in the same-sized glasses, the venue has proved highly popular. Not many such establishments manage a whole page article in *The New Yorker* magazine, with an interviewer revealing his bewilderment at the architect's ideas. The following is Leeser's response to being asked why the bar stools are all different heights: 'The Gold Bar was designed as a place where people couldn't sit down, because I didn't want them to be comfortable. But people complained. The bar stools are five-minute designs I drew on a napkin. This welder cut up scrap and made them cheaply. I wanted to make it clear that the stools don't really belong here.'

The entire range of materials used consists of raw steel (from junkyards), raw concrete and gold leaf. All furniture and lighting was created by Leeser (which perhaps explains how he worked to a budget of $62.5 per square foot despite using gold leaf). Besides the bar room itself, the only other spaces are the restrooms on the ground floor, and the area at the back of bar. In the basement is the ice machine, beer-cooling unit, general storage area, and a small workspace for repairs of equipment and furniture.

At one level, the idea of The Gold Bar is simply to attract attention. At another, it is to make a statement about the kind of stylish interior that has emerged from the once seedy East Village, a comment on the changing nature of a site. Leeser left the exterior virtually unchanged – bullet holes around the door frame remain, and when closed there is little to signal the presence of The Gold Bar. It is a place for the *cognoscenti*.

Bold patterns on banners help to divide spaces, while seating and tables emphasize the simplicity and strength of the materials.

Explosive paintings by McLean on the curved perimeter wall help break down the sense of an enclosed space.

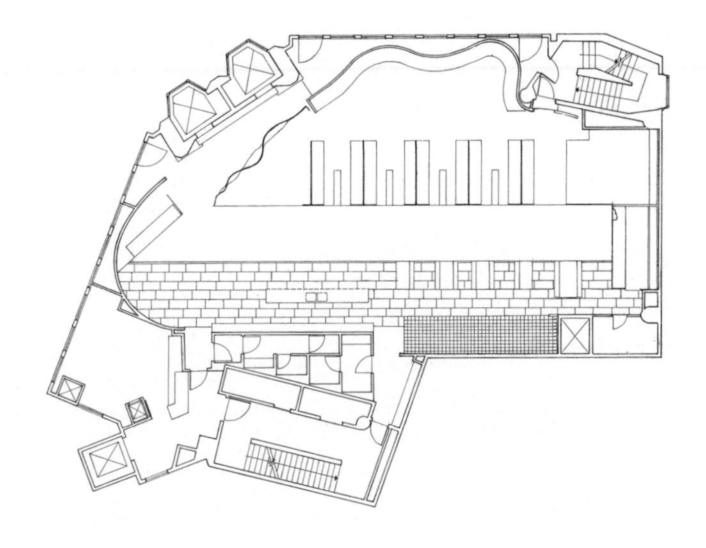

David Chipperfield & Partners

2.10 Bingo, Bango, Bongo

Tokyo, Japan

With a brief that required the creation of a 'light-hearted' space for a young persons' disco, the temptation of many serious architects might have been to hand over the project to a local graffiti artist and run. Chipperfield went one better: he sought to re-plan and develop the space to give it some rationale and then invited a group of artists and designers to contribute selected highlights.

The disco is situated in a seven-story building owned by the client Casatec (the design office of Cassina Japan). There had always been a club in the building, but it was no longer fashionable, and the intention was to revamp the whole profile of the building, including the club. The site was an area with three entrances, two escape routes, and seven columns dispersed around the floor.

Although the primary requirement was to produce a disco, Chipperfield wanted to achieve the atmosphere of a club, reaching beyond the basic approach to most discos, which suggests that interior design equals lighting effects and little more. His initial problem, however, was to find a scheme that gave structure to the space, making sense of the odd circulation and obstructions.

His inspiration for the solution came from a series of Picasso collages, which suggested a guitar shape. From this, he developed a plan with two parts: a plainer, linear form for the dance area, and a richer environment for the carpeted bar area.

There was also an awareness of a need to create a range of tactile experiences. The effect of the columns was softened by making them round with timber cladding. The artist Bruce McLean designed five banners that divide an area of tables and seating. Floors in the bar area vary from carpet to slate to a painted cement walkway featuring bold graphics.

At the perimeter of the club, curved forms break down the effect of the wall, making the space more indeterminate. Lighting also helps create a more sensual environment than is found in the box-like form of many discos: light sources vary from runway lights set into the skirt of the slate floor, to spotlights that pick up the McLean-originated faces and gestures that decorate some of the perimeter walls.

Other artists involved in the project included the fashion designer Georgina Godley and the graphic designer Peter Saville. Chipperfield oversaw a creative direction that ranged from his planning and servicing of the whole, through to such details as furniture design, staff uniforms and print graphics. While it is in stark contrast to his work on retail and office environments, and large planning schemes, this project shows how an unusual mix of creative contributors can often bring to a project the dynamic quality that may be lacking when orthodox experts are invited to design a particular job.

The total budget for this project was £350,000 ($560,000).

Dramatically different moods can be created, such as this quieter and more relaxed area at the edge of the club.

Floors vary from carpet, to painted cement, to slate, while timber-clad columns add to the tactile dimension of the disco.

Opposite The changing levels and materials of both floor and ceiling spell out the functions of different areas.

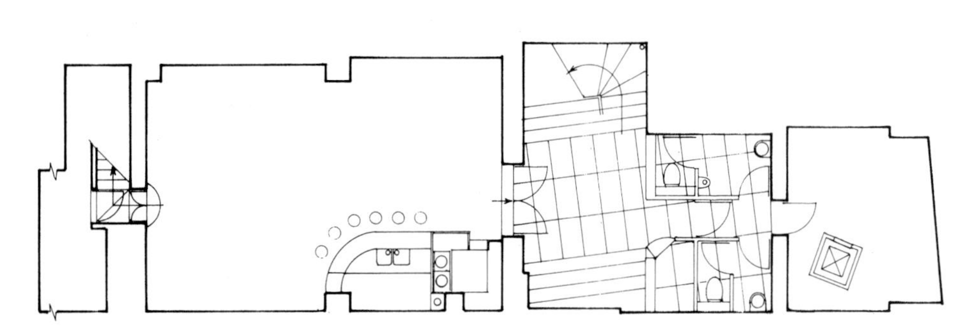

Upstairs, a horseshoe-shaped sushi bar is a less abrasive interior that provides space for art to be exhibited.

Bar lights sprout like flowers and an I-beam runs out across the ceiling seemingly unsupported.

Ingenious planning makes the most of the narrow site as seen here, with the entrance on the left helping to create a raised niche for tables, out of the way of people at the bar.

Chassay Wright Architects

2.11 Fred's

London, UK

'Soho is London's playground, we aim to be its most prestigious address.' Thus was the aim of Fred's club set down by the owners and designers in the initial concept document. Whether it *is* the 'most prestigious address' is open to debate, but it has undoubtedly more than met its target of drawing in the regular custom of 'glamorous 20 to 40 year olds in the film, music, fashion, design, art and literary worlds.'

The three stories of this members-only club are divided primarily into a ground-floor bar, an upstairs sushi bar, and a basement level disco/presentation area.

Chassay Wright Architects sought to create a form of the comfortable but artful interiors for which they have become known, notably with the nearby Groucho's club. With Fred's, the requirement was for a slightly more exciting, tougher environment that would interest a younger crowd. The eclectic range of elements that resulted is partly due to Chassay Wright commissioning other creative sources to design certain features.

The main structural work involved excavating the basement to form a full level, putting in a new metal staircase (fabricated by Henry Taylor), and installing air conditioning and other services. The front reception area was created by erecting a curved glass screen. The area behind the screen was raised and tables installed.

The ground-floor bar is the main focus of activity. It was originally intended to hold a maximum of 75 people, but the club is so popular that numbers must often exceed this. The cherry wood bar top was created by Matthew Marchbank, with tulip lights by Melanie Sainsbury giving a slight Art Nouveau feel. Chassay Wright had initially planned to have concealed lighting, but this proved unworkable. Sainsbury also designed the massive chandelier that hangs over the upstairs food bar, a feature that reflects the style of the clubs to be found on Pall Mall. The metal bar stools with green leather seats are by Jasper Morrison and are a further play on the club/bar heritage.

Merbau wood flooring and painted cement walls give a basic frame to the interior, the designers carefully working to restrict the palette of colours, and the range of materials and forms, to a scale and intensity appropriate to a very small space.

The stairwell maintains the simplicity of style with the steel staircase and cement walls. The stairs lead up to a smaller area where food is served around a U-shaped cherry wood bar (an allusion perhaps to the tradition of 'horseshoe bars' in English pubs), or down to the tough aesthetic of the disco floor: an almost bare, cement-lined box with a sprung wood floor and only the sound system to provide sensual experience. Restrooms and the kitchen are also on this floor.

The interior cost £200,000 ($320,000), approximately £100 ($160) per square foot. Its success suggests it is not only intriguing but appropriate. It also forms an interesting development from the building's previous use as a strip bar and drinking den.

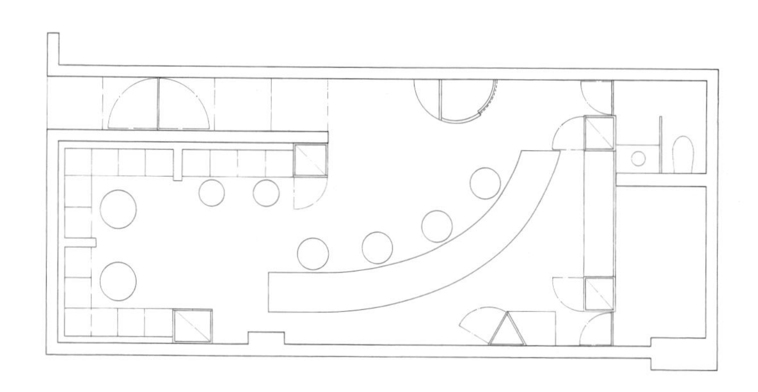

Fiber-optic patterns reflect so that floor, wall, and ceiling merge around the one fixed point of the door.

The underlit glass bar is a dramatic curve set into the grid patterns of the bar interior, and is the strongest lit element.

Satsuo Kitaoka

2.12 Bar Akasaka

Fukuoka, Japan

This is a small bar, merely 592 square feet (55 square metres), in a building housing many other bars and clubs. In it, Kitaoka, the designer, was met with a challenge presented by the density of space that often occurs in a dimly-lit and windowless area.

The design, as apparent on the plan, divides the space into a grid, with a dramatic slash through this structure provided by the curve of the bar. This intrusive element is made more so by its strange indeterminate form, a floating plane of thick glass which is lit from underneath. The glass tiles from which it is constructed are also used for the floor, which suggests a relationship between the bar and the floor as the only major horizontal planes within the space. The way in which the bar is lit reinforces its position as the key element, determining the use made of the space, while undermining the sense of the floor's solidity. Customers are made aware of the nature of the floor's construction, and of its indeterminate depth. This awareness of light is also stressed in the large wall relief designed by Plus-T textile studio. This is located behind the bar and is made from a fiber-optic cloth, depicting an abstract pattern and suggesting a three dimensionality that it does not possess.

Other design features are deliberately kept relatively simple to allow the two major statements of bar and wall panel to create the atmosphere. The ceiling is simply a painted finish.

The budget of Y330,000 ($2,350) per square metre was dedicated to maximizing the power of the statements made possible by the interaction of light and dark. The result is a bar with a unique design in a highly competitive environment.

DC3 affords excellent views out onto the airport, and this was considered in planning the restaurant.

Charles Arnoldi with Solberg & Lowe

2.13 DC3

Santa Monica, USA

Discussion on how art and architecture can be integrated often irritates designers. Architecture itself, after all, is an art – why obscure it, therefore, with other art forms such as paintings or sculpture?

While such discussion may continue elsewhere, however, here in Santa Monica is one marriage of art and architecture that presents a new aesthetic perspective. Client Bruce Marder already had two successful restaurants to his name in the Los Angeles area (one designed by Frank Gehry) when he embarked on adding a third by taking a 15,000 square-foot space (1,393 square metres) in the new Santa Monica Airport building, designed by architects Solberg & Lowe. Marder wanted to see a fresh approach in the design of his restaurant, and he therefore persuaded artist and friend Charles Arnoldi to give up 'a couple of hours a week' and help create DC3.

Arnoldi took some persuading, and, in the traditions of a true artist, demanded that he had final approval of the work. Over a lengthy period of design and building, he collaborated with Jack Highwart and Michael McBurnette of Solberg & Lowe in transferring his ideas from sketches into solid three-dimensional features.

The exploration of spatial and material values through the three-dimensional perspective is evident on arrival at the restaurant, with entry through a host station that is a black marble-lined cube set within a sphere of stucco. Customers may then choose to be drawn to the bar which has a counter 100 feet long, of solid aluminum, on top of a cowhide-lined front. A terrazzo floor and steel and leather chairs with aluminum tables lend support to the impression of a multi-cultural bar drawing its imagery from a wide range of precedents.

Alternatively, customers may go straight into the main seating areas. The restaurant can seat 150 people, a banquet room up to 250, a private dining room 30, and there is also a patio overlooking the runways. The bar seats 40. Much of the influence on the design of the seating plan came from the client. Arnoldi was concerned mainly with directing his attention to creating elements within the large space

Screen, bar and entrance sphere are contrasting yet complementary elements within close proximity to each other.

that would provide major points of stimulation. He is reported to have said that 'my main concern was that it would be frightening to have a restaurant on that scale if it wasn't really interesting visually. It had to be strong enough to carry itself even with nobody in it.'

The positioning of the restrooms illustrates this. Instead of tucking them discreetly into a corner, he puts them into the center of the plan: curious, almost abstract elements, which help break up the space and also have a functional logic in being most conveniently placed to lessen traffic through the various areas.

There is a boldness in the design of all the original features: the screen between the bar and the restaurant, for example, is a massive grid of maple that is not shy to declare both its structure and the quality of its material. This use of fine materials is evident throughout the $2.5 million project. Marble is used extensively as a wall finish, contrasting with a concrete ceiling. Lighting is partly carried across the ceilings in glazed box fixtures which appear like incongruous beams supporting the roof.

Although the intention was to avoid using any direct 'art' forms in the restaurant, there are in fact some works of art. These are present partly as a result of a surprise change to the plan that led to the creation of a large blank wall. On this wall now hangs a large work by Arnoldi, together with paintings by Billy Al Bengston and Ed Ruscha. There is also a sculpture by Robert Graham.

The mix of creative input – from Arnoldi through his client and collaborating architects to the craftsmen who made many of the unusual details possible – produces a highly eclectic interior. For architects Solberg & Lowe, who must be given most credit for realizing, developing and adding to the concepts behind this interior, there was a sense of experimenting with a different design process. Architect Highwart collaborated with artist Arnoldi when they sat together with a sheet of paper, exchanging ideas. Highwart sketched during the conversation and afterwards developed architectural drawings with proportion and scale. The architect's comment on the result is that 'In some ways the design of the restaurant reflects this fragmented process.' Arnoldi's hopes are to have created a venue that has some of the atmosphere of an old Hollywood nightclub: as he comments, 'I wanted to create a place where people would feel terrific.' Marder, on the other hand, has an immensely successful new restaurant and the biggest work yet of any collector of Arnoldi.

Fine art and sculpture merge into the interior, with the massive maple grid the dominating feature.

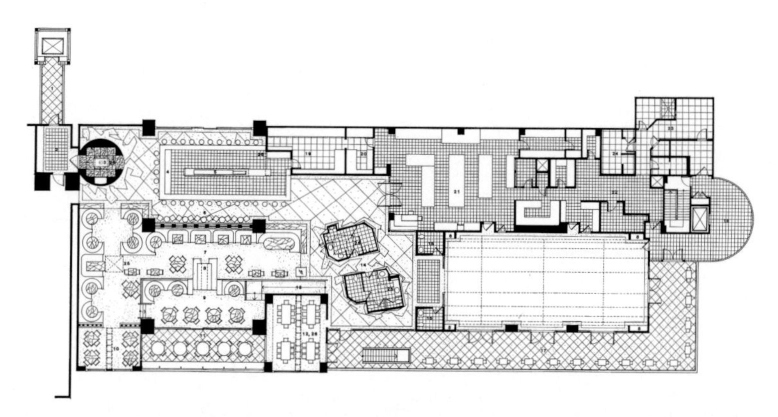

Furniture is primarily simple and functional: the art does not intrude on the eating.

The stucco sphere provides an introduction to DC3 that sharpens up visitors' visual sensitivity to the experience to follow.

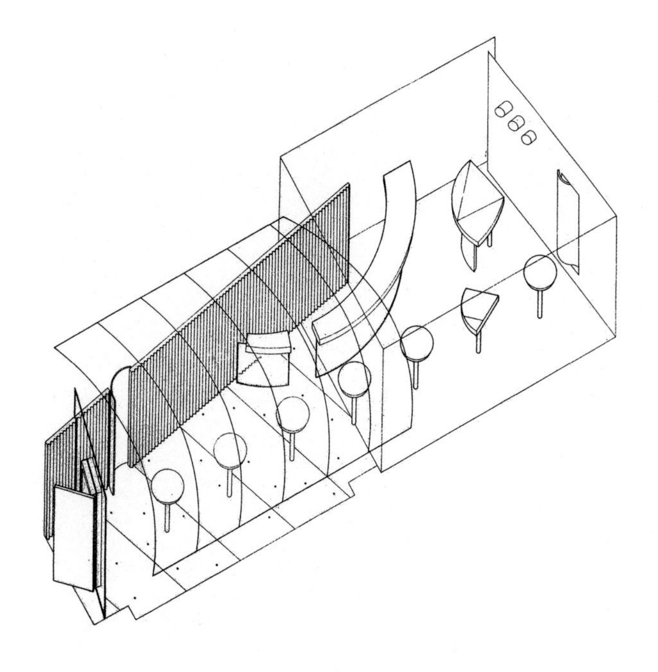

Shiro Kuramata

2.14 Comblé

Shizuoka-shi, Japan

The breadth of Kuramata's activities – from art to architecture, graphics to furniture – can be seen to underlie his approach to interiors. This small bar is as much a theoretical statement about the idea of place as a functional design: it has a beguiling simplicity that belies the innovation and precision of the detailing; it is concerned with metaphysical 'function' beyond the need to serve drinks in an enclosed space; it is refined almost to the point at which it is hard to see the interior working as a practical bar.

It is no coincidence that Kuramata should have worked with the Memphis group of designers, led by Ettore Sottsass. In Kuramata's work Sottsass sees 'rooms built by complicated systems of reflection and shadow, spaces designed not for substance but for allusions, surfaces crossed and worn away by flashes of bright neon, orders scanned by ambiguous rituals.' For Sottsass, Kuramata's work exists first and foremost as an intense three-dimensional essay on the climate of the times, presenting a form of self-consciousness in the interior where dreams, allusions and metaphors all play a part in realizing the purpose of the design.

This presumably explains why Kuramata is himself extremely wary of saying anything about his work. As to the brief, the purpose, the achievement of Comblé, Kuramata is reticent almost to the point of a vow of silence. As with the sushi restaurant Kiyotomo (see page 110), which he completed shortly before Comblé, he presents a neat backhander to any inquiries as to the particular practical issues involved in the design, saying 'all the conditions and obstacles are perfectly ideal for me.' But in the realization of the bar, in its warm colours and materials, its unassuming yet slightly strange forms, we can find a concern for engaging the user of the space in an awareness of an organic

The stark, hard surfaces of the bar are softened by the texturing and colouring of the materials.

relationship between people and the spaces they use. There is the suggestion of a soft, almost fleshy quality to Kuramata's materials: they confront our prejudices about the use and form of materials, the shape and texture of our environment.

In the treatment of walls and ceiling Kuramata worked partly with a material called OSB, a woodchip board transformed by the designer into a marble-like substance – from hard to soft, cheap to expensive – yet retaining a certain truth to material in that the chipboard remains clearly not marble. Anodized aluminum is also used for the walls and ceilings – a strange application that seems counter to any functional properties of the metal, yet the metal does not have the hard, engineered look of its more usual applications, but instead takes on a soft, decorative, and tactile appeal, a treatment accentuated by the semi-transparent polycarbonate shell that arches within the angular confines of the space.

The counter is another inversion of the expected in its use of materials. Constructed from a polyester-resin top and curved glass, it is a light, floating element where one might expect the kind of tough immovable form traditionally seen in a bar. And yet it is unmistakably the bar counter through formal allusions. The terrazzo, acrylic rods and LED display built into the floor similarly mix up traditional expectations and the unexpected to challenge our awareness of the components of an interior.

Such features see Kuramata stripping down elements of an interior to reveal the questions of identity within them, then recomposing the parts to retain enough distinguishing and functioning features while provoking the customer's sensitivity to the various elements. It may sound a complicated process, but, in fact, the result of such complex analysis seems to be a simplicity of forms, materials, and colours.

The use of transparent materials in the arched ceiling, frontage and bar counter lightens the bar and, with the minimal furnishings, creates a feeling of space.

The curving forms of the counter, arch, and tables give an impression of organic movement.

The clean lines and angles of the door are softened by the use of natural materials and a glimpse of the warm blue beyond.

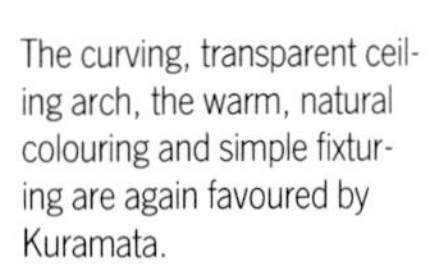

The curving, transparent ceiling arch, the warm, natural colouring and simple fixturing are again favoured by Kuramata.

The uncompromising exterior is very different to the transparent frontage of the Comblé bar, but the curving blue wall leads the customer inwards.

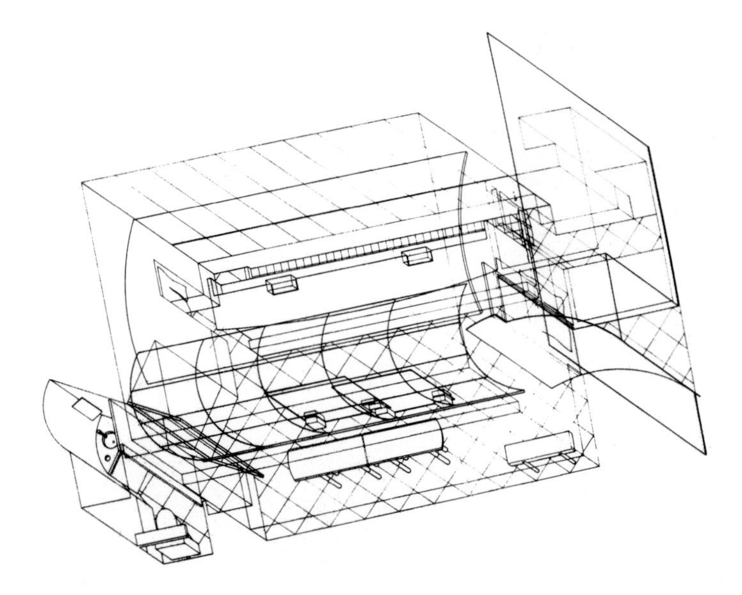

Shiro Kuramata

2.15 Kiyotomo Sushi Restaurant

Tokyo, Japan

Life is easy for Kuramata. His typical reaction to being asked what problems occur in a project is 'all the conditions and obstacles are ideal for me.' But how then does he know success? With this project the client was the chef Takanori Yoshioka, establishing a very direct relationship between the designer and the subject of the project. The brief was to create an environment in keeping with the nature of the food to be created by Yoshioka.

The results are at once both typically Japanese and yet reach for originality, a distinction from any other sushi restaurant. Even Kuramata may have a feeling that in some projects the requirements are more ideal than with others. The simplicity of the interior may disguise a refinement of detail, the search for the unique definitive form that seems to be involved in each aspect of Kuramata's project and tends towards the achievement of a rare clarity.

Here the floor is granite, the walls are straight-grained cedar, the ceiling cedar and acrylic, the partition opalized glass. The Ingo Maurer low-voltage lighting system YaYaHo provides the illumination; Maurer's pioneering work in developing the much copied bare wire and lightweight bracket being very much in the spirit of Kuramata's own interests.

The eclectic use of materials and styles typifies the restaurant interior. Here, hand-finished elements include the metal bar surround and the marble plaster effect.

Kalman's graphics provide lightweight amusement against the opulent elements of Beers' materials and forms.

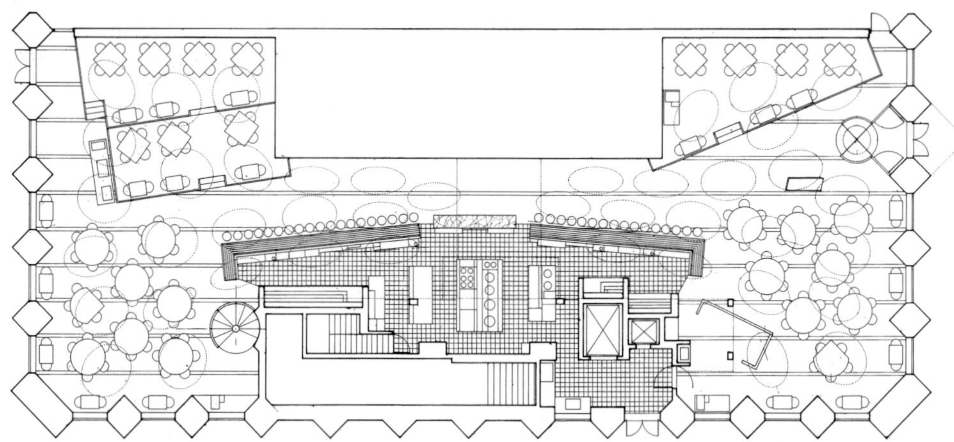

Beers' mushroom-shaped lighting canopies effectively disguise the massive beam that dramatically lowers the ceiling height by the bar.

Jeffrey G Beers Architects

2.16 China Grill

New York, USA

Situated on the ground floor of Eero Saarinen's CBS building in Manhattan, this Chinese/French restaurant had a design precedent to live up to. Unfortunately, it had to do this in a tunnel-like space that was almost split in two by a huge beam running across the center of the ceiling.

Previous restaurants in the location had been unsuccessful. They had tried having the bar in one half, the diners in the other. They had tried various cuisines. What was needed now was a radically different approach if China Grill was to attract a steady clientele and stay in business.

Jeffrey Beers' first, and possibly most significant, influence was to change the entrance from 52nd Street to 53rd Street, thereby picking up westbound traffic and attracting theater and museum goers. His approach to the interior was to treat the space as theatrically as possible, putting diners on different levels, and using the 'natural' split in the space by having the bar in the center. This neatly overcame the problem of the awkward beam.

The need to make a unique statement, to comment on New York art-culture sensibilities in an intriguing and rich manner, is displayed in numerous ways in this restaurant. The lighting and sculptural details were worked out at an early stage in the design. The 'cloud' light fixtures are made from airbrushed nylon stretched onto a rolled aluminum frame and change shape from round to oval as they appear to squeeze through the narrow central area. They also drop in height to help disguise the beam, as well as being at a height that has the effect of lowering the 20-foot (6-metre) ceiling to a more intimate level without losing the benefit of the natural light coming in through the tall windows.

There are many specially crafted features – indeed, only the chairs were not custom-made. Beers was influenced by the black granite elevator core wall designed by Saarinen, and sought to use this central feature as a guide in the selection of appropriate materials. Metal surfaces were hand finished with detail. The rubbed stainless steel kitchen hood, for example, has an almost three-dimensional pattern in its reflection of light. Six different metals with varying finishes were developed. Decorative and frosted glass was brought into the bar lighting, the standing screen and the purpose-built staircase. Saarinen's black granite was extended into China Grill's wall treatments, which also incorporated a number of special artist finishes.

This carefully crafted aspect is balanced by the more lighthearted side of China Grill's theatricality. The graphic design consultant Tibor Kalman introduced extracts from Marco Polo's travels (Marco Polo being the first Western sampler of Chinese cuisine) to decorate the lines that Beers had decided to run along floorboards. And the signs within the interior relate to the graphic program used for menus and other literature – a thoroughness of design integrity that is often missed.

The restaurant has been very popular since opening, overcoming the supposed 'problem' site and justifying the emphasis on a highly craft-conscious design. The costs were approximately $275 per square foot for this restaurant which covers an area of 6,000 square feet and seats 180 people.

Dramatic contrasts in colour and texture, and the bold separation of planes within the design distinguish the starkly functional nature of this bar.

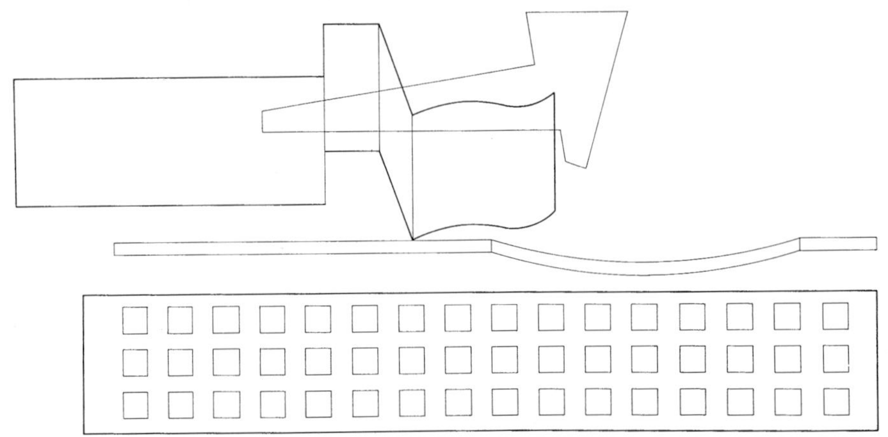

Lighting is used as a tool to reveal the precise sculpting of edges and to highlight elements, such as graphics, while drawing the eye away from less significant elements, such as the ceiling here.

Shigeru Uchida/Studio 80

2.17 Itchoh

Aoyama, Tokyo, Japan

This first of two bars designed by Uchida for the same client is located in the trendsetting Aoyama district of Tokyo where people in the fashion and design industries meet. The brief was to create a space for drinking and dancing.

The space seats 52 customers and is serviced by eight staff, four backstage in the kitchens. The design, typical of many innovative Japanese bars, maximizes the effect of comparatively small spaces – the coordinates that normally determine the feeling of the space are somehow stretched, while the quality of minimalist detailing draws attention to the richness of the particular rather than the whole.

Uchida created an aluminum partition at the entrance to set in motion this confusion of normal spatial relationships: both the larger architectural concerns of spatial character as well as the awareness of materials are intentionally disrupted by the intrusion of this screen. He says the partition 'is different from the simplified wall and furniture of the interior.' The screen displays an overt concern with exploring the relationship of the curve and the straight line, and also with bearing a clear presentation of tactile materials. Beyond, the environment is intended to be the opposite – a more neutral, elusive design that is a comfortable backdrop to the activities catered for within it.

For Uchida, the contrast between the entrance and the main part of the 'tavern' is a device that helps explore the relationship between order and chaos – the underlying abstract concern of any design. He believes that customers do not necessarily have much impression of the interior of this bar, as it is intentionally balanced to meet their expectations. But the introductory screen creates a moment of conflict that produces an awareness of the transition between order and chaos.

Despite the ambitious ideas, the design and materials are comparatively simple in their final execution. The floor is coloured concrete, walls and ceiling are sprayed paint, the benches and cashier counter are stained nara wood, and downlighting is used throughout.

Warm colours and heavy slabs of timber furniture produce a modern reinterpretation of the characteristics of the tavern.

Although the structural elements and furniture are over-scale they establish a basis for the tavern aesthetic.

The false wall-thickness is intentionally revealed with the carefully detailed inset around this beam, without compromising the sense of a strong, enclosed space.

Shigeru Uchida/Studio 80

2.18 Itchoh

Roppongi, Tokyo, Japan

This tavern takes further Uchida's work for the earlier Itchoh bar, with the aim of combining a highly populist aesthetic with more refined abstract ideals about space. The location is hugely disadvantaged – the building is set back from the street and the bar is on the third floor. The culture of the more usual basement bar was clearly inappropriate; Uchida had to find a way of exploiting the location of a bar that was above ground and within a larger structure, and that was popular.

Perhaps the most immediate strong elements of the design are the predominant colour of the interior and the playful 'structure.' The colour of the wall and ceiling of sprayed paint (somewhere between orange and yellow) provides warmth and is a radical departure for Uchida's previous almost total reliance on gray. The architectural elements of columns, beams and windows are brought into play by exaggerated (and partly mock) fabrication, as well as the faint suggestion of a classical form.

'Creating effective windows required ingenuity,' comments Uchida. 'The existing structural windows of the building were uninteresting, non-designed openings. Yet we were not allowed to make alterations to the structure.' Uchida sought to create a domestic feel partly by putting in double windows, and the deep sill helps create a protected 'cosiness' to the interior.

One important element in creating a friendly, domestic environment was to have an open kitchen, but this posed problems with revealed ducting. The way around this was to incorporate ducts into part of the structural grid of the ceiling, assisted by false beams. Thus, basic functional elements such as the water supply, air and sewage ducts are expressed as grand elements determining the spatial characteristics.

Materials are slightly upgraded from the earlier Itchoh bar; marble tile is used for the floor and partition wall, metallic silver paint creates an ambivalent cool/warm feeling to the columns and 'beams' – they are visually cool, but not in tactile terms. Nara wood is used for the benches and tables.

The three-dimensional structure and two-dimensional mural merge, as Iosa Ghini's interior slips in and out of its graphic extension.

Unexpected angles in all elements of the design suggest properties in items such as the chair that counteract normal gravitational forces.

Massimo Iosa Ghini

2.19 Bolido

New York, USA

The style of Italian restaurant and bars has provided an international architectural type: it calls to mind clarity and firmness of materials – terrazzo, metal, hard woods – with a functional rigour offset by such details as a bowl of fruit waiting to be squeezed for fresh juice. Moving down market, however, the straw-clad Chianti bottles hanging from the ceiling are the most powerful association.

Against these preconceptions Iosa Ghini's client, Co. Ge. Com. of Milan, owner of a number of clubs in Italy, wanted to open a distinctive club/restaurant in New York that promoted a recognizable yet original Italian image. The choice of Iosa Ghini as designer was an interesting one, supporting a vision of Italian design that was one of the most identifiable to come out of the last years of the Memphis group. The client wanted the new club to reject the classic Italian image abroad, and instead present a concept drawn more closely from the reality of contemporary Italian culture.

The location was previously a venue called Cafe Roma, that existed as a single space. Iosa Ghini knocked through walls and restructured the area to provide a small upstairs restaurant, with a dance area and bar downstairs. The curved staircase that descends dramatically into the middle of the main floor emphasizes this division of the space; the linking of the two levels is made to have an almost precarious quality, the staircase as a large curved ladder.

In executing the functional program of the club, this scheme can be seen to relate to what may be called the 'club type:' dividing up the louder and quieter areas with different floors, putting a bar under the mezzanine, having a conversation area wrapping around a long bar. But Iosa Ghini gives full rein to his own visions in the driving imagery of the environment. This is partly through the massive mural elements that present the designer's almost science-fiction view of a possible world: I say 'almost' because in Bolido Iosa Ghini has also begun to realize that world.

One of the major premises for the design of the club was for it to be a 'culture-orientated project,' with the club existing not only to present the new 'Italian' image but to serve as a base for the promotion of 'Bolidist' furniture (which is being sold in the USA through Palazzeti Inc.). Thus the questions of space, form and even time (what period is projected by the paintings – a past vision or a future world?) that are posed by Iosa Ghini's visions extend from two-dimensional art into three-dimensional actuality. The bizarre streamlined bar, for example, is suggestive of both Art Deco and 1950s sci-fi movies and yet is entirely at home in the late 1980s clubland. The bar stool next to it similarly seems to embrace a range of references to other stools while creating a unique form of its own.

When taken together, the paintings and the furniture present an artificial environment that unites a range of mechanistic and anthropomorphic aspects. The unpredictable angles, especially the break with the right angle, suggest movement rather than stasis, with a tension often set up against the force of gravity: the cantilevered edge of the bar, or the stools, along with other details extend the more adventurous distortions apparent in the mural.

The 6,458 square-foot (600 square-metre) project was completed to a budget of 1,000 million lire (around $695,000).

Exaggerated details are more than just decoration, in that they contribute to the constant sense of dislocation promoted by the design.

Right and opposite 1950s-style, science-fiction fantasies become real as Iosa Ghini streamlines and exaggerates a whole range of specially made furniture.

The Velvet logo glows mysteriously as an inset within the pavement outside one of the entrance doors.

Plan showing the two entrances/exits that give an unexpected depth and movement within the narrow shape of the site.

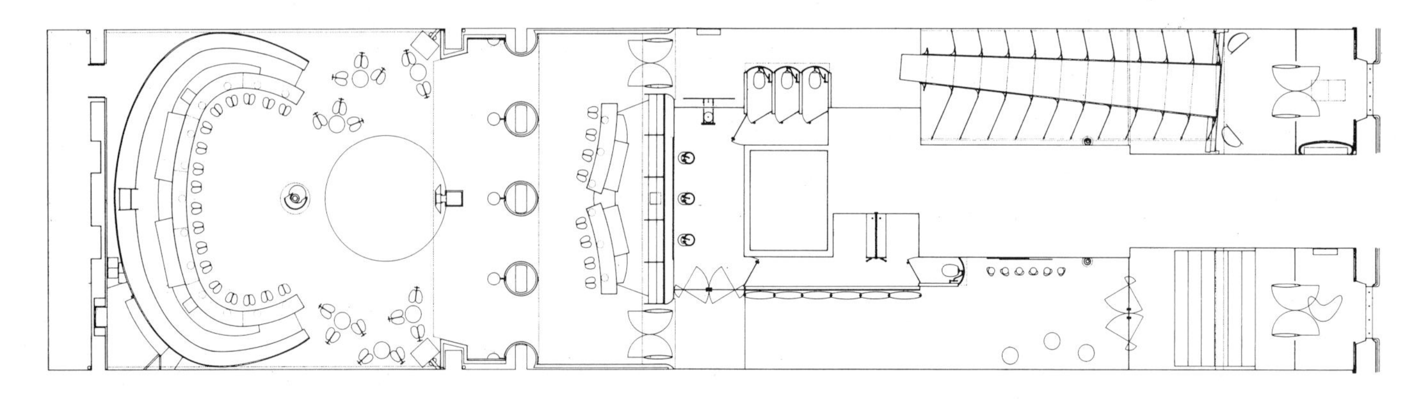

Light is poured over materials in differing ways to create a range of changing effects within the club.

Alfredo Arribas Arquitectos Asociados

2.20 Velvet Bar

Barcelona, Spain

If one of the motives of designers is to leave a memorable impression of their work on the visitor, Alfredo Arribas can claim to be setting the pace and a more memorable experience would be hard to conceive than a visit to the toilets in the Velvet nightclub. On entry, an infra-red light detects the visitor's arrival. It activates an electro-valve and water starts to flow into a glass box passing through thick coloured liquid. After a few moments, a stroboscope starts up, and if movement is continued in the toilets, the 'entertainment' is continued. The effect on the function of the space is unreported, but this interaction of form and user is an extreme of the whole design program.

Arribas describes Velvet as 'a game, a reaction.' It combines elements that suggest an atmosphere of space that is both nostalgic, a period interior, and yet is unseen, strange and new. There is a feeling of an old science-fiction movie, combined with a 1950s nightclub. It is self-consciously baroque, an amalgamation of influences, an entertainment in the design as well as in the function. Arribas admits to using the project 'as an excuse to wake one up and follow an ill-frequented path.'

The space is essentially in three parts: two entrance areas and the bar area. Yet the profusion of sundry objects and unpredictable forms within the design ensures that the vision of how the spaces work is fragmented. There is an overall impression, yet the experience of passing through is meant to change constantly as different details come to the attention. Curved and irregular forms, alterations in sections and floors, small optical tricks all collaborate in this.

Arribas sums up the effect as creating from this variety almost a sense of chaos but mitigating it by an attempt at an underlying architectonic orderliness. There is also the consistency of interest in the tactile nature of an environment. Materials such as slate, teak, different metals, glazed and gilded surfaces celebrate the idea of the joy in the skin of a place (in sharp contrast to most architectural approaches) and this culminates in the use of velvet as a material and a name.

The planning of the club is not so overcome with its celebration of the experience of space as to ignore the more basic physical requirements of the customers, however. There are two bars, one quiet and intimate, one more provocative with an oval dance floor that culminates in a central sculpture around a pillar. This plaster column is almost a totem at the heart of the club, a point of arrival and of reference.

The floors throughout the club are primarily slate and concrete. Walls are as found, painted plaster, with columns and fragments standing out in stone. The ceiling is in part as found as well, but painted, with a special curved plaster feature in the main room and perforated slabs elsewhere. Low-voltage spots are used in the lighting with specially designed supports, some featuring alabaster as the diffuser. All furniture was custom-designed, with a Carlo Mollino design being adapted and developed for chairs and stools. Graphics were designed by Juli Capella and Quim Larrea.

This entrance/exit contrasts sharply to the other, creating different moods and experiences for different times within Velvet.

The two cloakrooms share these specially designed wash units that draw on well and fountain imagery.

Below right The dance floor becomes a stage before the mini-auditorium of the bar seating.

Below Tactile and organic concerns in the Velvet aesthetic are displayed in the main dance area, with chairs that are split to reflect the symmetry of the body, while the column is wrapped in a timber cloak.

Comme des Garçons Shirt, Kawakubo, Kondo Mori (see p. 132)

3 Shops, Showrooms, & Retail Centers

1 **Eduard Samso**
Marcel, *Barcelona, Spain* 128

2 **Rei Kawakubo, Yasuo Kondo & Toshiko Mori**
Comme des Garçons Shirt, *New York, USA* 132

3 **Studio Citterio Dwan**
Esprit, *Antwerp, Belgium* 134

4 **Studio Citterio Dwan**
Esprit, *Amsterdam, Holland* 136

5 **Foster Associates**
Esprit, *London, UK* 140

6 **Building**
Ecru, *Los Angeles, USA* 142

7 **Din Associates**
Department X, *London, UK* 146

8 **Shigeru Uchida/Studio 80**
Conversation, *Tokyo, Japan* 148

9 **Nicholas Tedford & Claudio Nardi**
Sbaiz, *Lignano Sabbiadoro, Italy* 150

10 **Pawson Silvestrin**
Cannelle, *London, UK* 154

11 **Iijima Naoki**
Sonia Rykiel, *Tokyo, Japan* 156

12 **Eva Jiricna Architects**
Joseph, *London, UK* 158

13 **David Davies Associates**
Oliver, *Rome, Italy* 162

14 **Sanzin Kim**
Kenzo Homme, *Tokyo, Japan* 164

15 **Eva Jiricna Architects**
Joan & David, *Los Angeles, USA* 166

16 **Tadao Ando**
Galleria Akka, *Osaka, Japan* 168

17 **Christopher Connell**
Théâtre Végétal, *Melbourne, Australia* 170

18 **Katsuhiko Togashi**
Cinderella 12, *Tokushima-Ken, Japan* 174

19 **Stanton Williams**
Issey Miyake, *London, UK* 176

20 **Richard Rogers Partnership**
Magasin d'Usine, *Nantes, France* 178

21 **Setsuo Kitaoka**
The Body & Bath Shop, *Tokyo, Japan* 180

The main basement salon uses reflectivity and contrasting textures to break down the enclosed nature of the space.

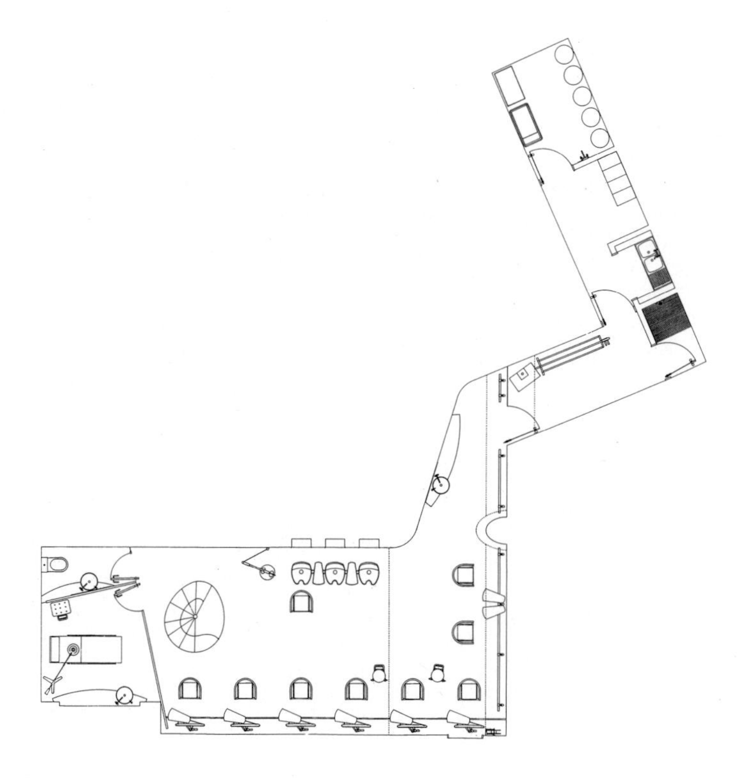

Eduard Samso

3.1 Marcel

Barcelona, Spain

The spirit of Gaudi lives on in this interior by Samso – although it is hard to imagine how that pious architect may have felt about tackling a project that involved giving an original identity to a hairdressing salon in a shopping center. But the requirements of the brief drew a confident response from Samso. In the unpredictable curves of the plan, and the use of broken ceramic white tiles on the walls, the Gaudi influence is apparent, yet there is much more than a borrowing of style at work here.

The location of the site made it difficult to conceive that such dramatic expression could emerge from it: its position in the shopping center meant there was only a small entrance at street level, with most of the space being in the basement. This position was deliberately chosen within the center as it had an unusual plan due to the fact that it was 'residual' space – a peripheral area that had been used to route a large number of service pipes for other parts of the building. Finding a way of either disguising or avoiding these pipes was a major problem.

Samso responded to this awkwardness by using the entrance point as a showcase that simply presented the atmosphere, the style of Marcel. With the shop located on Diagonal, a busy and fashionable street, the entrance area needed to announce Marcel as a distinctly original, intriguing and pleasing place to book into. The design of the reception suggests the environment of the interior, but makes a virtue of its small space by avoiding having hairdressing on show: most customers would prefer to have greater privacy than is often afforded in a salon, and here Samso provides it.

The strange fluid forms of the plan, and the roughness of materials used in finishing surfaces, are immediately striking. Samso aimed for a contrast of the smooth form with the rough texture, and planned a transition from a more 'upfront' tough appearance on entry to a softer environment in the basement. In his own words, 'The transition is shown in the shapes of the different spaces and the sophisticated forms of the movable mirrors.'

Walls are covered in a range of materials – broken white tiles, metal plates, plaster and mirrors. The ceiling is of metal plates and plaster. This represents a change from his initial design proposal in which he wanted the walls and ceilings partly to be painted dark blue. The floor was finally covered in slabs of white laminate, although Samso had originally wanted this to be covered in more broken white tiles, which would have created a much stronger, strange environment.

The consistency of the interior is a sophisticated response to a highly exacting brief. The client had specified requirements for a whole range of different spaces: besides the main hairdressing and washing area (which he wanted as large as possible), he also wanted a separate reception area, an area for selling products, a cabin for cosmetic application, a restroom, a shower, a laboratory, and an area for storage. All this in an awkward, leftover site. Samso's fresh thinking, from plan through to the numerous one-off specially designed elements, transformed these difficulties into advantages.

Brushed steel and stone for the staircase contrast with the lightness of the design which plays with the effect of which element is supporting the step.

Industrial styling and components are brought into the custom-designed furniture.

Riveted metal plates and broken tiles draw on the Art Nouveau tradition of Barcelona architecture.

Walls are left bare of fittings, with mirrors and shelving incorporated into freestanding units.

The sinks appear to be chained together by the metal fittings, from which the translucent trays seem to float free.

The narrow site is accentuated by the lighting and air-conditioning design, while the merchandising is presented as sculptural forms offering up a minimal display of products.

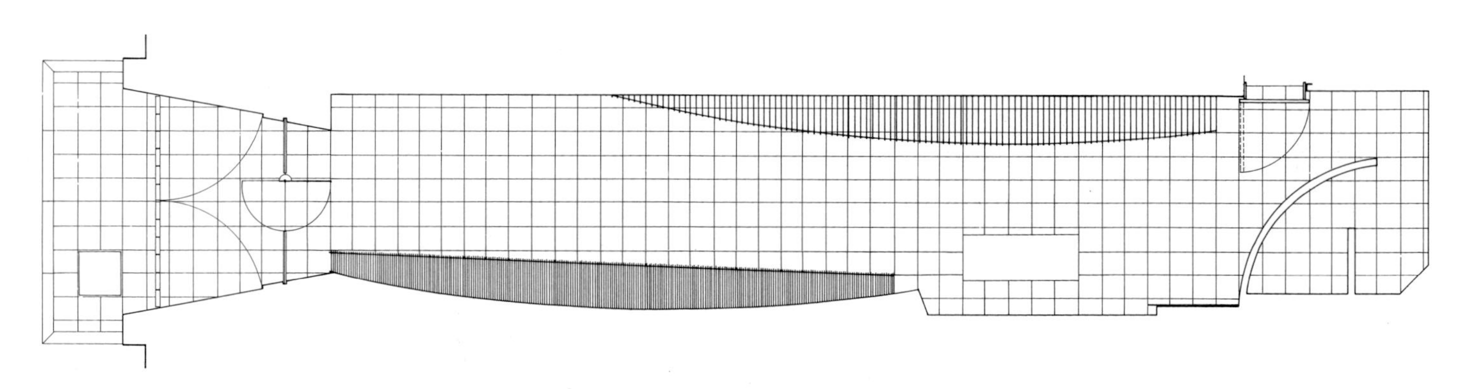

Starkly defined elements, including the clear bar-shape of the shop, present a coordinated and contrasting image, making an impact on the street.

Rei Kawakubo, Yasuo Kondo & Toshiko Mori

3.2 Comme des Garçons Shirt

New York, USA

The exacting standards of this client's requirements are displayed by the design credit: the concept derives from the creative leadership of Comme des Garçons' Japanese designer Rei Kawakubo, is carried through the Tokyo-based designer Yasuo Kondo, before being implemented by the New York-based Japanese architect Toshiko Mori. At the basis of the brief is the challenge of launching a new brand from an established image, in this case, of a store entirely devoted to just one item of clothing from the Comme des Garçons range – shirts.

Located on Broadway, the store provides a strong contrast with the bustling surrounding. The façade has a steel gate that covers the frontage when the shop is closed, and that, when open, relates to the space within by framing the form and accentuating the depth of the site. The gate makes the entrance narrower than the space beyond, emphasizing the extensiveness of the interior.

The long space within is developed as a series: the fixtures, shelving and hanging units are designed to be 'read' as a story that leads customers on. These are much more than simple, functional, display units, which often exist in a relatively unplanned relationship in many shops. Here, they create a passage through the store and an awareness of the interior as a form of sculpture.

The space is lit indirectly and softly, with the pools of light on the ceiling. Materials are kept simple, but are just different enough to create an awareness of the design decision. Flat-rolled latex on plaster and wood is used for the wall and ceiling finishes, with polished blue marble on the floor. This follows the white enamel of the façade and gate. The fixtures are sprayed aluminum.

Such simplicity and the self-conscious presentation of the interior details draw the attention to appreciating the design approach and, it would be hoped, the difference between an exceedingly expensive Comme des Garçons shirt from the more commonplace cloth found on most backs.

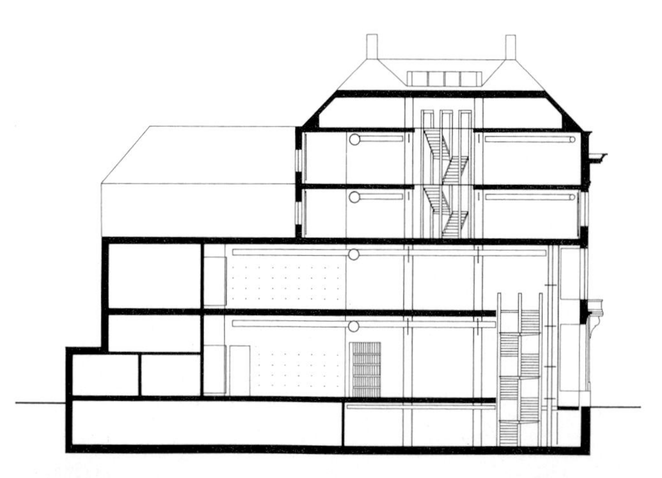

Citterio's perforated-metal stair system gives a consistent dramatic identity to the Esprit stores he has designed.

Concrete and steel create a furniture of the computer age, but the high levels of natural light ensure the environment does not become oppressive.

Studio Citterio Dwan

3.3 Esprit

Antwerp, Belgium

It would be easy to confuse this project with the very similar Esprit headquarters store in Amsterdam (page 136), or with the other Citterio-designed Esprit building in Milan (page 32): the overpowering use of perforated, zinc-coated steel mesh and structure inserted into the concrete building frame; the dramatic cutting away of floors to create double- and triple-height voids; and the large window areas and hard artificial lighting.

For some interiors, the sense of similarity with another project would be a criticism: here it can be seen as a virtue, at least in terms of satisfying the client. By having devised such a strong program of store design, which neatly reflects the modern, high-priced and elegant street-style nature of the clothing and other products sold by Esprit, Antonio Citterio and Terry Dwan have helped define the retail identity of the company. Earlier stores by Sottsass Associates gave a substantially different expression to Esprit, which was also appropriate to the products. Times and fashions change, and Esprit has thus moved onto a more mature style of neo-industrial aesthetic to reflect products that are themselves often derived from earlier periods of workwear and work accessories.

The Antwerp project has many similarities with the Amsterdam store. An eighteenth-century building on a piazza and major shopping street was gutted and fitted out to include a store on three levels (10,656 square feet; 990 square metres), a trade showroom and dining room (6,458 square feet; 600 square metres), and offices (2,260 square feet; 210 square metres). The new internal structure is devised around 400-millimetre steel columns and trusses that produce a three-dimensional grid. This is expressed outwardly in the layering of a new façade that allows the old façade to be perceived beyond, but creates also the drama of an entrance ramp with a huge display screen.

The adaptation of the façade was carried out to develop a greater awareness of the store from the piazza, giving it the two faces required of a corner building. This awareness in turn generates ideas for the circulation patterns predicted for the interior.

If Citterio/Dwan's intervention to an historic building seems abrupt, this is countered with the merit of being clearly readable: as they explain, 'Powerful gestures are expressed with the desire to contrast with the existing fabric.' Rather than echoing earlier forms, or presenting hi-tech arguments, Citterio/Dwan see their design as setting out to satisfy the client's functional needs and to pose questions about the relationship of elements, and the relationship of the store to the street and piazza.

Great attention is given to refining details, to honesty of materials and to achieving a 'high-build' quality. Citterio and Dwan describe the approach as that of 'engineer philosophers' rather than being hi-tech.

The project was carried out in collaboration with local architect Werner de Bondt.

Citterio's use of perforated metal sheeting achieves a dramatic expression here with a massive, yet light-weight staircase structure.

The main entrance features a ramp over a void that runs between three floors of Afrikahuis, with the principal cash desk beyond.

Studio Citterio Dwan

3.4 Esprit

Amsterdam, Holland

Esprit Afrikahuis has swiftly become a key point in central Amsterdam, so well does it meet the need to provide a powerfully theatrical store and cafe that address both a major pedestrianized shopping street and also a square.

The client began with the need to have a launch and general headquarters for Esprit Benelux. This called for a multipurpose building, which needed to provide a strong reference point for the development of the Esprit image as more stores were planned in Benelux countries. A handsome, later nineteenth-century building, originally a furniture showroom and workshop, was acquired with a site of importance to Amsterdam's shopping area: Afrikahuis is close to the main pedestrianized Kalverstraat and faces onto a space formed from a canal filled in in 1882 and a deep piazza. This piazza was the scene of student protests in the 1960s; this, together with the transient, youth-orientated nature of the area, clearly influences the design. Further influence is provided by the fact that the steel-frame structure takes its name from the West Afrika Line steamship company that occupied it in the 1950s.

As is so often the case, a rich, assorted past often means the retention of a few scars: in the case of Afrikahuis, the steel structure had been coated with cement. The division of floors and some of the external expression had also lost any honest meaning for Citterio. He claimed that, initially, 'it was impossible to capture the old "memory" of the building with its structure made of iron, its columns. Then I came upon the idea of restoring the iron frame on the inside. And right away I could envisage the design of the building.'

The building encloses 32,292 square feet (3,000 square metres) on seven floors. A basement, and the ground, mezzanine and first floors comprise the public area of the store. The second and third floors are designed for buyers' use, showroom and affiliated offices. The top two floors are Esprit Benelux headquarters. All three areas are linked by the dynamic steel forms of the circulation structure – stairs, catwalks and ramps. But the store area is the showpiece of Citterio's dramatic contribution: appropriately, he also sees the store as 'a kind of stage on which performances are given, according to the changing seasons and the changing fashions.'

The use of a three-story screen, 12 metres high, in the store is an example of this approach. It floats past the footbridges and elevators, carrying small mannequins that play on the scale of the structure. It can be changed easily to dramatize new collections. The cement wall on which shoes are placed is another out-of-scale element, massive and more reminiscent of a factory aesthetic (indeed, it was manufactured by a firm that prefabricates panels used in constructing factories).

Citterio sees his partnership with American architect Terry Dwan as highly influential in developing ideas on how to exaggerate design and experiment with out-of-scale elements. He cites, as reference for their exploitation of this play on scale, references from architectural history, and 'the

Varieties of finish and fixing give a wealth of character to the insistently metallic interior of many areas within the store.

hands, the feet on Michelangelo's paintings are always out of scale.'

The staircase and ramps perhaps most strongly exploit this method of creating dramatic tension: they have a massive structure and yet are heavily perforated – absence of matter is, ironically, one of their strongest ways of expressing their substance. A modernist concern for the clarity of individual elements was also a major factor, the junctions of ceilings, walls and floors being made as deliberate and clean as possible. It is a celebration of jointing, however, that has more in common with Scarpa then with Mies.

The small space of the Esprit cafe onto the piazza illustrates the ability of Citterio and Dwan to scale down the elements while retaining the qualities of design. Here the purpose is not to display goods, but, rather, to display people – relating them to the piazza and to the youth culture outside, thus making the cafe an advertisement for the store and an incentive for customers to enter.

Purpose-built furniture and display systems reinforce the distinctive design. They are not only appropriate to the aesthetic, but also have a quality of individual detailing that fully demonstrates Citterio's strong record in furniture design. The forms of the air conditioning 'mushroom' diffusers suggest the allusion to the factory, but have been executed with a care that exceeds the design detail quality found in most store interiors.

The Afrikahuis project crystallizes a heightened industrial aesthetic that Citterio has made his own, diverging substantially in character from the hi-tech work of, for example, Foster and Rogers. Citterio is a connoisseur of the design detail of the industrial age: in Afrikahuis he explores its potential as an altogether appropriate backdrop for the drama of youth culture and youth-culture products that, themselves, draw on industrial clothing and materials for expression.

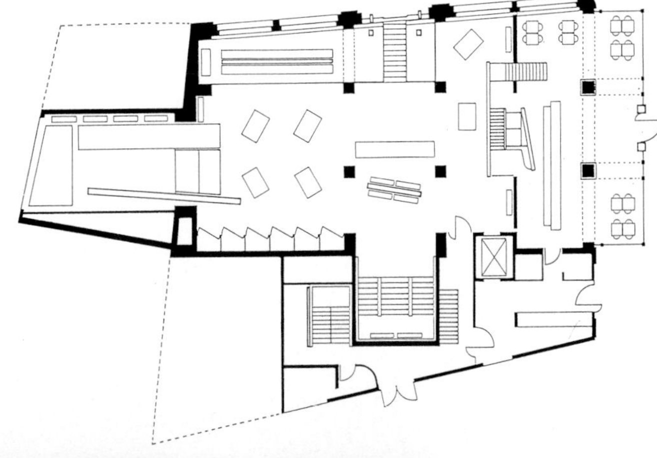

Office areas keep the core drama of the steel staircase and industrial air conditioning funnels while softening the environment with carpeting and less obtrusive lighting.

The identity of the main store extends into the adjoining cafe, although Citterio's chairs soften the industrial aesthetic.

The surfaces of polished concrete, steel, and glass are given texture by precise lighting.

The incongruously 'industrial' construction for the display and storage system creates an entertaining character for the shop.

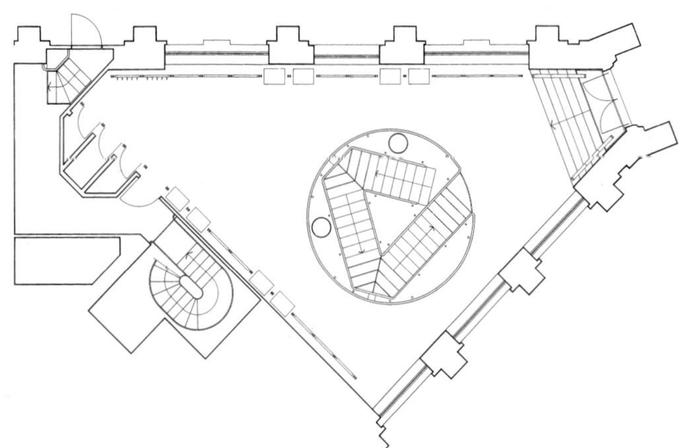

By the time Esprit asked Norman Foster to design its first London store, there existed a formidable image that had to be maintained. How would Foster's 'hi-tech' approach fit with the earlier tradition of exotic Memphis-style interiors set up by Sottsass Associates? Not only was there this distance between the image of the architect and that of the client, but the site of the new store provided a further irony: Foster was being asked to convert the very same space that he had designed for the first Joseph store a decade earlier. If nothing else, the result would give an interesting perspective on how Foster Associates' work had developed.

The teaming of Esprit with Joseph and the prime Sloane Street location provided a range of intriguing problems as to how to express the identity of the store, making a new statement and yet building on the brand values of the clients. There was also the not inconsiderable task of getting any innovative ideas passed by the landlords and the planners. Furthermore, there was the basic design challenge in

Upstairs the store displays are kept to the perimeter, where they also function as window displays, and permit customers to walk around unobstructed.

Foster Associates

3.5 Esprit

London, UK

making the most functional use of the tight triangular floor space generated by the corner site, with ground floor and basement combined amounting only to approximately 2,000 square feet (186 square metres).

Foster Associates' response to these demands centers on a dramatic use of the staircase linking the two floors. The dominance of the stairwell void on the plan, its central position as a core cut out of the triangular store, is so intrusive as to make the elements of construction become more clearly readable to any visitor. Instead of there being a main space with a basement below – a great problem for many retailers if they want customers to circulate throughout – this design breaks down the differences between floors.

This is aided by the staircase being a carefully crafted, one-off work fabricated from glass, stainless steel and mild steel. The mannered design takes on an almost sculptural significance: stairs of 25 millimetre thick, sandblasted glass are silicon bonded to stainless steel frames that are in turn bolted onto the main painted steel structure. Stainless steel tube hand rails complete this strong but elegant focus point of the store.

The display system specially developed for the site is a bold solution to the unusual location. Tall windows extending around two thirds of the store's perimeter could be considered a drawback when it comes to finding storage space, but this design ensures that they are instead an asset. Display and storage are pushed to the edge of the floors and contained in a steel racking structure carrying birch-faced panels. Great flexibility in the arrangement of the elements allows varied interior displays and window dressing (which are one and the same in the way the windows work). This gantry exists as a form of set construction, a theatrical element enabling the maximization of the display potential of the clothes for sale without allowing interior space to be used solely for window dressing.

The theatrical analogy can be extended to the appreciation of the benefits of Foster Associates' strict palette of colours and textures for the basic elements of the structure. Natural finishes, raw concrete, unpainted metal and timber help provide a simple stage setting in which the clothes become the performance. The introduction of a new season's goods into the store can have the effect of the opening of a new act. The highly adaptable lighting system reinforces this potential for creating varied effects, staging the show.

With such flexibility and durability the comparatively high cost of the project, £775,000 ($1,240,000) – leaving little change out of £400 ($640) a square foot – may be justified. And if Esprit lasts as long as Foster's Joseph, it should outlive many other fashion interiors.

Angled wood screens are simple dividers of the space and the lighting marks out patterns for circulation.

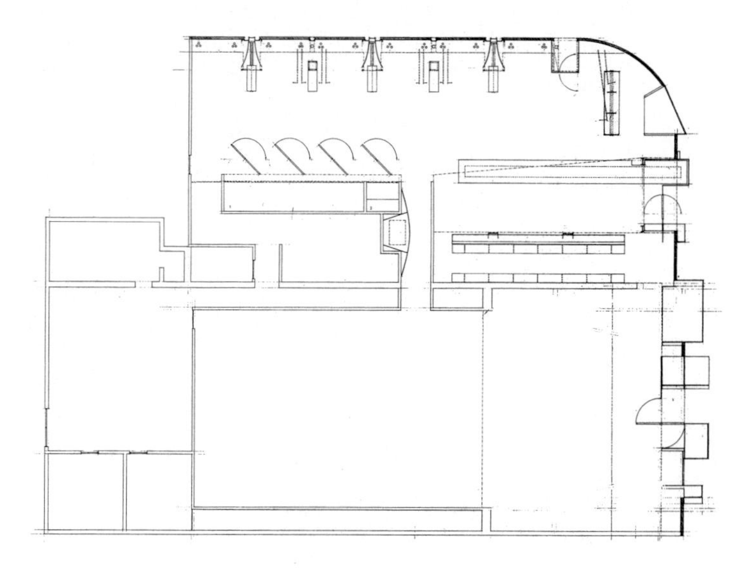

Building

3.6 Ecru

Los Angeles, USA

Successful retail design involves an awareness of architecture as advertising. From the outside the 'unique selling proposition' must be apparent, and inside this must continue, through to the point of purchase. From then on, the products must be responsible for their own persuasion. Such awareness is well displayed by the designers of Building in this shoe and clothing store that sits on the fashionable Melrose Avenue.

Designer Michele Saee describes the road as 'one of the few walking streets of L.A.' and he and his colleagues Richard Lundquist, Max Massie and David Lindberg took full advantage of this position in producing a frontage that shouts the presence of Ecru at the same time as integrating the exterior with the interior and drawing visitors in. Co-owner of the shop, Ken Fasola, gives testament to the success of this storefront: 'Everybody who walks past, walks in.' The secret appears to be in having made the front window an event in the street; its construction of letters 16 feet (5 metres) high, spelling out the store name, is three-dimensional, a sign that is a sculpture and, on entry, also a piece of architecture.

Inside the store the reverse volumes of the steel and glass window help form the interior expression, the construction merging into display counters and also making a conscious impression on shoppers by its control of the light from outside.

The strategy of strong, almost brutal forms extends throughout the 7,000 square-foot (650 square-metre) store in the specially designed display cases and lighting fixtures, the steel and glass aesthetic being maintained. The cost was finally $420,000.

The inspiration for the design was derived in part from the idea used to manipulate the view from within the store: a decision to reduce a side window to mere slits, that revealed nearby trees rather than cars, seems to have fueled the whole concept to invite shoppers to have a 'blinkered' view. Ironically, so radical was the method of constructing this narrow view on life for this store that the contractors refused to tackle the installation of the main window. It was left to the designers and their helpers to execute this idea by their own hand.

Building's work on this project comes as a development of ideas displayed in the Trattoria Angeli restaurant (see page 72). There the designers saw as important the task of relating a space to a street that people did not walk down; with Ecru it was the converse. Both display an understanding of the importance of controlling perception of the world outside an interior.

The dramatic staging of minimalist product displays is a feature of this environment.

Saee's seats further explore the relationship between timber and metal that occurs throughout Ecru.

In this design, steel becomes a soft element that seems to work in a similar way to timber in texture and function.

An open floor space allows Saee to overlay different forms – lighting fixtures, display cases, and screens – without creating clutter.

Cracked floors and welding burns are happily incorporated into the scheme, alongside burnished wood finishes and the traditional design of 'imported' oriental rugs.

The double-height glazing and massive logo, together with a mechanized window display and massive door, give the shop a unique impact in the already busy Oxford-Street context.

Industrial materials – such as steel floor plates and walkways – are combined with new display devices designed by Din Associates, that play with the industrial aesthetic.

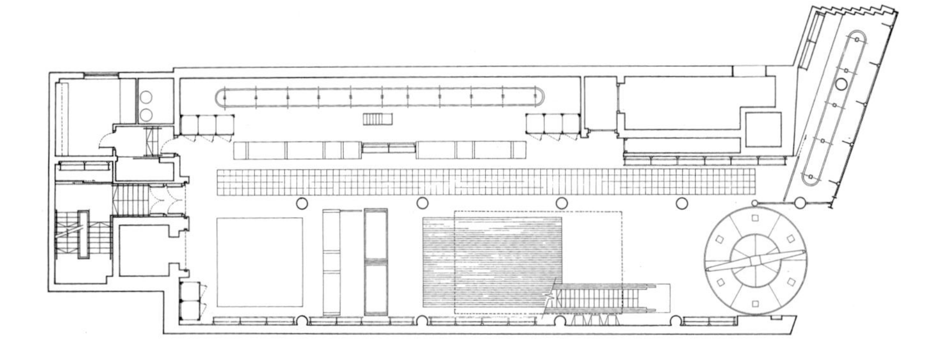

Innovation was the brief for this project. In order to develop a method for retailing that was startlingly different, and to target it at the volatile mix of young shoppers who parade along Oxford Street in London, designer Rasshied Ali Din and his team were inspired to rethink how the fashion store works.

Din had already carried out a number of prestigious projects for the client, Next plc, and had helped develop the identity of their various chains of stores which seem to have a place on every major high street in Britain and have been influential on other retailers. But in this project he was being asked to explore and produce what would become a new step in retailing.

The result draws on ideas from the whole process of product distribution. Department X presents an industrial aesthetic that takes many of its key design elements from warehouse systems. The 13,000 square-foot space (1,209 square metres) comprises two floors in what was a featureless 1960s building. It is signalled from the street by a giant double-height

French galvanized chairs and ceramic tiles give a slightly different style to the upstairs cafe, without breaking the aggressive and fun style that is the shop's identity.

Din Associates

3.7 Department X

London, UK

steel 'X' in the window. A massive revolving wood and metal door with windows inset is also a distinguishing feature: when closed it produces a sense of great solidity, when open it provides a large entrance, through which to draw shoppers in. On first-floor level the partly open, partly glazed terrace cafe is visible as a further attraction for passers-by.

Once inside, the industrial flavour is set by several computer-controlled stock systems that are lifted from warehouse usage: many of the clothes are carried on two huge revolving tracks, one on the ground floor for menswear and one on the first floor for ladies. Shoes are displayed on a paternoster rack that revolves between floors. Besides giving a striking image to the store, these systems also ensure highly efficient use of space: a lot of stock can be carried, and the need for stock rooms is obviated.

Side benefits of these systems include a low rate of theft. This seems to be due not only to the fact that items have to be obtained via staff from the systems, but also to a reduction in opportunity for staff to steal from the stock room. A further benefit is that expensive high street square footage is not given over to stock rooms. Thirdly, saving is also made through the efficient distribution of goods, which requires fewer sales staff.

The industrial concept is reinforced by the materials used, without loss of awareness of the need for an attractive and warm environment. Din Associates designed a range of shelving and freestanding units from mild steel that pick up on the factory aesthetic, and oak-paneled fitting rooms that provide a more friendly, intimate and quality-orientated atmosphere for the customer who is trying on clothes and is considering buying.

Essentially, however, the environment is tough, bright, and active. The floors are primarily concrete screed with merbau hard wood and mild steel tiles inset, as well as terrazzo. Structural elements, concrete and steel, are revealed. The walls are either raw pink carlite plaster or covered with the coarse industrial feel of acrylic paint. Glass elements introduce a sense of lightness – reeded glass for screens and glass walkways bridging gallery areas on the first floor. The cafe maintains the aesthetic with features such as galvanized chairs that are ideal for the mixed indoor and outdoor use.

Besides the moving storage systems, there are also large revolving graphics, videos and flashing lights. As Din remarks, 'The environment as a whole offers a fantastical shopping trip.' He adds that the designers' initial ideas had been 'less mechanical' than the final results as they had not been confident that all the machinery could be obtained on time and to budget (some was from overseas). However, delivery did keep to schedule, and costs were actually reduced by duplicate orders for a follow-up Department X in Glasgow. The project cost approximately £80 per square foot.

Most stock is cleared away from open display to be stored in the wall, so requiring interaction with the store staff.

Uchida's grand oversized shelf running through the middle of the downstairs provides a feature for display that also helps determine the circulation of customers.

Shigeru Uchida/Studio 80

3.8 Conversation

Tokyo, Japan

What is a store but a place in which goods are housed and presented in order to be sold? This basic approach to the nature of the retail space appears to underline the simplicity of the interior of Conversation in Tokyo.

The client had specialized in children's wear, but with this development wanted to launch a new brand of products aimed at the working woman. The basic, clean and bright approach associated with children's retailing seems to have been carried over in the client's brief to Uchida to create an environment that blends the imagery of the fashion store with that of a more cost-conscious form of selling.

The unit combines the retailing of casual clothing for children from about six years old with that for adults. It has ranges that continue right through all the age groups, using the same styles and colours. Matching socks, shoes, umbrellas and other accessories are available, and other product lines include dishes and towels, also colour coordinated.

This one-stop, one-style, no-frills but fun approach of the client's marketing strategy clearly underlines the fresh environment. A strong grid of shelving is the most dominant feature, responding to the need to relate the ranges of merchandise carefully and to allow flexibility for new ranges.

Uchida sought to step beyond the merely functional, however, and to achieve a grander statement from the references inherent in the structure. He refers to the architecture of 'Neo-Rationalism' as an influence. The shelving grid, with its orderly repetition, appeared to him to be linked to the window articulation of a Rationalist structure.

Uchida also found a need to reach out from the particularities of the small space of this store and relate it to grand spaces: for him, the space surrounded by the shelving grid 'is almost like the relationship between Piazza San Marco in Venice and its surrounding buildings.' Not a reference most would spot, but the concept of how a strong wall grid enhances awareness of the open space as an opportunity to promenade and try on clothes is an understandable one.

The solidity of the merchandising and structural elements aims to form the architectural frame that Uchida refers to. This approach underlies his attitude to all elements of the design: 'Often when designing wall fixtures I come to realize that I am designing the wall instead of the functional fixtures.' His use of the chunky, thick-framed shelving structure is partly to bring out this sense of architectural frame, of windows around a square. In the case of Conversation, the effect is heightened by the use of colour – the red backing to the shelving units suggests a warmth appropriate to the enclosure, while the cool lighting picks up the green on the central units that are, in Uchida's frame of reference at least, out in the open.

Materials used in the store are restricted: a marble tile floor, painted walls and ceiling, and lacquer-finished plywood for furniture and shelving.

A timber façade and loggia frames the corner site store, disguising the original undistinguished building.

Curiosity is provoked by the discreet presentation of products on shelves, well away from the entrance area and checkout (on the left).

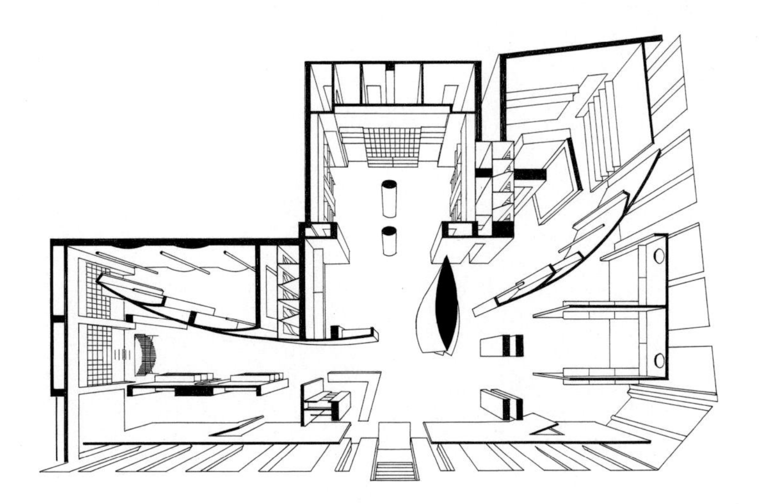

Claudio Nardi & Nicholas Tedford

3.9 Sbaiz

Lignano Sabbiadoro, Italy

The first remarkable aspect of Sbaiz is that it is not where you might expect it to be. Instead of being the latest stylish addition to a fashionable street in a major city, it is located in a seaside town in a little-known resort in north-eastern Italy. And the dramatic depth and sweeping forms of the interior are quarried out from an entirely unprepossessing building shell.

The requirements of the client were for an interior that matched the quality of the high-fashion clothing to be sold within. That Nardi and Tedford achieved what they did on a budget of 700 million lire for the 7,319 square feet (680 square metres) of space (about $720 per square metre) required ingenious exploitation of the dramatic properties of comparatively low-cost materials.

The designers begin their transformation of an undistinguished 1950s building by cladding it with a timber façade and loggia. Customers enter onto a white terrazzo floor (here a relatively economical finish due to its traditional craft base) and are then drawn around the spaces created within the store by a dramatic curving wall. The store occupies a corner site in the building, and this wall, constructed from plaster board, is a dynamic expression of the odd floor plan. It provides a means of shielding storage space on one side, and displaying products on the other. It creates a basic structure for the floor layout, enabling different areas to be created for the different fashion lines and categories, and enabling the discreet slotting in of changing rooms and back stock room areas.

The unusual geometry and the deceptiveness of many of the finishes are crystallized in the central staircase, which provides access to an upstairs area intended to be used as a bar and exhibition space. The staircase has clean lines that on the one hand have modern connotations, but on the other, with the slight sweep around a rusty metallic (actually timber) column, also have an Art Deco flair.

The intention of this interior was for customers to experience the store as a series of almost theatrical stages, yet its stark whiteness allows it to avoid competing with the merchandise. Similarly, the store systems and furniture both express their 'designed' nature and yet are light enough not to compete with the clothing and accessories.

There is a clear disregard for any purist fears of seeming fake here. The comparatively cheap materials are exploited to look almost precious, and the manipulation of space is definitely architectural: a grand scale is given to the store from the outside by exaggerating the heights of windows with fake awnings and louvres. The justification for such trickery is provided by an interior that matches expectations with new visual deception. The 'truth' that emerges for visitors is straightforward enjoyment in the ebb and flow of space around the displays.

Rusted metal is the effect, but wood and paint are the materials on this staircase feature, rising up to the first-floor gallery.

Freestanding, specially designed display cases complement the shelving system and add to flexibility in the retailing. Changing rooms stress the concern for detail.

This striking, curving wall is surprisingly low-cost – simply painted plaster board, with a carved pattern providing flecks of light and shade.

Varieties of wood, glass, and plaster finishes are behind the ingeniously crafted spaces, producing a warm effect from a predominantly white interior. The products themselves supply the colour.

The showcase display of the cake in this store promotes the idea of confection as art.

A stepped screen conceals necessary equipment and services, heightening the impression of a space devoted to presentation.

The best cakes are rarely eaten to satisfy hunger. The more delicate and delightful the confection is, the less likely it is to exist as mere food: it becomes an item to be savoured, to be looked at, a presentation of the *pâtissier*'s skill and a comment on our desires.

Although the making and consuming of such cakes may reflect such a relationship, the actual selling often differs little from the 'pile-'em-high' approach of the common bakery. In designing the Cannelle patisserie, however, architects John Pawson and Claudio Silvestrin broke with this vernacular and set out to establish a model of retailing for their client's products that may be applied to a chain of similar stores.

The project aims to create a clear, unfussy space that allows customers to concentrate on choosing from a simple presentation of the range of goods on sale. Instead of all the stock being presented in a manner which devalues the purchasing of particular individual items, here the emphasis is on presenting the products for their quality rather than for their

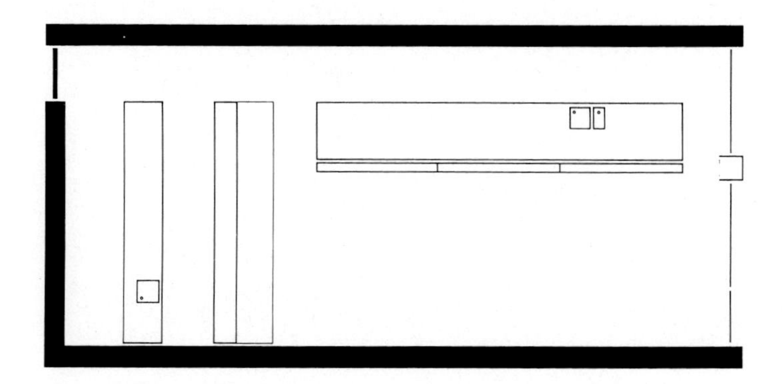

Pawson Silvestrin

3.10 Cannelle

London, UK

quantity. The approach, in merchandising terms, is equivalent to that of the most expensive jewelry stores rather than to the high street or chain-store boutique.

The architects had an entirely unremarkable 1,000 square-feet (93 square-metre) space with which to work, and a budget of £45 ($72) per square foot, which is extremely tight for the quality of materials they would ideally work with to achieve the minimalist style for which they have become renowned.

The basic space was a featureless cube in a 1970s building on a busy road. Now, the first unusual element to stand out is the opaque acid-etched window, which features just one small display box set in the middle. This contains just a single piece of cake and provides the only view from outside into the store. From inside the store, this box appears as a glass box that is merely attached to the window with invisible adhesive. The occasional passer-by staring in becomes a neatly framed entertainment for customers. At night, back lighting changes the effect of this window from a neutral screen to a more mysterious and bold statement of the store.

A concern with the interior was to ensure that no equipment was visible, despite the requirement for refrigeration units and ice cream and espresso equipment. These facilities are thus hidden behind a stepped screen.

On the main wall are four display boxes similar to the window unit, each containing an example of the patisserie's range of products. Most of the merchandise is kept hidden from sight in order to maximize the effect of this minimal display. This serves to draw more attention to the particular items of food on sale and to the detail of the skill involved in the design. Simple, high quality materials are used (wherever the budget allowed) to reinforce this devotional image. The floor is oak, the walls are white plaster and the counter top is white marble from Carrara. In addition to the natural light entering through the front glazed wall, there are also low-voltage downlighters.

Pawson and Silvestrin have little time for criticisms that such an interior is difficult to maintain in the highly refined form of cleanliness and display that they intend. They argue that the simple, uncluttered environment promotes an awareness of the subtlety of form from visitors, and that the maintenance requirements encourage a sense of responsibility in the staff.

The entrance area features the staircase and demonstrates the dramatic use of the restricted palette imposed on the designer.

Minimalist displays maximize the perceived value of the objects displayed against the precisely detailed interior.

Iijima's exploration of the circle and ellipse generates this distinctive display desk and unit beyond, while the simplicity of line exaggerates the sense of space.

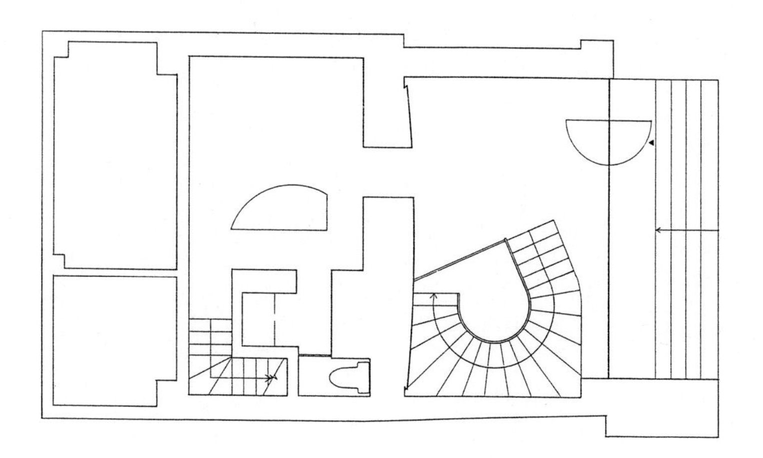

Naoki Iijima

3.11 Sonia Rykiel

Tokyo, Japan

The breaking down of cultural boundaries in design is demonstrated in this neat fashion boutique interior in the Roppongi district of Tokyo.

Iijima cites as an influence on her concept for the interior, 'the important role that circles played in the montage of much of Spielberg's film *Empire of the Sun*.' It is hard to know where to set the limits on interpreting symbolism derived from an American film of an English book about experiences in China under the Japanese occupation. At the same time, she also drew on the use of circular shapes found in early twentieth-century modern design – a reference which could lead to forms ranging from Art Nouveau to Constructivism. A design using similar ideas may be seen in the Sbaiz boutique interior produced in Italy at about the same time (page 150). There, too, the minimalist aesthetic is combined with a plan that incorporates the dynamic of curving walls and furniture.

Iijima uses the circle and ellipse in plan and motif applications, thus carrying them from the experience of three dimensions to the clearly perceived two dimensions. The curves exist in the flow of the staircase, in the ceiling beams and in the rotating displays, and are taken through into the exaggerated sweep of the arms on a specially designed chair. The circle is seen also in the effects of the spotlighting.

Such play of abstract form would perhaps not be unusual in a large single-space store. But part of Iijima's brief was to create three individual rooms with different characteristics. The space is divided into a ground floor and basement: an entrance hall and sales floor, with the main salon for viewing merchandise below.

Another initial requirement of the brief was to restrict the colour palette to black and white. Iijima explores this well, with black granite, terrazzo and aluminum used in the flooring alone. The client was particularly pleased with her treatment of the walls, Nextel paint giving a particularly hard consistent finish to the sheetrock. The specially designed furniture and display units are constructed from aluminum.

This project is the third boutique that Iijima has designed for Sonia Rykiel. It develops the aesthetic of the earlier work, most significantly in the exploration of the forms created by inserting circles and circular movements into the standard box shape provided by most store units.

From a brief to create a very clean, uncluttered store with a low level of merchandise on display, Iijima has produced a design in which the abstract formal composition is highly accessible.

Changes in floor level are made into an asset with the curved steps softening the shape of the space and providing an element of contrast in the white environment.

Eva Jiricna Architects

3.12 Joseph

London, UK

The stores that Eva Jiricna designed for Joseph in the 1980s have probably been the principal defining statement of the hi-tech interior: they advocate an honesty to materials and a joy in structural expression, with exquisite detailing being brought increasingly to the fore as an almost decorative element.

'Decoration' would not normally be a word found in the Jiricna canon. However, this latest addition to her work for client–patron Joseph Ettedgui introduces a new richness of expression that appears to break with the hard line of her earlier work. A key reason for this was the brief from the client to look to the Italian palazzo as a model for the desired atmosphere. For Jiricna there was 'nothing more foreign to my way of thinking,' but she found connecting points between the aesthetic of her Joseph work and of the palazzo, from which to develop a design that was still innovative. A budget (inflation adjusted) of £750 ($1,200) per square metre was probably less than the Medicis may have spent, but was still a base for high-quality finishes.

The 10,764 square-foot (1,000 square-metre) store is both the biggest store Joseph has yet opened and perhaps also the most irregular in plan. The entrance is at the more narrow 'end' of the shape, where a bay of windows wraps around a busy corner of the highly fashionable Brompton Cross location. Within the shell, the design team had to work out how to cope with a number of obstructions: there are various pieces of structure and servicing relating to the floors above, and featuring, in particular, four huge columns.

The reaction in some treatments of this space might have been to disguise these central obstructions behind a partition wall or enclose them in some other way. But Jiricna chose to celebrate them, if anything drawing more attention to them, by cladding them in a corrugated sleeve. At the same time, this cladding does not disguise the feature as something it is not, as it is cut away at top and bottom. The effect is to create a curious floating quality to these massive obstructions, the fluting lessening the impression of solidity as well as adding a sense of height. The fluting also has a more basic

Large windows surround the corner-site building, requiring an interior that displays products for shoppers both inside and outside.

The detail of the stair structure shows the complicated requirements of carrying the load at the top of the stairs rather than at the bottom.

functional benefit in that it disguises wear and tear better than would a smooth finish.

While these columns are a major feature, the *pièce de résistance* is the staircase that dives in front of the columns, linking the ground floor of womenswear with the basement, where menswear is located. The staircase is positioned in relation to the entrance on an axis, the eye being drawn through by the circulation route and the columns beyond. A raised ceiling at this point and a mirrored end to the perspective channel the flow of space.

Jiricna has increasingly developed and refined the elements and the imagery of the staircase in stores she has designed in recent years. By using chromed-steel structure with glass treads, a catenary of rods and cable suspending the main load of the structure from the floor slab above and supporting each glass step with the apparent minimum of material, she has transformed walking down a store staircase into a major event. As ever, there were functional pressures that prompted this design in that there was no position to brace the load back, so the structure had to be suspended.

The elaborate expression of details, with the hand rail and foot guard having the generous stylized curves associated with Art Deco, helps make this functional element of the store express the nature of the interior: along with the columns, the staircase says 'this is how this interior works, this is how the spaces relate, this is how we move through it.'

Downstairs, a low ceiling height restricted potential for manipulating the oppressiveness of an area without any natural light. But the use of high-quality, light materials throughout the store – Spanish marble on the floor, plaster of Paris finished with wax on the walls – reduces the impact of the heavy structure. The comparatively low level of stock required to be on view enabled a range of jewel-like displays to be created, with the merchandising systems paring away structure to float as temporary, freestanding elements within the store.

With such an indeterminate space, the designers have worked hard to give it a form and movement. The curving step that puts the back of the ground floor onto a slightly higher level is one technique for doing this; the maintaining of the sense of natural light as much as possible is another. In addition to the extensive glazing at the front, and a new window put in the side of the store, Jiricna also chose to combine bright metal halide lighting with tungsten halogen to give a variety and softness to the spotlighting that would merge with natural light.

The client was concerned that there was perhaps too much lighting. But the designer pointed out that the merchandise – particularly the tendency towards black clothing and accessories – would effectively balance this out.

Heavy timber shelves hang from the wall on hidden brackets in a break from Jiricna's hi-tech style.

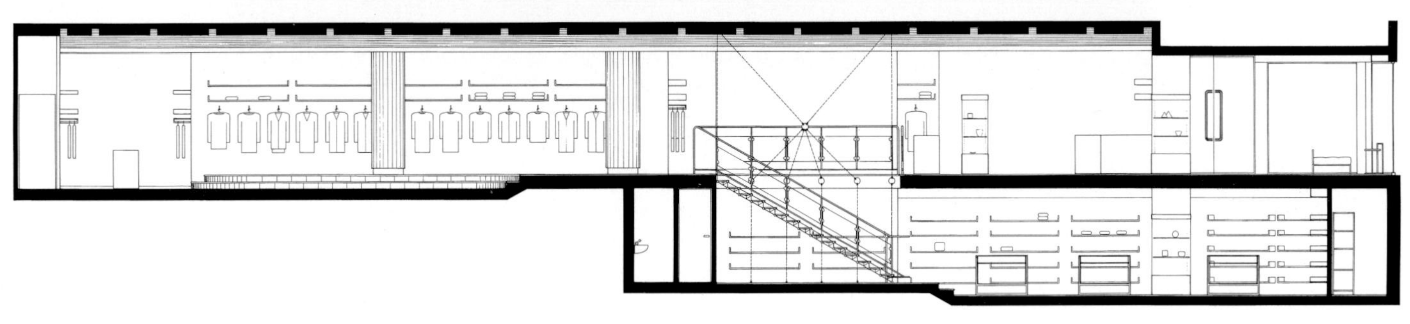

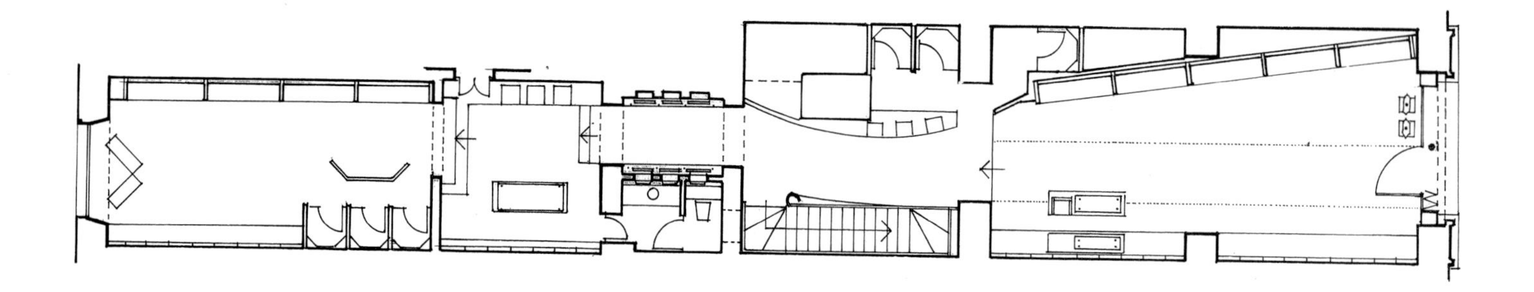

Original details such as this gothic stone arch were discovered in the restoration of the building and incorporated into the design.

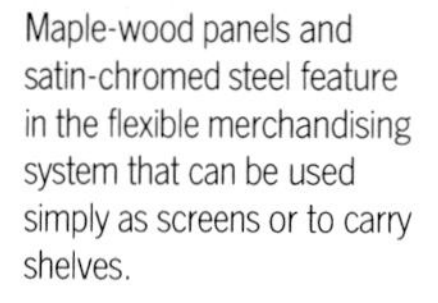

Maple-wood panels and satin-chromed steel feature in the flexible merchandising system that can be used simply as screens or to carry shelves.

This venture by the couture house of Valentino into a younger market sought to find a distinctive position in a competitive market while enhancing, rather than undermining, the main company identity. In Italy, where there is a great precedent for jewel-like fashion-shop interiors, David Davies Associates (DDA) were under considerable pressure to make a distinctive mark.

Oliver is located in a former art gallery in an eighteenth-century building on the Via del Babuino, a prestigious address in the main shopping district. The space consisted of a series of vaults, some high and some very low, progressing through to a rear access on the Via Margutta, a street of a slightly different nature, characterized by antique shops and restaurants.

Stringent planning requirements were placed on what could be done to this historically important building in an historically important area. For DDA, such tight controls were seen as an opportunity to

Ladies- and menswear both have to be presented within the narrow store frontage, while the views inside suggest the length of the store.

Glass-fronted, inset cabinets in the narrow central corridor display accessories opposite a bank of monitors showing the latest collections.

David Davies Associates

3.13 Oliver

Rome, Italy

test their objective of reconciling traditional values in store design with contemporary requirements and tastes. At the same time, the design team of Peter Kent, Steve St. Clair and Louis Hosker had to ensure that it was creating a retail environment that could be adapted to other locations internationally.

The initial design ideas involved injecting an element of classic 'English style' into the interior, a quality much favoured in Italy. This is not so incongruous with the traditional building as might be thought, as the mix of stone and wood and neo-classical forms is very much a part of the English club tradition, supplemented by softer elements, here provided by the merchandise.

The store is entered through massive metal-studded black walnut doors that serve as a screen when folded back during opening hours. Within, the space is divided into three areas, partly using the existing change in height of the space.

The first room houses menswear. The major element introduced by the designers is the merchandising unit made from maple panels and satin chromed metal, with an adjustable halogen lighting system cantilevered off. These materials, plus black walnut, are used again for the shoe and hat racks. Folding mirrored screens pull out to reveal silk ties.

The space then narrows, with a large metal-studded walnut wall curving inwards and carrying television monitors which display the latest collections. Opposite, in this barrel-vaulted corridor, are glass cabinets holding accessories. The floor changes from wood to green Westmorland slate.

The passage opens onto a room in stark contrast to that which has gone before. Here there are more shoes, ties and other accessories. It has a soaring ceiling, but attention may also be drawn to the tall, stone gothic arch which leads into the final area of the store. This feature was revealed during the restoration – and presumably is one aspect not carried in the extensive design manual that DDA has produced for the franchising of the store. The final room contains womenswear and jeans, with a window looking out onto Via Margutta.

The investment of time and money in DDA's designs for all the fixtures can be seen partly as investment in designing for a range of spaces other than this specific location. Part of the function of this design had to be to launch the concept of Oliver as a chain. The quality of this retail scheme is that it can be appropriate in this application as well as giving the retailer a firm identity.

Yellow American pine dominates the character of the store, creating a warm and welcoming environment with only a minimal range of materials and colours.

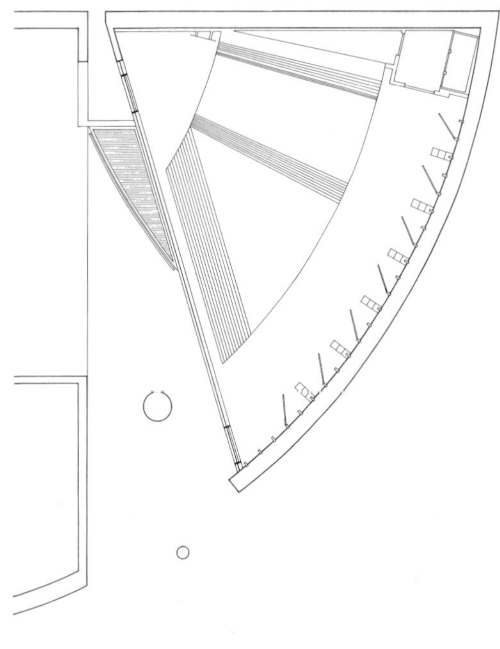

Displays of clothing are mounted on a peg-board of hooks set into the concrete wall providing a consistent grid, yet offering flexibility as well.

The shape of the display feature derives from the unusual and constricted dimensions of the store that demanded a response capable of drawing attention to the interior rather than its boundaries.

Sanzin Kim

3.14 Kenzo Homme

Tokyo, Japan

The value of concentrating on one, clear design statement is exemplified in this fashion boutique interior in the OXY Building in Tokyo.

The client wanted a store that appeared more as a showroom than a place for selling. Importance was placed on creating a distinctive display image that would draw attention to the attractiveness of the clothing as a high fashion item of great value. All else – notably sales – follows on from the achievement of this presentation of the clothing.

A bold and conspicuous design is not sufficient in itself, however. It must be appropriate, both to the culture of the client and to that of the space it occupies. In the case of this building, there were a number of problems that Kim managed to turn to advantage. The 560 square-foot (52 square-metre) site is in a curious segment shape, a quarter-circle. This is an interesting architectural form, but an unusual one into which to fit the functions of a showroom and store.

Kim's response is to use this curiosity to generate the main feature, a striking display and storage unit that echoes the segment plan in its form. By taking over the center of the store, it creates a dominant image to look in upon, while also determining the circulation route and activity area within the store. The structure, built from warm yellow American pine, contrasts with the black granite floor and unfinished concrete walls. The unit actually flows across the floor and up the wall, providing another display area, and the pine finish continues over part of the ceiling. More hangers are created by steel pipes and wooden hooks protruding from the concrete walls.

While the store has no obvious representation of human forms to help model the clothing, the central display suggests the fluidity of clothing by its wave-like stepping and softness against the hard finishes of wall and floor. The concentration of warm light on this area highlights the merchandise.

For Kim, one of the major problems was how to create an effective entrance to the store. The boutique is on the second floor of the building, and access to the space was across an open area that was four stories high. Kim dramatized this element by adding a bridge; the display table then follows almost as an island, first perceived from afar and then reached after the journey. Thus, Kenzo Homme provides the experience of a sense of passage for the visitor.

The curving form of the staircase and detailing is taken up by the sinuous shape of the seating.

Exquisite detailing is at the heart of the polished feel of the Joan & David interior that ensures it is more than just glitter.

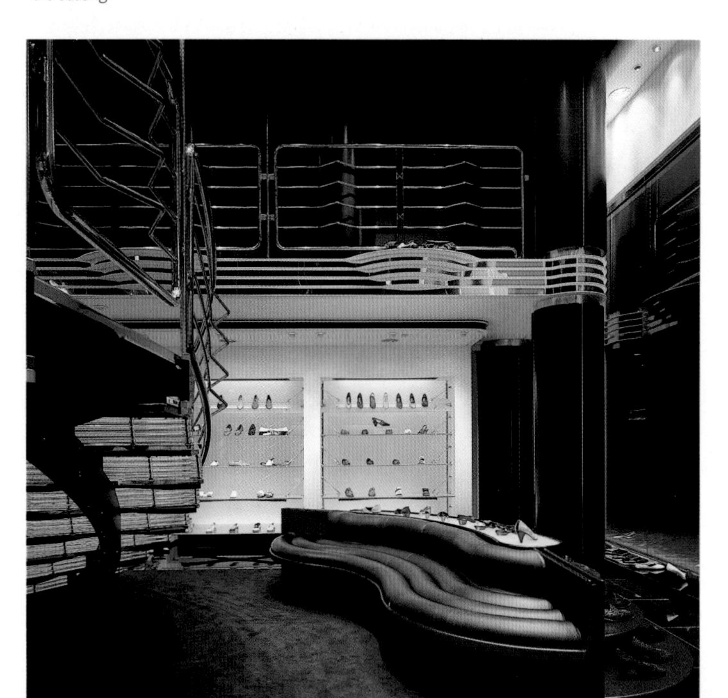

Shoes become objects of desire, displayed on delicate glass shelves held up by wire suspenders.

Polished stainless steel and clear glass treads give the staircase a jewel-like quality that seems at odds with its function.

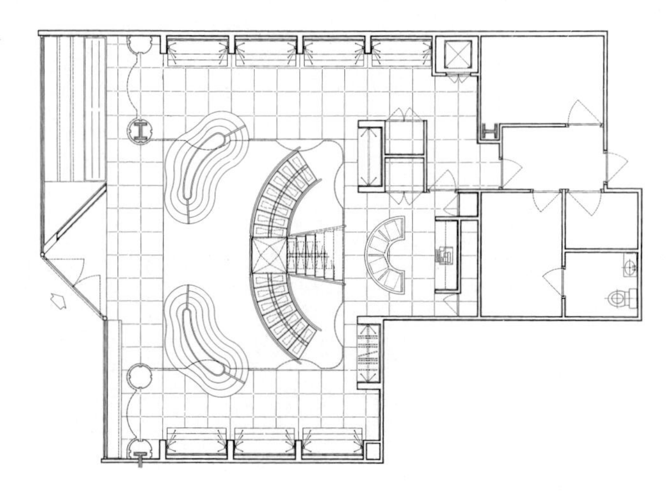

Eva Jiricna Architects

3.15 Joan & David

Los Angeles, USA

An interesting irony forms the central feature of this shoe store: an extravagant staircase that draws one's attention through the double-height glazed storefront on the South Coast Plaza mall in Costa Mesa. It is an element of such glamour and style in its own right as to give a brilliant luster to the high-priced and stylish products displayed within. But the staircase is out of bounds to shoppers, and is simply to provide access for staff to the mezzanine storage areas.

Such a twist is all the more amusing in the knowledge of the great difficulty that always exists in capturing the interest of shoppers to go up or down a staircase. Jiricna has repeatedly used this dynamic expression of the interior to develop her ideas (note also Joseph, page 158), but here the feature moves almost entirely away from its obvious function to become a sculptural, symbolic element. It articulates the two-story space and sets the pace for the aesthetic through its use of polished stainless steel and clear glass treads on a central black, powder-coated steel structure, with a curving stainless steel banister as the most dominant aspect.

This design solution is not simply for effect, however. It may be a stunning design idea to create a staircase of splendour and just use it to serve what would normally be a back-of-store area. But there was a further generating factor behind this decision: local regulations prohibited the use of the upstairs space for little more than storage. The staircase is hung from what was an existing roof structure at the mezzanine level. Around this level a gallery was created by the design team of Jiricna, job architect Jon Tollit, Duncan Webster and C. J. Lim. At the main floor level this gallery is reflected with display units and seating. The main shoe displays exist as recessed areas within the side perimeter walls. The brief involved generating a form of store design that could be carried on to other sites as a common identity (Jiricna was simultaneously also working on a Joan & David shop in San Francisco). Display systems and finishes had to be adaptable, yet of a quality and appropriateness that would not in any way suggest the standard chain store.

A rich yet monochromatic palette of materials and colour tones is used, which is intended as a base for use in other outlets. Floors are covered in black granite or carpet, depending on the position in the store: granite provides a hard perimeter that reflects the lighting and accentuates the sparkle of the displays, while the carpet provides a warmer and more comfortable surface in those areas where customers may be walking or sitting.

Walls and recesses are clad in plaster and finished in a sprayed off-white paint. Counters and seating display areas use a deep red-stained timber. A 'hot' point in the colour scheme is provided by the red leather, upholstered furniture designed by Matthew Marchbank.

The ceiling is a distinct profiled plaster unit that carries most of the lighting, and takes on a suggestion of an independent structure floating over, and illuminating, the space, in the way that stage lighting is not immediately perceived as part of the stage design. The glazed storefront provides the equivalent of a proscenium arch, through which passers-by have the whole store 'event' presented to them.

Daylight floods in from above to cast stark shadows and produce a dramatically changing environment throughout the day.

The staircase runs down between a massive, blind, concrete wall and a curved inner 'wall' behind which the stores are located.

Ando creates a sculpture gallery where his uncompromisingly minimalist palette provides a neutral situation for the art.

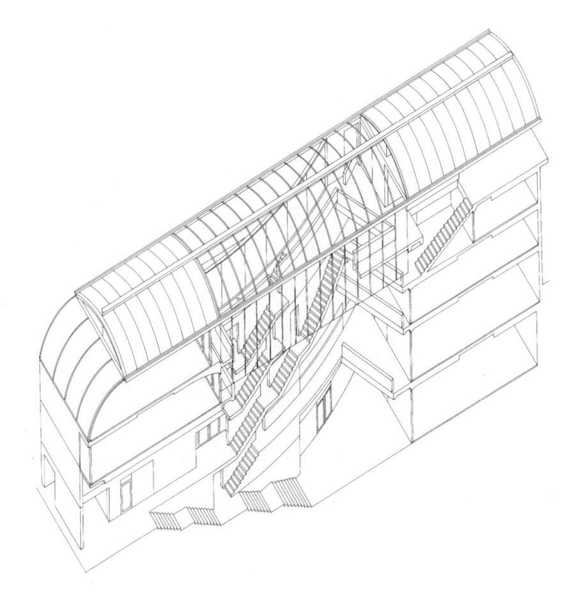

Tadao Ando

3.16 Galleria Akka

Osaka, Japan

The severity of Ando's work in its insistent use of unfinished concrete as a surface material for interiors is stark even by the standards of Japanese minimalists. But in this project, the rationale behind this use of the material is substantiated. Ando claims that, for him, concrete is the most suitable material for revealing a space when it is lit by natural sunlight. He aims for a look to the concrete that is not solid, but has a lightness and consistency. When it loses the sense of weight, as he intends, then walls simply become the parameters of a space, rather than an oppressive sense of mass.

In Galleria Akka, a five-story development (four stories above ground and a basement), Ando had to give a distinctive character to an exclusive set of four stores topped by a gallery. This is boldly achieved by giving half of the 40 × 8 metre site over to the atrium area, which is bounded by a curving wall on the outside and by stores on the other. Stairs run down in a dog-leg on the curved outside wall.

Such a description of the scheme does not do justice to the almost maze-like complexity of the circulation then viewed from within. Although the way to reach the different floors is apparent, moving through the three dimensions of space is designed to be an exciting experience.

Giving over so much of the site to circulation space rather than to retailing area may seem a pointless luxury to a hard-headed property consultant. But it is the making of this scheme. Besides allowing the complex play of the staircase and landings, it also enables a high level of natural light to reach the basement area. The mass of concrete walling does not take on an oppressive quality, but, as Ando claims, it becomes more of a screen, decorated by its grid structure and reinforcements and reflecting light without ever having the hardness of a bright finished surface.

Crowning the whole development is a roof of curved, frosted glass, maximizing the potential for natural light, while not allowing any exterior distractions into the calm, enclosed world of the court.

Ando is an architect rather than an interior designer, but his concern for never separating the interior from the exterior of a building is exemplified by the distinctive expression he gives the interiors of his buildings. 'They seem to me to be vitally connected; the nature of the interior depends on that of the exterior,' he argues. Although this may have been a truism once, some of the retail developments seen in the UK and USA bear no relation whatsoever to the building structure. Ando's comment may therefore be worth reconsidering.

THÉÂTRE VÉGÉTAL

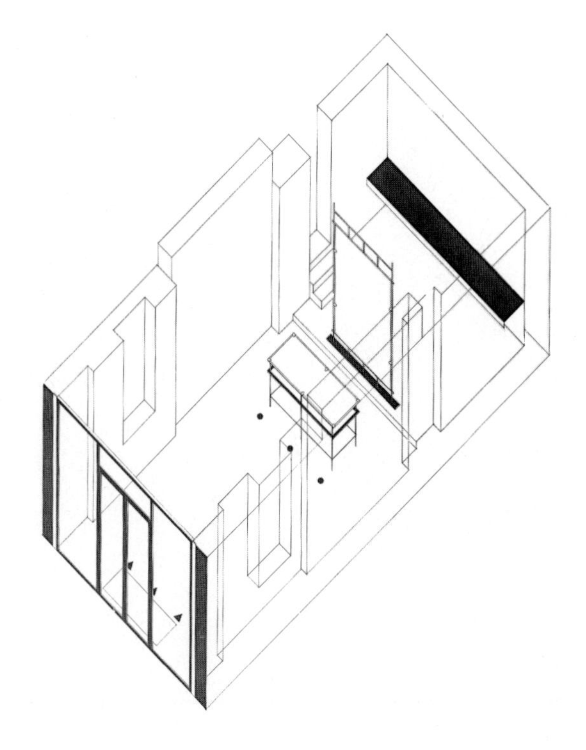

Christopher Connell

3.17 Théâtre Végétal

Melbourne, Australia

The art of the still life is transformed into reality in this dramatic presentation.

This approach to creating a florist's shop seems so obvious that it is surprising that more florists do not take note and copy. Instead of a space full of flowers and plants, with little to distinguish one florist from another other than location and the exotic nature of the products and prices, this shop finds a powerful form for dramatizing the content: the *théâtre végétal*. This is the proper name for the set that forms the basis of many a still life in seventeenth-century and later paintings.

The clients, Michele Doherty and Ian Cook, had the idea of presenting flowers in a clearly staged manner; designer Christopher Connell found the means of translating the fine art reference into a workable environment. The clients were friends of the designer, which perhaps helps explain the detailed links between initial concept and final design, all to a tight budget.

While always aiming for the theatrical, Connell abstracted this into a concern for creating a sense of space, light and strength to the small rectangular shop unit (645 square feet/60 square metres).

Although a fairly standard space, there were awkward problems: the existing ceiling height varied from front to back, the walls created conflicting widths within the space, and the existing floor timbers had deteriorated. The façade was also unstable and unsafe.

Connell took the model of the theater as an opportunity for providing a shop that would be the simplest of frames, the activities seen within the space being the main point. At the same time this 'stage' would be one that the audience would step into – thus requiring that the materials and details present alongside the drama of the flowers were of the finest.

The façade suggests the stage and the stylish low-key approach by its use of charcoal-coloured rendered cement as the frame for a glazed frontage. The black aluminum frame of the glass and the oxidized copper leaf-shaped door handles provide the quietest of intrusions into this presentation of the

The interior 'stage set' display is clearly seen by passers-by, with no further explanation of the store's function felt necessary.

event within. The eyes are drawn through to the back of the shop where the name and logo are carried on the rear wall, rather than being prominent on the outside.

There is a strong symmetry intended for the arrangements within; a formality that has echoes of a monumental setting, even of a memorial. The black cement floor and stone-effect painted walls and ceiling aid this association.

Distressed materials have been widely, perhaps excessively, used in many environments, but here they gain a sense of appropriateness when placed in the context of flowers; oxidizing metals and rough stone/cement finishes suggest an outdoor environment and a natural process of growth and decay. The furniture, counter and the logo are all produced in distressed mild steel by Mark Douglas. Against this there is a precision and control within the shop that can be attributed to the staginess of the lighting: from outside it helps frame the centered perspective. Inside, it spotlights the detail of the 'product' quality and brings out the texture of the contrasting hard materials of the design and the softness of the flowers.

That Connell describes his ideal project as a gallery where the work of young and innovative designers could be shown reveals a lot about his approach to this project. It is a design which has rewarding details, which has a distinctive voice, yet is generous enough to give the lead role to the stars – the flowers on display.

Lighting is a key factor in the dramatic display of subtle compositions in colour and form.

The use of rusted metal details suggests the material's subjection to the laws of nature.

The swirling, organic form of the door handles presages the plant life within.

Floor, walls, ceiling, and displays are clearly articulated elements within the single-floor store.

Unique display units express the idiosyncratic nature of the store, while meeting functional needs for product display and table surfaces.

The flexibility of the merchandising units enables easy changes in the form of the display, while always retaining a strong identity.

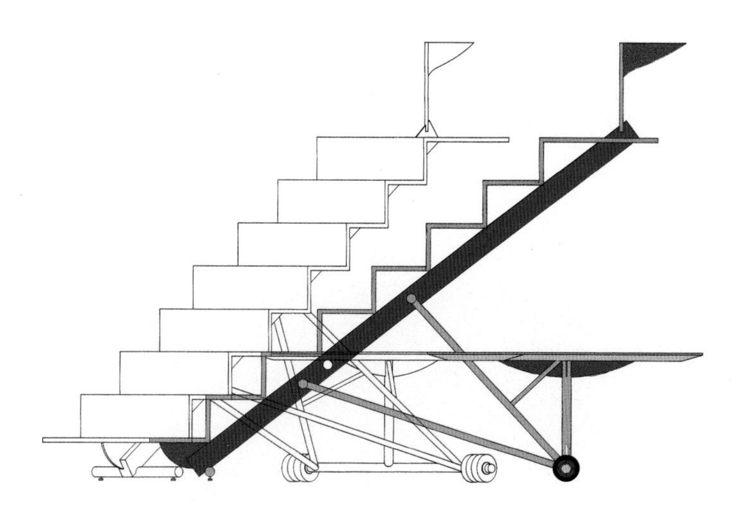

Katsuhiko Togashi

3.18 Cinderella 12

Tokushima-Ken, Japan

If Cinderella could ever visit this store using her name, she would not be able to find any glass slippers, but might be pleased with the elegant, lightweight effect of the interior.

The purpose of the design of Cinderella 12, however, is not to allude to the fairy tale. Rather, it is a way of handling the vast, deep space of the shop floor and the need to adapt it from time to time for different uses.

The main area is a ladies' shoe store carrying different ranges that need exclusive displays. There is also a stationery store and a cafe included in the development.

Togashi developed the striking stepped and movable display units in response to the need for an interior that could be altered extensively with the changing merchandise over the fashion seasons. His design had to advertise such changes clearly when viewed from the outside. The store is in a highly competitive location and this added to the need for a design that would promote and sell the range of merchandise (each shoemaker has, in effect, their own corner) and prompted the idea of drawing in more customers with the cafe and stationery store.

While being extremely lightweight, the display structures are strong enough to be stepped on for decoration of the upper ledges. They are made from aluminum sheet pressed over wooden steps, reinforced in the center by a steel beam.

A source of inspiration for Togashi was the treatment of airport interiors. He saw the need for 'a space that is vast and should be flexible as well as dramatic.' This store therefore had to be a space in which the store itself was read as almost 'nothing,' while the incessant movement of an airport interior is echoed by the customers and by the displays, the latter of which bear some resemblance to airport trolleys.

Togashi wanted to make the airport metaphor read much more clearly. He initially proposed insetting runway taxiing lights of red and blue into the Taiwanese marble floor, but cost constraints meant this detail was omitted from the completed project. This witty approach is realized in the display units, though, which are designed not only to show merchandise but also to express the floor space both dramatically and humorously, providing staircases to nowhere.

Merchandise is mostly out of sight of the street, discreetly displayed at the bottom of the narrow, triple-height space.

Precise detailing and the slightest suggestion that the shop sells clothes provide the invitation to explore a space which concerns itself with the abstracts of fine clothing – form, texture and finish.

Stanton Williams

3.19 Issey Miyake

London, UK

How do you tell a customer that a shirt costs £300 – and that it is worth it? You could try sworn affidavits from rich pop stars, but in commissioning this jewel-like interior for his London menswear store, Issey Miyake has taken a characteristically much more original and creative path.

Shoppers do not need to be told about the store from the outside: here the name is carved in the door sill by the sidewalk, but otherwise the narrow store appears to be virtually empty from the street. It is seen as a high, lit space with a descending staircase taking a large part of what little floor space there is. Visitors either know of the store, or know that this is the design language of a stylish and elegant environment, where fashion retailing enters the realm of the art gallery. Indeed, objects of art are sometimes used to reinforce the allusion to an art gallery and to give a more unusual expression to the ground floor. Shoppers rarely see any merchandise from the street. The entire ground floor is presented as the store window: a statement of cool quality.

In this particular store, this quality is almost obsessively applied in the materials and the detailing, apparent from standing on the entrance step. The glazing is exquisitely detailed where it meets its stainless steel frame. Two massive English oak doors, with purpose-made stainless steel bolts, open onto an interior where the creamy walls and gray floor have a plainness that is clearly not achieved simply. The finish and depth to the surfaces are achieved by a highly skilful (and expensive) coating with *marmorino*, an Italian plaster made from crushed marble.

Stanton-Williams removed two floors from the original building to create the dramatic, narrow, empty entrance floor. At the rear of the store a roof light brings a shaft of daylight down through the entire store to the basement level – which is the only place to go once the visitor enters. The basement level is approached down a wide portland stone-step staircase. Once in the basement, the true identity of the place is revealed: a series of alcoves runs along one wall holding the merchandise. Recessed lighting in the ceiling and walls picks out the clothing and accessories. If one were to count all the products in the store – every item of clothing, every belt or pair of socks – the total would probably not exceed much more than one hundred.

Furniture in the form of a till desk and chairs is again in English oak. Display brackets are the most minimal of hangers.

The detailing is immaculate and is noticeably so, not because it is grossly enlarged but because there is very little else to notice: the interior draws the visitor's concentration to the materials and how they are put together to function beautifully. This is the best possible introduction the design of the store could make to the presentation of the refined products within it.

Huge servicing elements within the basic shed structure give a form and overall character to frame the various retailers.

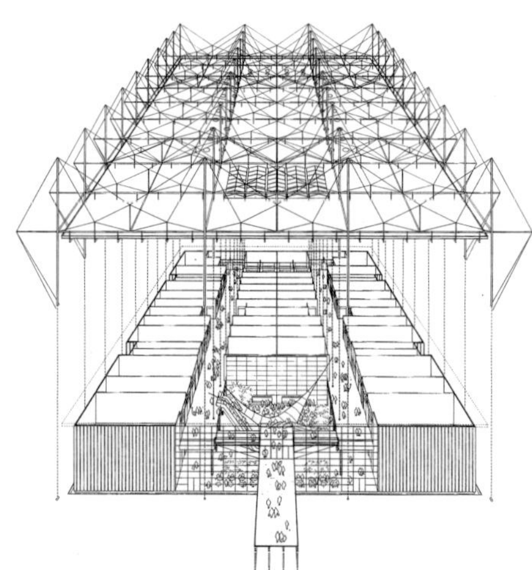

Structural and servicing elements are picked out in bold primary colours and natural lighting is maximized in the circulation areas.

The exterior of Magasin d'Usine is distinguished by the suspended structure and the long bridge approach to the glazed entrance wall.

Richard Rogers Partnership

3.20 Magasin d'Usine

Nantes, France

This out-of-town shopping center attracts shoppers on the basis of selling direct from the factory. The merchandise of furniture and clothing is not sold on the basis of 'added value,' but on the marketing of lower prices. It is the first of a number of similar buildings that Richard Rogers Partnership is due to design for the client, and follows the principle of architectural quality and honesty which is rarely seen in such retail sheds.

The 226,044 square feet (21,000 square metres) of shopping space are spread over two floors within the building in a simple but bold factory-like environment, which proves to be highly functional both in its manipulation of circulation and in its uniting of the various retail outlets within a strong frame. The basic building is a suspended structure, the roof masts giving a distinctive expression to the center, with profiled metal walls. Within this frame sits a concrete structure giving a substantial 21-foot (6.5-metre) slab-to-slab distance to work in. Entrance is across a moat on a bridge coming in at first-floor level. Once inside the center, the analogy with a factory interior is continued in the conveyor belt-like passing of the customers before the various opportunities to spend money: shoppers are obliged to walk around most of the shops in order to reach the exit, taking in the various kinds of outlet and the restaurant facilities. Such a reductivism could seem offensive, if it was not so honestly done: the building does not pretend to be anything it is not.

A powerful primary colour scheme on the structure and exterior shell is carried through to the interior. The building's parts are effectively colour-coded, the elements read in the clearest possible way and there is no disguising of the nature of building components. Not only is there a design purity to such an approach, but here it also serves to give a strong identity to the center. Remaining in the visitor's memory as a center with a spirit of place, rather than just an amorphous mass of shops, is essential for an out-of-town shopping complex that cannot rely for its character on being located in a particular town or street.

A further benefit of Rogers' renowned approach of expressing the structure is that it also helped, in this context, to meet the client's budget requirements: the whole complex was built for £6 million ($9.6 million), about £290 ($464) per square metre, including all structure and servicing, which would have allowed little for the additional smarter surfaces that are often used in shopping centers. Here the expressed structure reinforces the suggestion of basic qualities while giving a visual excitement that 'cheap' finishes would never have provided.

In addition to the celebration of building structure and technology, Magasin d'Usine also maximizes the exploitation of another essential and cheap element: natural light. In contrast to many large centers where all awareness of the outside environment is lost, this center allows daylight in at many points. A glass entrance wall reveals the basic configuration of the center to arriving shoppers, while domed roof lights above the malls keep an awareness of the outside world alive.

Solid elements in the main entrance area contrast with the strikingly lightweight design elsewhere.

Light, water and materials are given a common fluidity in a project that aims to celebrate the experience of bathing.

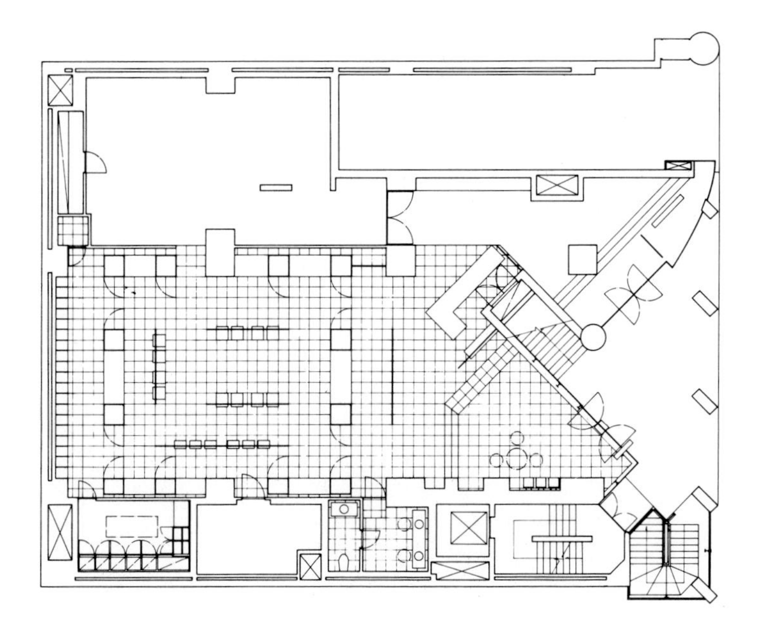

Setsuo Kitaoka

3.21 The Body & Bath Shop

Tokyo, Japan

The stark, clean abstract qualities of this showroom have some shock value when placed against more everyday retail environments, and yet are perfectly understandable when put in the context of their purpose. The brief from the client, Uchino Co., was for an experimental 'bath boutique' to encourage interest in the 'bath lifestyle:' the client is the largest wholesaler of towel products in Japan.

The store, in a prime location in the city, is a form of advertisement for a company that has had a low profile: it is not a store intended to sell large amounts of product directly or even to attract all passers-by. Rather, it needs to promote to retailers and other people of influence the corporate image of a company that is quality conscious and design orientated. By doing this, the showroom also helps test new products and gain sales information on how to develop in fashionable and high-priced directions.

Kitaoka's response to these requirements is not a conservative wheeling out of the expensive materials and traditional forms that might be seen as the more usual techniques for creating a luxury market image. Instead, he claims that the basic challenge he set himself was 'to embody the abstraction of the shimmer of heated air:' highly fanciful, but highly appropriate as a linking factor in any comfortable bathroom environment.

This effect is achieved by a refined, limited range of materials and controlled palette of colours. The white marble floor has familiar reference as a bathroom material, but the painted metal sheet used on the ceiling and some wall areas plus the stretched cloth panel (using fiber-optic strands) on the 'powder room' wall suggest a more innovative and abstract treatment. Yet they, too, could be seen as having traditional associations: a development on the grid of the Japanese screen.

Custom-made fixtures add to the unique atmosphere of the space. A showcase of strengthened glass is finished with a suede coating that emphasizes the tactile nature of bathing. A chair contrasts leather with different metal finishes, enamel paint and chrome. Large mirrors add to the sense of spaciousness in the showroom as well as providing further allusion to the bathroom environment.

Kitaoka claims that a major obstacle to achieving his design objectives was that the ceiling height (8.5 feet/2.6 metres) was too low. It might not allow for the grandeur of gesture he hoped for, but there is room enough to create a setting that engages in a surprising discussion of the qualities of the 'bath lifestyle.'

Grids are a repeated device helping to unite floor, display areas and ceiling in a coherent whole.

Underlit display cases use different glass finishes to play with light and suggest the misting of the panels.

Developing corporate image rather than fast-turnover custom is the underlining requirement of the store's identity.

La Cigale, Philippe Starck
(see p. 214)

4 Cultural & Public Amenity Buildings

1 **OMA**
Dance Theater, *The Hague, The Netherlands* 186

2 **Murphy/Jahn**
United Airlines Terminal, O'Hare International Airport, *Chicago, USA* 192

3 **Mitchell/Giurgola & Thorp Architects**
Australian Parliament House, *Canberra, Australia* 196

4 **Alsop & Lyall**
Splash, *Sheringham, UK* 200

5 **Kisho Kurokawa**
Museum of Modern Art, *Nagoya, Japan* 202

6 **Bach & Mora**
Josep ma Jujol School, *Barcelona, Spain* 206

7 **Morphosis & Gruen Associates**
Cedars-Sinai Comprehensive Cancer Center, *Los Angeles, USA* 210

8 **Philippe Starck**
La Cigale, *Paris, France* 214

9 **Kiyonori Kikutake Associates & Keikaku-Rengo**
Kawasaki City Museum, *Kawasaki City, Japan* 218

10 **Behnisch & Partners**
University Library, *Eichstatt, West Germany* 222

11 **Evans & Shalev**
Truro Crown Court, *Truro, UK* 226

12 **Christoph Langhof Architekten**
Public Baths, Kreuzberg, *Berlin, West Germany* 230

13 **Barton Myers Associates, BOOR/A & ELS Design Group**
Center for the Performing Arts, *Portland, USA* 234

14 **Santiago Calatrava Valls**
Cabaret Tabourettli, *Basle, Switzerland* 240

Within the auditorium, little is spent on disguising the basic black box of the space, but a curving ceiling relates it to the rest of the building.

OMA

4.1 Dance Theater

The Hague, The Netherlands

From the outside, this dance theater complex designed by Rem Koolhaas and his colleagues is a curious sight. It is a range of forms – blocks, cubes and a cone – brought together in a clash of different materials: brick, cement, corrugated metal, reflective glass, and the golden cladding of the cone, where a restaurant is located.

Inside, the excitement of the design is heightened further by the almost wilful distortion of spaces, the creation of circulation areas around the auditorium seeming to have been carved by a sculptor determined to bend the role of architect to his first craft. But this is no criticism. OMA justify their play on forms, volumes, textures and colour by creating (on a tight budget) a fascinating response to a complicated brief.

The project is the third that OMA were commissioned to carry out by the Netherlands Dance Theatre. Previous work had been on housing performance, rehearsal and administration functions in new buildings near The Hague. But this brief required the architects to take an awkward city-center site, part of the Spui complex where a hotel and concert hall already existed. OMA had to link the new dance theater and its facilities with the concert hall. Their commission included offices, costume workshops, three rehearsal studios, a sauna and swimming pool, and a restaurant and bar. To unite all these elements required the evolution of a distinctive character and clarity. Despite – or perhaps partly due to – the complexity of OMA's three-dimensional imagery, this has been achieved.

The foyer, with its strange play of bisecting planes expressed in differing materials and colours, develops from the more subdued exterior both to express the building functionally and to suggest the use of the space: the dance is not only confined to the stage, but is evident throughout. The foyer is connected on three levels with the neighbouring concert hall. This merging of buildings is exploited in the design, the concert hall wall of pink and green on one side of the foyer facing the hot red of the theater wall on the other.

Dynamic interaction of planes and forms defy expectations of traditional spaces and theater layout.

1 Dance Theater

Underneath the raked seating of the theater, Koolhaas has extended the lobby space, playing games with perspective and with the sense of structure.

Juxtaposition of unusual forms, materials and colour is a strong theme: above the foyer float two apparently almost unsupported forms while the whole circulation space dips down into a curious, seemingly purposeless large space. This has been created by releasing the area under the raked theater stalls, a neat use of an awkward area to provide a place in which to promenade outside the auditoria. The intriguing nature of this area is added to by different coloured columns puncturing the space, rising through the floor and into the ceiling without base or capital. The design of the speckled ceiling and terrazzo floor is such that they are seen as related planes, contrasting with the gray-green wall, while the lack of sharp angles makes the flow of space deceptive and intangible.

The bizarre ovoid that floats over the main foyer area is in fact a bar. This is reached by a route of discovery, on which the visitor ascends different staircases and walks over different surfaces, the floor passing from terrazzo to rubber and wood. There is never any confusion about where the route leads, however, and from the top there is a view out.

Koolhaas's use of a wide range of materials and colours, some rich, some minimal, fulfils the need for a theatricality, a sense of some luxury, without ever appearing retrospective in design or too aggressive. There is a sense of conflict, but only in a playful way.

In contrast to the excitement of the circulation and other public areas, the backstage area is spartan. This may be partly for cost reasons, but is also appropriate in terms of expressing the different use of space. The theater itself is also kept subdued, with emphasis given to providing an informality for performance: simple materials, a stage that projects out towards the audience with a soft curve. Even though it has the atmosphere of a small theater, the auditorium can seat up to one thousand people.

Levels collide or float against each other with a drama of structural ingenuity that conceals the fact that Koolhaas had to work with a tight budget.

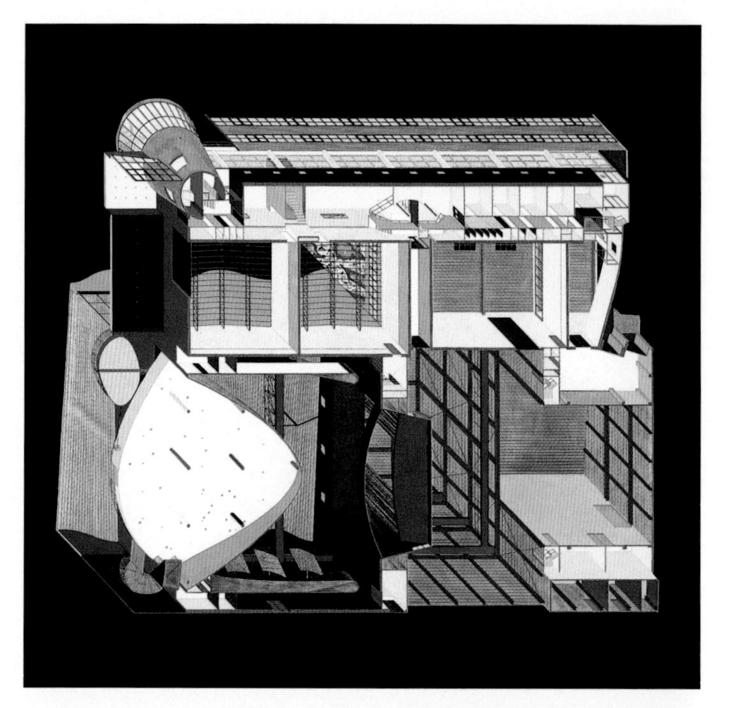

All the elements of the building – from floors to ceilings, furniture to staircase fixtures – are exploited for their dramatic properties.

Opposite This provocative contrast of functions – balcony floor becoming a light source – is a dramatic capping of the dynamic features within the lobby.

BAR
DANSTHEATER
BOVEN RECHTS

B16
B17

Patterned glass allows high natural light levels yet reflects heat during the day, while at night it reflects the light internally.

Murphy/Jahn

4.2 United Airlines Terminal, O'Hare International Airport

Chicago, USA

To design the terminal for the biggest carrier at the world's busiest airport is to be invited to perform in front of as big an audience as an architect is likely to get. Helmut Jahn met the challenge at O'Hare International Airport with a scheme that breaks new ground in airport design in both the rigour of the planning and the fun of the execution.

Jahn is better known for a number of speculative office skyscrapers (including as yet unbuilt attempts on the title of the world's tallest building). With the O'Hare commission, he was working in both a public realm and that of private enterprise: there was obviously a need to produce a terminal that would satisfy a vast range of users and carry out many complex functions. At the same time the development was all part of the sales pitch of United Airlines, and to create a pleasantly memorable place to fly into or out of would clearly benefit the image of the company.

The Murphy/Jahn scheme rethinks terminal design from its initial plan. Instead of having a 'Y' configuration to the concourses, a supposedly efficient way to park as many aircraft around the building as possible, here there are two 1,600-foot concourses separated by 800 feet of taxiing area. Underneath is a moving walkway that links the buildings. This enables more aircraft to be accommodated and a faster turn-around of flights.

Departing passengers check in at a hall that precedes the first of these concourses. Here, one of the most striking achievements of the design is immediately apparent: the building is substantially open, with views almost from the point where cars drop passengers off, through to the planes. The openness extends to the arrangement of check-in facilities, which are booths rather than a forbidding bank. Bags are taken directly down out of sight behind each counter, rather than running along a continuous belt.

The effect of this arrangement is that passengers can proceed in a clear, logical way forward, from check-in, through the security screening area and into the departure concourse. Here the initial effect of being in a highly spacious, light environment becomes more dramatic with the concourse, which is formed by a powerful barrel-vaulted structure of steel clad with fritted glass (the 'fritted' aspect is an innovative use of ceramic glaze on glass that reduces solar loss, can be patterned, and produces a reflective surface for artificial light). The architects claim that with the use of this glass, 100 percent of daytime lighting is now natural, and that energy bills will be up to 50 percent lower than those of other terminals of a similar size.

There are a number of crude elements to the detailing of the structure, but Murphy/Jahn emphasize the economy of their hi-tech expression when compared with more refined buildings: here many of the fixtures are standard items ingeniously used.

There are a number of areas that display greater sensitivity to the effect of the building, however. Having devised a dramatic and functional structure, the designers refined such details as the columns to a more human scale, breaking down the load over a clutch of columns rather than constructing one

All opportunities to open out the interior to the exterior activity are taken: here the descent into the sub-runway walkway is made more exciting by the views of the airfield.

massive pile. The patterning of the glass is seen as a way of reducing scale (as well as its functional aspect of heat gain), and the punching of holes in the massive I-beams of the vaulting reduces the impact of the structure, changing what would have seemed a very heavy roof to a light open structure. The height of the structure also adapts to the amount of activity within: it is highest at the central busiest point and lower at the quieter end areas.

Approximately 40 percent of passengers depart from this first concourse: the remainder are treated to the most exciting moment of the interior, by passing down escalators and traveling on the under–the-runway walkways that lead to the island concourse.

As passengers enter the walkway they are struck by the colour, sound and movement of light and structure. Above their heads is a light sculpture traveling the entire length of the corridor. Devised by artist Michael Hayden, it is computer generated to produce random patterns that are synchronized with an original music composition by William Kraft, and the soundtrack relates to the dramatic moving patterns of neon light. These 'toned-down disco' elements are not only applied as 'art' but carry through into the architecture, the sculpture being multiplied in the reflective ceiling and echoed in the coloured lighting behind the wave-forms given to the translucent walls, breaking down the oppressive feeling of being in a tunnel.

The island concourse is similar to its twin, in that it has a pedestrian walkway 50 feet (15 metres) wide and 1,600 feet (487 metres) in length. Most flight transfers are handled here and (as with the first concourse) the space includes a range of facilities in the way of shops and restaurants. All public furniture and fittings were designed at the Murphy/Jahn office.

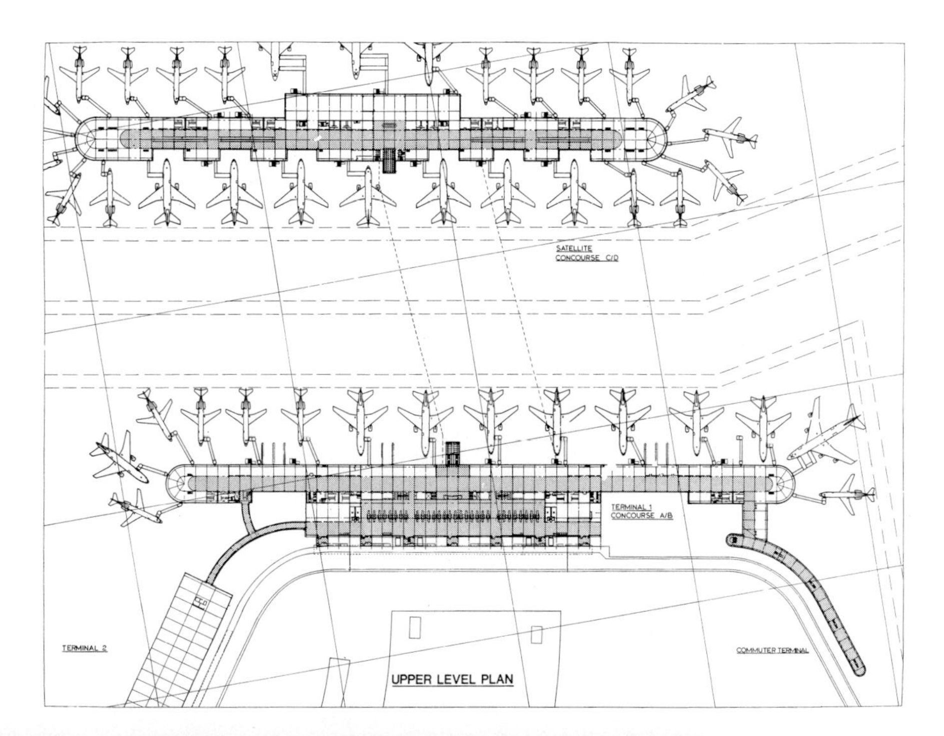

Sound and light envelop travelator passengers in a computer 'sculpture' as they travel under the runway to the island concourse.

The massive scale of the inlaid-stone flooring-pattern balances the monumentality of the entrance lobby where paired staircases lead up to the Senate offices.

Fine craftsmanship in a wide range of materials is demonstrated by the detailing between surfaces in the many exacting geometric forms.

Mitchell/Guirgola & Thorp Architects

4.3 Australian Parliament House

Canberra, Australia

On sheer size alone this project lays claim to being considered one of the great buildings of the late twentieth century: with a gross floor area of 2,700,000 square feet (250,000 square metres) distributed in buildings set on an axial plan across an 80-acre (32-hectare) site, the architects created 4,500 rooms specially designed to accommodate the range of functions required to govern a nation. The budget topped 1 billion Australian dollars.

Both in the whole and in the parts there was a need to symbolize national unity and the commitment to a democratic process. Through the works of art displayed, the crafts, and the furnishings, the buildings aim to reflect the history, cultural diversity, development and aspirations of the Australian people.

But this rich concept had to be worked with an exacting list of specific spaces with their specific environmental requirements. Australia's bicameral system of government required the following:

– accommodation for the House and Senate chambers, committee and party rooms and office accommodation in close proximity for all Members and Senators;
– a series of major public and ceremonial spaces to accommodate public education and State occasions;
– accommodation for the Executive, including the Prime Minister's suite, Cabinet suite, and offices for ministers and staff;
– multiple dining rooms, bars, and cafeterias for Members, staff and the public; multiple recreational facilities;
– service facilities, primarily for staff, such as banks, post office, shops, travel agency and hair care.

With such a program, it is clearly impossible to attempt a detailed summary of the interior – or, rather, interiors – in anything less than a very long book. But a run through of some of the elements does give the character and quality of MGT's handling of the project (the interiors were designed by the architects' Canberra office).

The range of materials used in the project suggests the diversity of Australia's mineral and industrial wealth. Internal floorings include marble, granite, timber parquetry and carpet. Ceilings are, typically, of suspended acoustic plaster tiles, metal tiles and timber panels, both painted and natural. Internal walls use pre-cast concrete panels, prefabricated timber and fabric panels, or plaster on metal studs. A notable feature is the predominance of skylights in the deep-plan building, custom-designed as laminated, double/triple glazed units. Indeed, custom-designed elements range from the lighting to door hardware, timber paneling to entire suites of furniture. This enabled the architects to display a whole range of Australian crafts and materials.

While showing diversity was one objective behind the design program, there was also the need to unite the whole with a clear architectural imprint. MGT sought to do this through creating 'a balanced and unforgettable geometry.' That partly derives from the plan that already existed for the site, one of intense order and geometry, but which also had a sensitivity to the landscape. Giving shape to such a massive interiors program required a careful balancing of

Simple, white-plaster walls are contrasted by the rich native Western Australian jarrah parquetry floors and joinery timbers providing a warm red-brown colour scheme in the Senate Office area.

Controlled natural light bathes the main committee room, where soundproof galleries allow visitors to watch without disturbing the proceedings.

human-scale elements while representing the massive overall concept within the constituent parts.

Another unusually demanding, although pleasing requirement for the designers was to create a building with a projected 200-year lifespan, capable of achieving a timeless integration of the changes in function (and, indeed, design) in the decades of use ahead. This further encouraged the use of materials already tried and tested over many years – such as granite, native timbers, wool fabrics, leathers, and bronze for both internal and external fittings.

The constant desire also to be aware of not losing the human element in such a large project is expressed by MGT's comment that 'the high standard of craftsmanship throughout the building is intended to convey the importance and dignity of the work of the individual in a democracy.'

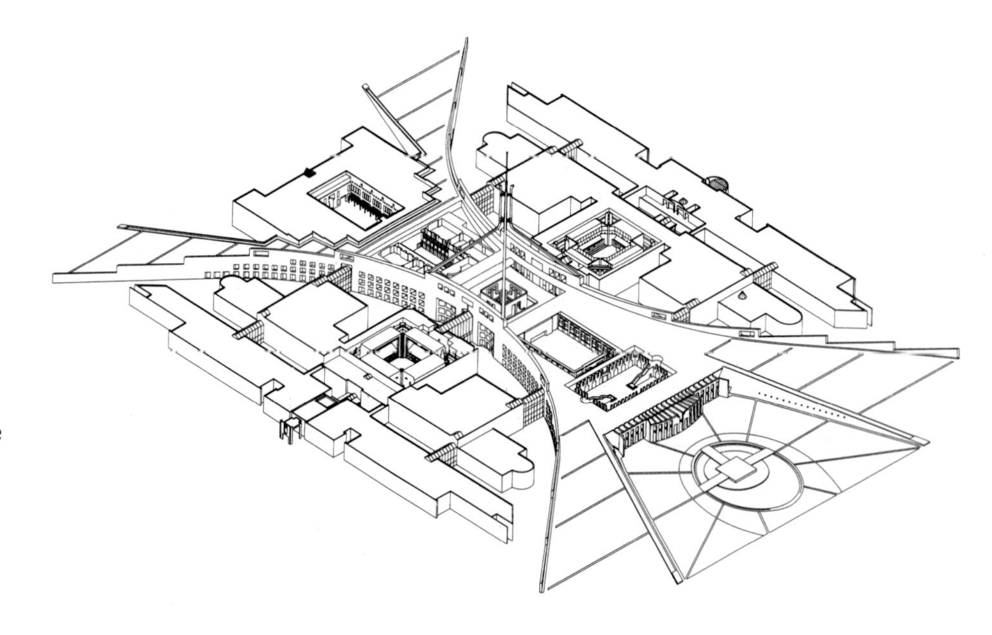

MGT designed the carpets, furniture, and light fittings throughout the complex in a range of different forms that aims to avoid institutional uniformity.

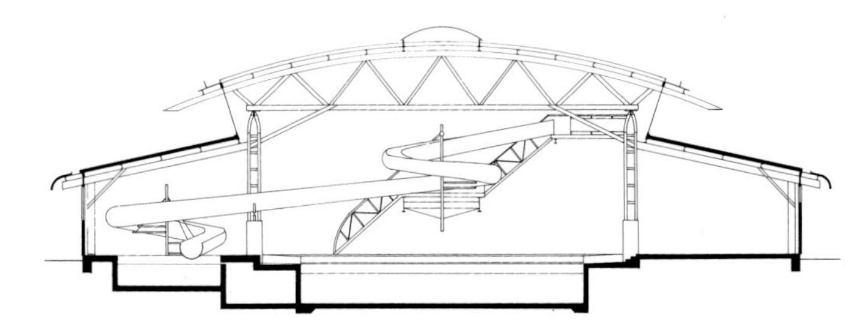

The main pool is kept free for serious swimmers and is suitable for competition, despite being part of the overall 'leisure pool' concept.

Ship-style features, such as this staircase to the head of the water slide, add to the nautical allusions of the design.

Changing pavilions and lockers with tables and chairs at the poolside suggest the beach rather than the functional single-sex changing rooms usually seen at swimming pools.

Massive sums of money are spent on creating places for public pleasure, yet few of them ever get within range of consideration for design magazines and books. The new architectural type of the leisure center rarely rises away from being a summary of its parts –its facilities lumped together with no more interrelationship than goods in a warehouse.

The contrast between recent leisure centers in Britain and their predecessors of Victorian and Edwardian swimming pools is often a sharp one: the mono-functional aspect of those buildings leading to the rigorous devotion of the interior to the water, while the variety of pleasures being promoted in the modern leisure hall all too often results in a confused and insubstantial interior.

An exception is the pool designed by architects Alsop and Lyall for a private developer on a site in the seaside town of Sheringham, Norfolk. It unites the clarity of the earlier mode of the swimming pool with the sense of fun and more relaxed activities associated with the modern pool. At last the concept of 'the interior beach' finds a clear form.

From the approach the visitor is prepared for the sense of the large space within and for the sense of carefully wrought humorous details. The form echoes both the grand hall of the pool type and also the barns that stand out in the flat landscape – the architects had the plywood paneling of the exterior specially developed – while the rainwater is channeled through oversized funnels and the entrance door handles are wave-shaped.

Once inside, the large, light space of the pool hall is immediately apparent. Ahead is the 'beach,' a curved shallow area of the pool, separated from the main area of water by a series of concrete blocks that serve also as starting blocks for races. On the side away from the entrance area is the 'orangery,' a place for sitting and consuming refreshments, and all this area is dominated by the glazed wall that allows in an unexpected intensity of natural light. Next to the 'beach' is a conservatory and indoor garden, which further help to create a summery environment. These areas can also be used for functions.

Alsop & Lyall

4.4 Splash

Sheringham, UK

Visitors will tend immediately to turn to the side of the pool, where the facilities are conveniently placed to enable changing. Modern pool design often involves the bather entering a closed-off area to disrobe before being admitted into the pool hall. But Alsop and Lyall avoid this formality by building not a series of changing rooms, but opening out an area to this usage, avoiding discrimination by gender. Instead privacy and security are offered with lockers and, notably, tents that are reminiscent of the Victorian bathing machine or the beach hut. As with the beach proper, families can stay and change together.

The most dramatic single feature of the pool hall is the water slide. Yet it is not the crude intrusion into the space seen in many other similar leisure centers: its first spiral forms a focal point to the head of the pool, and its splashdown is in a small pool off to one side, thus keeping the 25-metre-long main water area free for swimmers.

The main pool is not just an open area of water, however, as it includes the 'fun' element of a powerful wave machine. (And this has a serious purpose, too, in lifesaving training.) The plant room is situated behind the only blank wall in the hall, which is behind the head of the pool and is thus enlivened by the slide and the staircase which feeds it.

This use of basic structural and functional elements to capture a sense of fun and express the purpose of the building is crucial to the interior aesthetic and is most clearly expressed by the main structure: the single span, large beamed curving roof held up by timber lattice columns mounted on concrete stubs. The timber elements play heavy beams against a web of lighter woodwork.

From the tile-clad concrete bases three platforms are cantilevered, providing a position for the lifeguards and two balconies for the cafe. They introduce a level above which the eye is guided to see the hall as one virtually uninterrupted space, following the roof form. The timber structure thus becomes more of an expression of the lively activities than any part of a solid built form. The exposed services similarly express activity rather than being hidden in more weighty structure.

There is a significant predominance of white finishes – timber, tiling, steel and plaster. Initially, the client wanted more colour in the environment (drawing on experience in developing a similar pool), but the architects held firm to the scheme of white and blue. Colour is provided in plenty by the people, and by temporary elements within the cafe area, or the graphics (which were not of the architects' choosing).

In time it is intended that planting will grow up parts of the laminated timber structure, further interweaving the sense of indoor and outdoor environments.

The project was completed on a tight budget of around £2 million ($3.2 million) for the total building costs.

The building as art: Kurokawa explores relationships of form and space with regard to the expression as much as the function.

Approaching the museum, the unusual form suggests this is a place for meditation, for reflecting on questions posed by the unpredictable form of the building as well as the contents.

Kisho Kurokawa

4.5 Museum of Modern Art

Nagoya, Japan

The development of the Japanese museum as a place for meditation on culture takes a very different form in this project than in that carried out at the Kawasaki City Museum (see page 218). The priority behind Kurokawa's design was not to create a strong public space, like the interior piazza/ amphitheater of Kawasaki, but to take advantage of the unique location provided for the Nagoya museum. It is situated in a park at the center of the dense city, and clearly has a role as a haven, a place almost of silence. Again, the analogy of the modern museum as a place of worship is stressed.

To this Kurokawa also brought his own message of the need for 'symbiosis' between nature and architecture. This is evident in a range of symbolic forms in the exterior expression of the building; architectural forms and references range from an abstract pergola to 'quotations' from Le Corbusier's monastery at La Tourette.

Inside, however, the building's integration of Modernism and Japanese tradition, together with concern for interaction with nature, is not so self-conscious. The outside world is acknowledged by the introduction of as much natural light as possible, both direct and indirect. It is also acknowledged by the use of architectural forms that are more often seen outside: bridges link galleries, the lattice frame seen on parts of the outside extends inside, materials connect from the exterior to the interior. With substantial glazed areas apparent from outside, particularly the main entrance lobby, the visitor is able to experience a mirror image of a space, first from outside, then within. This adds to the 'readability' of a complex building. This atrium or lobby is at the crux of the interior, being a space three stories high, from which every exhibition can be reached.

There is an honesty and clarity about the use of materials. White marble, rubber tiles, painted cement, aluminum and acoustic board are clearly articulated surface elements. In some of the formal decorations, however, Kurokawa's work suggests ironic comments on other modern museums: there is an oversized column and capital familiar to Stirling for instance. There is also a crude neo-classical door frame that could be a reference to a number of contemporaries – or indeed to none, but merely another example of the 'intercultural' architectural language that Kurokawa sees as succeeding the International Style.

Relationships of materials and their properties are particularly significant in Kurokawa's achievement of contrasts without conflict.

Substantial glazed areas and flowing geometry suggest the interrelationship of exterior and interior, with contrasts in light level and volumes accentuating the effect.

The design uses doorways, bridges, columns, and many other elements in a way that is both cool – through the colour choices – and yet exciting in form.

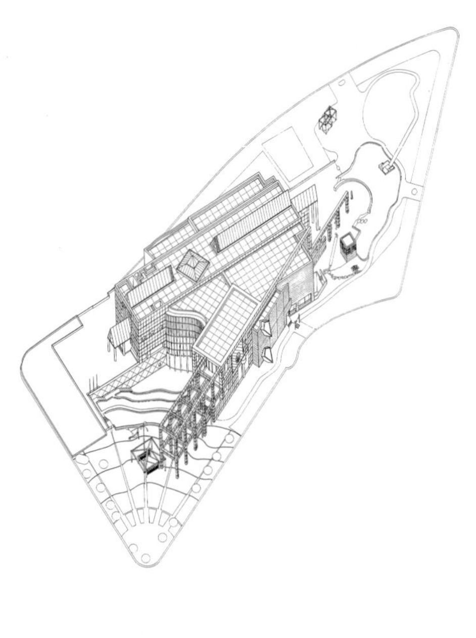

Traditional Japanese design elements are reworked with lessons drawn from various architectural styles to create Kurokawa's distinctive environments.

Structural bays of the former Manach factory become porches that protect the pupils' recreation from summer sun and winter rain.

The plan shows clearly the division between the remains of the Jujol building and the multi-rise new school with gymnasium on top.

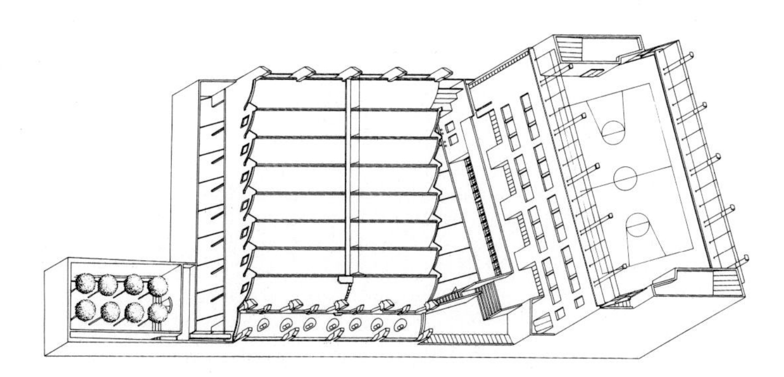

Bach & Mora

4.6 Josep ma Jujol School

Barcelona, Spain

This award-winning conversion project combines a highly respectful rehabilitation of a 1916 work by the noted architect Jujol with a strikingly original program for a new school.

Architects Jaume Bach and Gabriel Mora, working with collaborating architect Roberto Bruzau, began with an unpromising proposal to convert the former Manach factory building into a multisports center. This they rejected in favour of creating a school within the highly irregular rhomboid structure, set within an irregular site created by the street plan.

The structural bays, all that remained of the original building, were a major problem: how could they be included within a new building without either being lost, adapted or compromising a new structure? The architects' ingenious response was to use them as a series of porches that break down the barriers between interior and exterior, and provide a distinctive low-rise feature at the center of the new, high-rise school.

The Jujol bays become an *objet trouvé*, a place for recreational activities and unplanned events outside the main building. The new is thus separated clearly from the old, while at the same time the old links the new with the site and with its environment.

The formality of the Jujol structure, the historical character celebrated in the project, is complemented by a restrained architecture in the school interior. The new building is bisected by a corridor with classrooms either side, and the odd spaces at the points of the rhomboid are taken up with stairways and services.

The architects opted for open brickwork for interior walls for reasons of durability and economy, and because of a concern about escaping the 'curse of plasterwork' by which they mean an indiscriminate use of this finish in most buildings in the city. Brickwork was also seen as a material that was a solid, 'noble' component that helped display the angles within the construction. The inter-relationship of interior and exterior spaces is also brought into focus by using a material that works for both environments. In contrast, artificial stone surfaces are occasionally used to point up the significant use of brick and its contrast to the prevailing aesthetic in Barcelona.

The porches are given a frame and protection from the uninspiring environment around the recreation area.

Brick and tile provide surfaces that are hardwearing yet have a soft character for interior spaces, while curving forms in the columns, steps and ceiling profile also suggest organic qualities.

Interior corridors without natural light were a result of the multi-rise scheme, but decorative tiling relieves any oppression.

Bold colours and soft forms express the unusual junction of old and new and develop an aesthetic in keeping with both the rigour and play of a school environment.

Meeting rooms and other facilities draw natural light and a sense of activity from being located around the central waiting area.

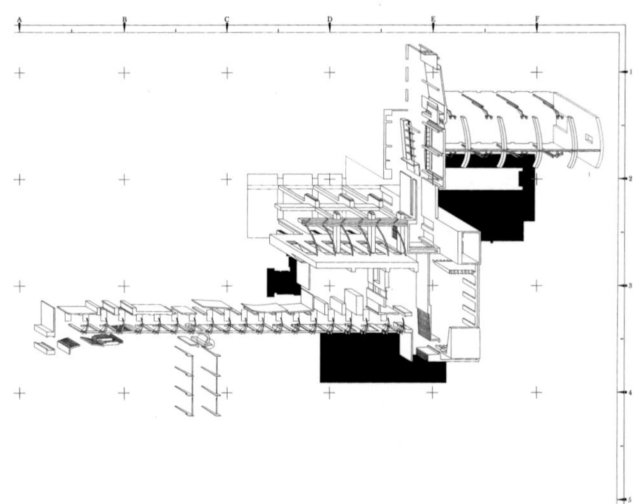

Part play, part sculpture, the twenty-four-foot-high central feature of the waiting area reaches up to the light to be topped by a tree: a symbol of life.

The cancer center's semi-underground position does not encroach on the light or views of neighbouring hospital buildings and generates the top-lit form as an essential design element.

Morphosis & Gruen Associates

4.7 Cedars-Sinai Comprehensive Cancer Center

Los Angeles, USA

If you are the intended user, then design will not succeed in making your day at a cancer clinic, but it might help to put you a little more at ease. When client Dr Bernard Salick wanted to open a 24-hour center for treating the disease, and to do it in such a way as to provide a flagship for other such enterprises, he was concerned that, despite his own self-confessed 'traditional' views on design, the architects should develop an appropriately innovative solution for this new kind of building.

Part of the brief required that the building should be 'dramatic but warm.' And drama, humour and a lightness of touch seem to have been key factors influencing the environment created. To achieve this, Morphosis partner Thom Payne reported that the design team set out to change the conventions in health care design, which tend either towards the antiseptic functional and neutral style, or towards the false tone of trying to be seen as a 'home-away-from-home.' 'If frightening things go on here, then the architecture should reflect it,' says Mayne. In this way, the building would avoid being coldly clinical or condescending in its design, and could instead perhaps be made to encourage patients in their struggle against cancer.

These were, however, high hopes, especially given the site requirements: the new unit had to slip in unnoticed in the general hospital plan, and was to incorporate a basement level wing of the Cedars-Sinai Hospital. The attempt to be uplifting first had to overcome being underground.

The entrance makes clear the tough stance of the designers. A corridor with granite floor and upholstered steel benches sets a stylish but stern atmosphere. This terminates at the balcony overlooking the waiting room: a dramatic space, 45 feet high, introduces the drop to the lower floor and is dominated by a structure that is part play and part pure sculpture. Crowning this 24-foot (7.3-metre) structure is a tree reaching up to the light, below is a chair with a series of stylized steps leading up to it: the tree being a symbol of life and of the patients' fight against illness. At the base is a play area.

Full advantage is taken of natural light in the waiting room, and this bringing of natural light into a partly subterranean interior is a priority throughout. The other major space in the building is the chemotherapy atrium, where a barrel-vaulted skylight produces a sense of relief. Where there is no natural light to exploit, clever use of indirect sources helps maintain the softness of the atmosphere. This softness is accentuated by the hard-edged nature of some of the fixtures and the minimal palette of colours used.

High-quality finishes, contrasting light levels and planting help break down the institutional feeling in this lobby outside consulting rooms.

Long corridors can be overwhelming in hospitals but Morphosis relieve the experience with contrasting lighting, textures and colours plus the incorporation within the wall design of positions for pictures.

Exam Rooms
Day Hospital
Day Hospital

A tight budget called for almost utilitarian sparseness in Starck's work without compromising the rich period flavour.

New graphics link the early cinema origins of the building, 1920s style, and more current enthusiasms to give a low-cost flourish to the entrance.

Philippe Starck

4.8 La Cigale

Paris, France

This is a project in which a high standard of design appears to have been achieved despite all that fate could put in its way. The brief was to create a multi-use auditorium from a building that is seen as housing the first French cinema; thus, a delicate knitting together of old and new was required. At the same time, the budget for the project was at times a tight one. In addition, Starck found that, at times, he lost control of the project during the construction due to major management problems. Nevertheless, the combined flavour of a period interior and Starck's distinctive approach appear to have survived and flourished.

The design team had a complex range of uses to cater for in the conversion. The technical requirements of rock bands, fashion shows, classical music concerts and cinema had all to be provided for, without losing the original character that has been treasured by, amongst others, the Surrealist movement. Starck's use of rich materials, such as gold leaf, marble and velvet, maintains the turn-of-the-century opulence, while avoiding the mere reproduction of period details.

Starck's approach is expressed in the way he sees the modern technological requirements as an opportunity to introduce 'avant-garde forms' into the design. The hi-tech appearance of contemporary sound and lighting is not something to be disguised, but to be celebrated as an addition to the rich mix of elements that has always been a part of the interior of La Cigale.

The auditorium exists on three levels: the orchestra level (4,305 square feet, 400 square metres), the ground level (8,611 square feet, 800 square metres), and the balcony (3,230 square feet, 300 square metres). An important functional development of the auditorium is that an area of the orchestra pit and stalls has been made adaptable to allow the seating capacity to vary from 917 to 1,500 seats (standing and seated). But it is perhaps in the surrounding circulation areas that Starck's contribution is most clear: in the green marble bars and the dramatic black and white granito flooring. The overall effect of some of these areas is to appear like the naive spaceship visions of 1950s *bandes dessinées* artists: a not altogether surprising image, considering Starck's interest in the forms of space architecture.

The designer's enthusiasms, however, appear to have been a little stretched by the difficulties of completing this project. When asked to suggest what he would like to design next, Starck commented: 'To stop the design, and to go into politics,' which perhaps reveals the area of skill most necessary at times in design.

La Cigale's grand interior is retained while incorporating the sound and lighting equipment to stage a whole range of demanding spectacles.

The red velvet of the richly decorated auditorium contrasts with the cool, more spartan lobby surrounding.

Opposite The traditional flooring pattern is twisted and stretched with a characteristic Starck sense of humour in the meeting of forms.

8 La Cigale

Concourse areas present the museum as an open and welcoming public space.

In the normally neutral box of an auditorium Kikutake uses lighting symmetries and tricks with a mirrored wall to both entertain and focus attention on the stage.

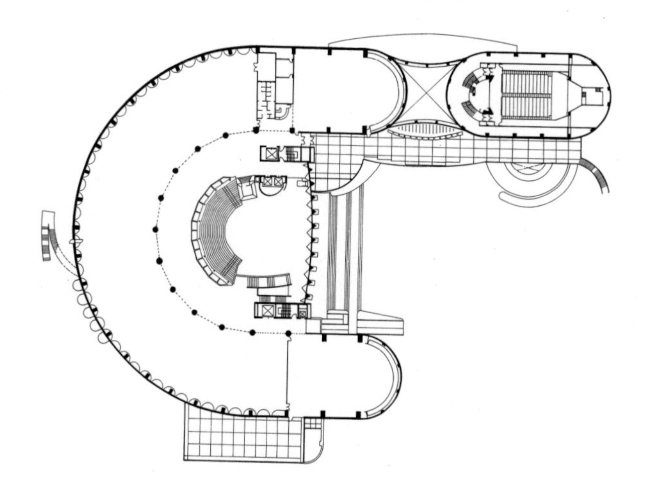

Kiyonori Kikutake Associates & Keikaku-Rengo

4.9 Kawasaki City Museum

Kawasaki City, Japan

The decline of religion and church-going has been seen as a phenomenon linked to the growth of interest in museum building throughout Europe and in the United States. Museums and art galleries, with their collections of our cultural treasures from the past and expressions of ideas in the present, are seen as a logical development from churches, loss of faith being replaced by a search for signs of meaning.

This experience has not been evident in Japan to quite the same extent, but in the Kawasaki City Museum Kikutake and his team have tackled just such a major search for communal meaning through the built form. As Kikutake comments: 'The functions of museums these days are as a mirror that reflects various urban situations. People visit museums just as they look into their mirror every day and find therein the "looks" of their city. It leads them to think over the past and contemplate a future. It also encourages them anew and reminds them of the joy and perspectives of life, or simply comforts and relaxes them.'

These are the attitudes with which the designers interpreted the brief from Kawasaki City's planners. They wanted a series of spaces that would create more than just a place for displaying exhibits and would be more than just a research laboratory for scholars. The museum had to be a public facility that united the exhibits with such related areas as a museum store and restaurant. The designers extended this to take account of the need to provide channels for communication between the museum and its visitors. Thus, interactive temporary exhibits, seminars, study groups and other conference activities are provided for – even wedding ceremonies may be held in the museum, strengthening the analogy with a place of worship.

At the center of all activities is the 'promenade space,' a lobby that is like an amphitheater in its curving, tiered form facing onto the main glazed entrance façade. Temporary exhibitions and performances can be staged here, and above and nearby are the store and restaurant facilities. It is a focal point, providing quick and clear reference for the location of the permanent collections.

These permanent collections are extremely diverse, ranging from archeology to folk culture, from graphic arts to photography and comics. Rather than attempt some false association between the disparate elements, the designers have planned the building to reflect the user's activities: the three stories are allocated the functions of 'see something,' 'do something,' and 'think.'

On the top floor are the 'things to see.' This floor comprises an information area, a video library, and a range of interactive areas where users learn through visual experience. On the middle floor, visitors can take part in various activities, visiting one or other of the several exhibitions that may be mounted.

On the ground floor, the promenade space with its seating provides visitors with the opportunity to meditate or discuss and thus completes the function of the museum by provoking them into thinking about the experience it provides. It is a brightly lit, airy space with a vast glazed wall allowing in the natural light and a bank of stage lights providing spotlighting for events. A slightly domed ceiling and pavilion entrance/exit doors allude to classical forms. The building thus appears less as a 'traditional' museum 'type' than as an egalitarian 'culture palace' or city hall.

At night the main entrance lobby becomes a showcase for the museum experience, giving glimpses of its temporary exhibition.

More neutral spaces provide the main gallery areas, but the curving plan suggests the activity of the central amphitheater.

Circulation, exhibitions and simply promenading are activities catered for in the main lobby area, the hub of museum life.

Romanistik
Geschichte
Klassische

At night the library changes to being a warm, inward-looking environment, in contrast to the day when natural light dominates.

Behnisch & Partners

4.10 University Library

Eichstatt, West Germany

The grand Baroque buildings that distinguish the small town of Eichstatt in Bavaria are the backdrop to a careful integration of a number of new buildings that form the only Catholic university in a German-speaking country. While the diocesan architect Karl-Josef Schattner had to work hard to fit in the new with the old and convert existing buildings for most of the university, when it came to the centerpiece of the new library there was an opportunity to develop more freely on a site at the edge of the old town, in the meadows by the river.

This freedom is important in considering how Behnisch and Partners (project architects Manfred Sabatke, Christian Kandzia and Joachim Zurn) were motivated and were able to create such an open, and apparently free-form series of spaces.

Two directions can be seen behind the aesthetic. First, the awareness of the Baroque precedents provided an opportunity to produce a modern development that presented the same *joie de vivre*, achieving this, however, through light and colour rather than structural extravagance.

Secondly, there is a statement of the architects' philosophical approach. Formal harmony, or any imposed linking of the various parts of the building together, was avoided in the belief that 'the individual elements, and the spaces between individual forms are the most interesting; the points where larger units come into contact and don't quite harmonize. Just as, in a cultivated landscape, the borders of the fields, with their heaps of stones, hedges, trees, bushes, animals and so on are more interesting than the larger areas of the fields themselves.'

An example of this dynamic discordance is the space between the library proper and the faculty rooms where many things come together – staircases, lift, fanlight, glass wall, galleries, foyer and more. Through the overlapping of the parts an exciting view through and relationship between elements is achieved. From different perspectives, in different lights, these relationships change.

This approach was taken through to the handling of the technological systems, marking a departure from the 'hi-tech' aesthetic that might have been

Lightweight structures provide a functional framework for storing books that echoes computer circuitry in the complex engineering of the system.

Stacks are set back and above the main reading floor with a choice of study areas providing different degrees of privacy.

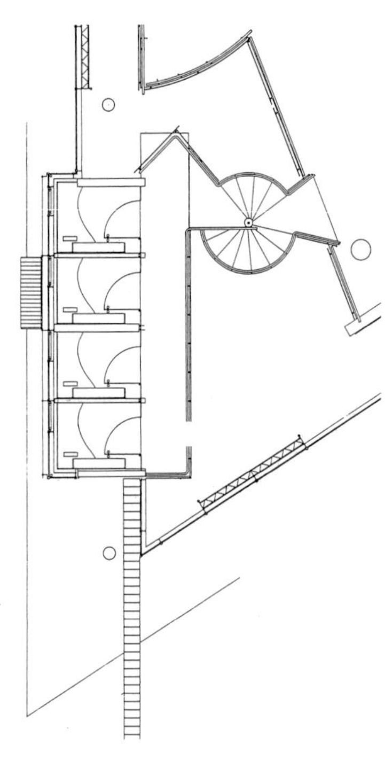

initially construed as a part of the approach. Here the structure, the cladding, the services were each allowed to obey their own 'laws' rather than being forced into assisting in the presentation of some master image. Altogether, the approach seems almost anarchistic in relation to the traditions of architectural thought.

Clearly the degree to which such a free-form of design is allowed to go is in some tension with the final resolution, in that some parts of the building program cannot be allowed to contradict others (for example, servicing running across windows or through a doorway).

The basic brief required a building complex that provided central and specialist libraries with a common reading room (49,806 square feet/4,627 square metres). Along with this there is a language laboratory (1,830 square feet/170 square metres), the languages and literature department (8,557 square feet/795 square metres) and the history and social science department (4,854 square feet/451 square metres). Underneath the library are located most of the stacks (11,302 square feet/1,050 square metres, with potential for doubling).

The reading room is the central feature, a location that acts as a symbol and focus of the university life. It is very light, opening out towards both the river and the town. A large gallery, akin to a theater dress circle, is partly above the reading room, with the two faculties opening out of the back of the library room. The library administration is on the main ground floor level, with reading carrels along the glass wall facing the river. Many of the key axes within the library radiate out to specific points in the town and surrounding country, adding to the sense of the building being a central part of the landscape.

Many materials are used throughout the complex, but Behnisch and Partners achieve their objective of making light and colour the main attraction rather than the solid elements. There is an interplay of concrete slab and column with steel staircases and with the shelving system; against these solids the lighting – natural or artificial – throws shadow grids and illuminates the insubstantial structure of blinds and perforated metal. Floorings range across all kinds of surface – from stone and linoleum to parquet and carpet.

For all the architects' concern with colour, intriguingly they avoided using much bold colour. Many of the surfaces are in white or natural tones, such as the wood and metal furniture, or concrete structure. This is appropriate in creating study areas that must be calm, neutral, and not distracting. The books and students themselves provide a spectrum of colour. However, bold features such as the striped exterior blinds or the blue and yellow surfaces on the major interior junction of spaces accentuate the dynamic and refreshing qualities of this major non-commercial building. It does not stand on ceremony, but succeeds in creating an image of the importance of its role by the very bold way in which it avoids any traditional, formal stereotypes.

While white is the dominant neutral colour within study areas, circulation space is enlivened with bold graphics and more contrasts of lighting than would be desirable in reading areas.

Light and space are the all-important features of the design.

The detail of the rotunda clerestory illustrates the use of contrasting colour and natural lighting within a strong architectural framework.

The courtyard outside retains a clear relationship with the central rotunda, both in its function as a waiting area and in the bold black and white tiling and wall treatments.

Evans & Shalev have created a hierarchy of spaces denoting public and private, formal and informal, circulation, and waiting areas.

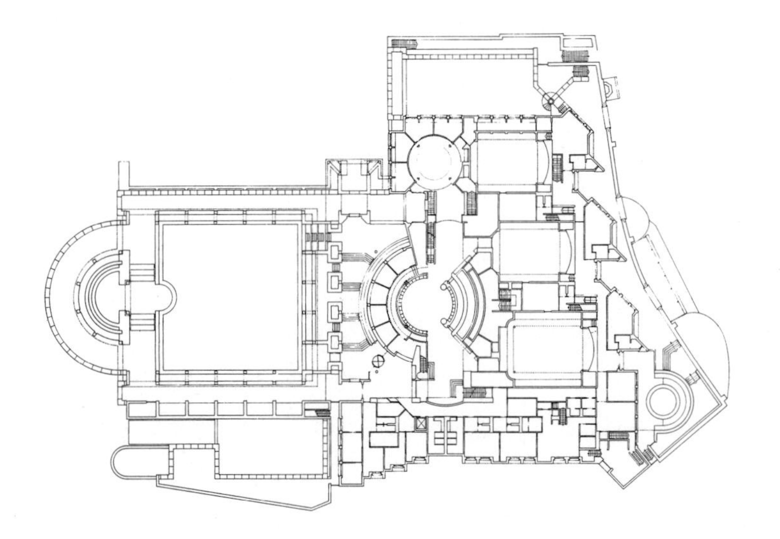

Evans & Shalev

4.11 Truro Crown Court

Truro, UK

In England there is a saying that 'justice must not only be done, but be seen to be done.' It is an axiom of public morality that perhaps can be seen to underlie the traditional approach to the design of court buildings: not only are they places where grim judgements are often handed out in response to tales of grim events, but they often give the impression that the architects think the worst of all who pass within.

This is, of course, grossly unfair in that much of the life of a courthouse involves people who work in the building and any number of people who visit and do not depart 'in chains.' At the same time the designers of such buildings do have unusual problems to contend with, in particular the security requirements for handling prisoners. But at Truro Eldred Evans and David Shalev managed to ensure that such pressures did not result in a building that suggested guilt before innocence. Instead, they created an elevating, open, and light building.

The complex is erected on the cattle-market site where Truro Castle once stood. It is a hilltop near to the town center, with views around. The basic building requirements were for two Crown Court rooms, a dual purpose courtroom with accommodation on three floors, and a public concourse. There are related judge and jury areas, waiting rooms, consultation rooms and other administrative facilities. There is a public dining room and a courtyard within the complex for the use of the waiting members of the public or lawyers.

The most striking space is the dramatic rotunda, the hub of the building where the two waiting spaces of the courts meet. Besides taking full advantage of all available natural light and ventilation, this feature creates a scale and dignity within the building often lost in modern court complexes. Yet it is not an element that is too weighty in the manner of older courthouses, where neo-classical architecture becomes a symbol of state power. Here, Evans & Shalev have taken just the scale and suggestion of

importance that goes with a rotunda, while adding a sense of drama and even decorativeness with the black and white tile scheme and colourful fabrics.

They describe their aims in the rotunda as producing the following qualities: 'Vibrant and serene. Full of light. Comfortable. The outside brought into the building. A meeting place.'

Details, such as the glazed courtroom doors, bold contrasting colours and forms, and a cheerful restaurant, all of these help to break down the tension that normally rules in a courthouse. 'The process of law is made more accessible, humanized,' claim Evans & Shalev.

Consider the integration with the outside environment: the jury deliberation room commands a view over the neighbouring park, the judges enjoy a small enclosed private garden, and the visiting public have a garden area that is a natural extension of the main building and reaches out into Truro. Only the defendants have no open space, lament the architects.

The cost of the project was £660 ($1,056) per square metre. Some of the furnishings, such as the courtroom benching, were designed by the architects, while the rotunda seating, courtroom seats, dining and canteen tables and chairs were from Hille Ergonom. The Crown Suppliers provided other movable furnishings.

Light tones on the furniture and strong basic colours, plus varied lighting, reduce the intimidatory character of the main courtroom.

At the heart of the building is a rotunda with light, planting and comfortable seating, in stark contrast to many English court buildings.

Pools of water replace windows as the points of relief, with semi-enclosed areas between pools creating a sense of depth and movement.

Christoph Langhof Architekten

4.12 Public Baths, Kreuzberg

Berlin, West Germany

There are several things that are apparently wrong with this building. And Christoph Langhof would be the first to tell you what he thinks they are. The reason why they are 'wrong,' and why he will happily explain them, has much to do with the character and quality of the work.

With his colleagues Thomas Hanni and Herbert Meerstein, Langhof had to overcome a number of problems that would normally badly compromise a project: the building had to be squashed into a sensitive situation on the edge of a new urban park; the brief asked for much more than the budget appeared to be able to stretch to comfortably; and, during planning, circumstances changed, requiring major cuts in the size and form of the project.

The response to these difficulties was made in a number of ingenious ways. A substantial proportion of the building is hidden under a hillside in the park – this is not only environmentally sensitive and energy efficient, it also adds the element of surprise in discovering a building that seems much larger on the inside than it is outside. The sports pool, diving pool, learners' pool, sauna and gymnastics room are below ground, but natural light is brought in through small glazed courtyards cut into the turf. This gives a particular quality to the light and to the orientation of the building: things are not quite as they might be expected to be.

The factor of surprise is carried through to awareness of the proportion of the rooms. They are too small, in conventional terms, for what is in them. The pools are more dominant than usual, the circulation space smaller. The reason for this is two-fold. First, it was done to save money without compromising the provision of pools of the stipulated size. Secondly, it is Langhof 's idea that each pool and each function should have its own specific area over which it will dominate. The water is 'the object of desire,' set in a simple tiled space and glowing with the underwater lighting.

To pass from one pool to another is to go from one room to another, with doorways and ramps signalling the passage. The constant linking factor is the ceiling height which remains the same

Reflections, grids, and contrasts in lighting and dimensions are used to break down the oppressiveness of the many enclosed spaces.

With tight budget restrictions the design makes the most of the heavy structural requirements by turning them into a bold decorative statement.

throughout and allows the eye to travel further. Thus, visitors are made aware of a sense of space, but are moved through this by the passage to new areas and new spaces.

With such a tight budget, it was not possible to give high quality finishes to all surfaces. This restriction helped generate a further rationale in the design: the entrance block becomes an almost forbidding fortification-like area, with narrow slit windows on the outside giving onto a spartan, unrelieved interior. But from this area, the entry into the pools becomes a point of delight, the more pleasurable, luxurious textures, colours, materials and lighting being emphasized by the contrast.

The proportions of the hall that houses the wave pool and three paddling pools are criticized by Langhof. It is 'too long, too wide and too low,' he says. He suggests that the solution would be to increase the height of the hall in order to correct the proportions, but cost prohibited this. Instead, he opted for an architectural solution, drawing attention to the golden girders and pylons that support the roof, and thus drawing the eye away from consideration of the formal proportions of the area. That, combined with the heavy servicing plant, sets up a different perception of order in the space, making the actual roof seem without weight compared to the structure.

At the heart of Langhof's approach is a belief in creating 'jewels' within architecture. He argues that it is not necessary to put everything on the same level of detailed design excellence: as with a favoured street, just a few points of real quality will satisfy the perception. In his own words, 'If the architect can succeed in recognizing the strategic elements, the ones which are important for the space, then it obviously suffices to concentrate on these elements and design them in such a way as they dominate the whole.' At the Kreuzberg pool he decided to make 'gems' of the main hall, with the golden structure, the ceiling, the lighting in the blue rooms, and the entrance façade of the white monolith which anticipates perception of the interior.

Views through the building are like windows onto other scenes with the water creating a play of light.

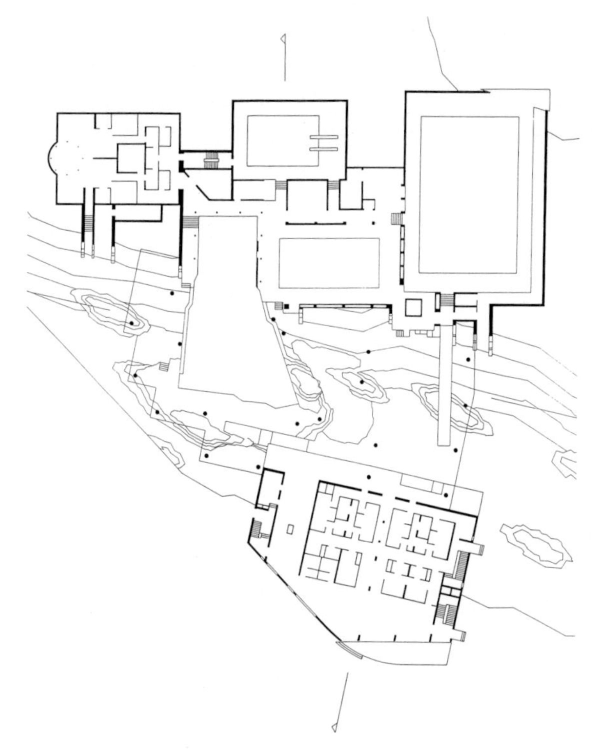

A structural steel frame and stainless steel clips hold up glass bands to create a striking glass sculpture over the foyer.

The eclectic nature of the new theater façade is a bold response to the mix of imagery in adjoining older buildings.

Barton Myers Associates, BOOR/A & ELS Design Group

4.13 Center for the Performing Arts

Portland, USA

The eclectic interiors to be found in this partly new, partly restored theater complex reflect – and perhaps derive in part from – the rich mix of designers involved and the source of the commission. The decision to invest in the center was backed by a bond put up by the citizens of Portland, Oregon, and a whole range of local issues went into the brief that preceded the initial design competition.

Out of that came success for a design drawn up by designers Barton Myers Associates, architects Broome, Oringdulph, O'Toole, Rudolf Associates and ELS Design Group. Their $27 million scheme proposed a manner of meeting the requirements of restoring the existing 1927 theater and building two new auditoria in a way that both suggests a new building of integrity and yet gives character to the individual parts.

The first phase saw the restoration of the old Paramount Theater, originally designed by Rapp and Rapp, and the conversion of its interior into a 2,750-seater concert hall, renamed the Arlene Schnitzer Concert Hall. But it is across the street from this hall that the more intriguing modern design contribution is made in the creation of the new halls; one a 900-seat intermediate theater for drama and chamber music, the other a 360-seat 'showcase' theater designed with highly flexible stage and audience arrangements. (Barton Myers was the design lead for these theaters.)

From the outside, the nature of the building is clearly apparent: it is stagey, reflecting materials and details from neighbouring buildings in a way that both acknowledges the context and yet proudly announces the newness and theatricality of the place. Inside there is less reserve. The design draws on the typology of theater, its glory in the effect and showiness of design, and the bold embracing of different styles and different periods in the one project. The larger theater leans most towards turn-of-the-century style – and yet is undoubtedly a theater of today. There is seating on orchestra and two balcony levels, with the curved balcony fronts defining the main auditorium, and side balconies and boxes bringing the audience close to the proscenium arch. The most dominant elements in this space are the grand steel frame – structural yet decorative – and the brass balcony rails set against the basic blue and green palette.

In contrast, the smaller theater is planned more in the round, the great flexibility of elements reducing the richness of the design. Yet the two theaters are still obviously related. Perhaps the boldest gesture from the designers here is to take the idea of the basic 'black box' theater and furbish it almost entirely as a red box – strong red walls of stained cedar lattice and acoustic red backdrops providing a hot interior when the lights are up, but one that is just as neutral as black when the lights are directed only on the stage.

Any relationship of the two auditoria is ultimately expressed in the multileveled space of the lobby that feeds both. This area alludes to the classical opera house, presenting a grand stage for the audience to show themselves before each other – a gesture that is a long way from the often miserly circulation areas provided in many theater complexes in the recent past. The 'stage' nature of this lobby is enriched by the perimeter boxes that provide interval seating. And the performance opportunity of this space is

fulfilled with the proscenium-like opening of suspended glass that further reinforces the grandeur of the lobby and provides a platform for informal performances.

The topping of the five-level foyer space by the James Carpenter glass sculpture is contrasted with the solidity yet richness of the terrazzo floor, and cherry wood panels on faces of the lobby rotunda are further 'anchors.' This integration of more informal theatrical functions into the building is taken even further in the plans for the space between the new building and the old: a glass canopy covering Main Street and providing an outer lobby that is literally outside, making a stage of part of the city, and yet is integrated with the interiors. The outside covered lobby is the final frame for approaching and viewing performances and for realizing the role of culture in the life of the city.

Grandeur without oppressive formality was aimed for in the creation of the dramatic major spaces.

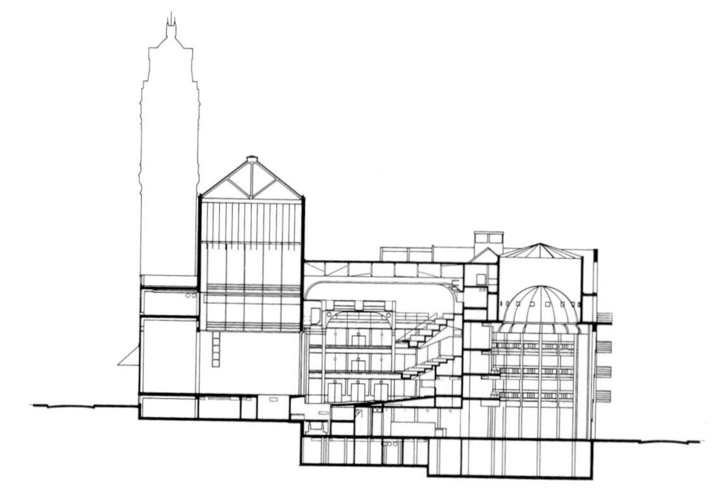

Classic theater architecture was reinterpreted with modern planning and materials but with a concern to retain character.

Startling bold colours break with obvious traditional choices while still developing the aesthetic of the period theater.

Looking up through the 'spectral light dome' from the foyer reveals the dynamic light play of the glass and steel construction.

A combination of the classic horseshoe-shaped theater and the more modern banks of seating maximizes the viewing and seating flexibility while establishing a distinctive character.

The staircase makes a feature of the engineering challenge of providing a load-bearing structure.

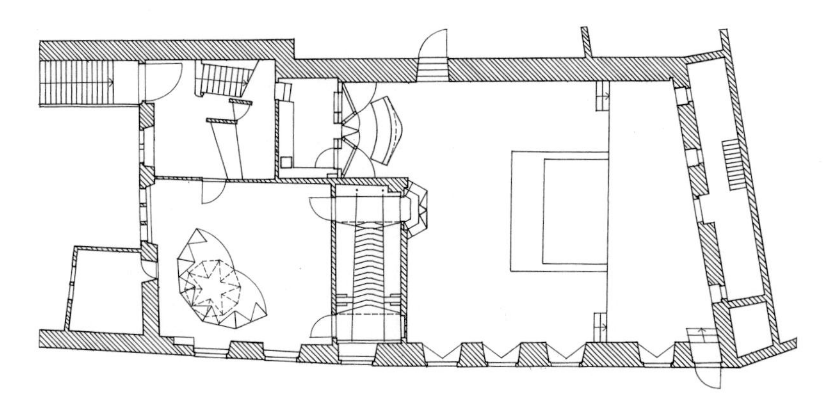

Santiago Calatrava Valls

4.14 Cabaret Tabourettli

Basle, Switzerland

The combination of architectural and engineering knowledge with a sensitivity of a sculptor typifies the work of the young Spanish architect Calatrava and gains perhaps its fullest expression in the interior of this small cabaret theater.

The project is part of the restoration of the medieval Hinterhaus, a building in the heart of Basle, where apartments and other facilities are also located. The first-floor position of the Tabourettli theater was a commission that came to Calatrava as a result of his engineering expertise: the building had severe problems with structural movement (there were virtually no foundations), and there was concern over how any loads could be placed during restoration.

Calatrava's response to the building's structural problems generated the major feature of the interior – a striking staircase that concentrates the load into a single point which steps over the ancient parts of the building and focuses the load where heavy bearing members could be placed. The new staircase acts to improve the structure of the whole building, while at the same time opening up much better distribution within the building and for the Cabaret Tabourettli in particular.

This overtly engineering-driven element of interior design is unusual in such a sensitive restoration context, being at first sight totally out of keeping in form and materials to the medieval tradition. Yet the sculptural eye of Calatrava manages to integrate the new by ensuring the clear readability of the new and old elements. His staircase is not only a bridge within the structure, but is a bridge between old and new. The organic form is expressive of the same forces that determined the original structure, and its character is also carried through into other interior fitments, expressing the new building program as a clearly identifiable element within the whole.

The small theater is split between two floors of the building: the first-floor entrance level housing the pay booth, restrooms, and other facilities, with the cabaret theater, bar, and performers' wardrobe area upstairs.

The furniture and other furnishings extend the aesthetic of the staircase in metal and wood. The curious folding wardrobe on the performance floor is a solid feature, yet also has a portable nature. Other elements – the bar, the wooden shutters on the windows, the seating and tables – also display an original detailing and aesthetic that sits apart from the medieval fabric and yet complements it.

There is a celebration of materials and their potential in Calatrava's design. The light elements of the stairs stretch and tease the potential of steel, the glass steps are ironic fragile elements that belie their appearance by taking the load of all traffic in the theater. The pear-wood furniture and screens are often flexible where one might expect firmness, solid where lighter elements would be more usual. The overall effect is to create an environment that is itself part of the experience of the cabaret performance.

The bar carries through the stark use of metal and wood, which is then enlivened by the sharp detailing on counter and stools.

The portable, folding wardrobe demonstrates the flexibility of the design to meet the multiple requirements of the space.

Old and new work together in the performance area, with the wooden and metal structure of the ceiling echoing a medieval aesthetic.

Further Reference & Acknowledgements

Lucy Bullivant

BIOGRAPHIES OF DESIGNERS

Alsop and Lyall was established in the UK in 1980 by William Alsop (born in Northampton in 1947) and John Lyall (born in Essex in 1949). Both trained at the Architectural Association from 1968–73, and currently teach there. They have worked for architects such as Cedric Price, Piano and Rogers and Rock Townsend, and are visiting professors at architectural schools in the US, UK and Europe. Their major projects vary greatly in scale: a new museum and urban planning in Hamburg; Butlers Wharf Loft; housing in London docklands; the Real World leisure park in Sydney, Australia; the refurbishment of the Leeds Corn Exchange; a retail, housing and office development in Normandy, and the Sheringham Leisure Pool in Norfolk. International competitions such as the proposal for a media park in Cologne, have built up their profile.

Tadao Ando was born in Osaka, Japan in 1941. He is a self-taught architect who in 1989 was awarded the Medaille d'Or de l'Academie d'Architecture. He became well-known in the 1970s for small-scale residences such as the Horiuchi Residence, Osaka (1979) and Azuma House, Osaka (1976), which used traditional Japanese features with Late-Modernist structures. The Rokko housing project of 1983 won international acclaim, as did the Kidosaki Residence of 1988. Ando has lectured and exhibited widely (Intercepting Light & Nature; Breathing Geometry), and his recent work – the Bigi Building, Tokyo (1983), Galleria Akka, Osaka (1988) OXY Unagidani, Osaka (1987) – shows continued use of simplified concrete forms to create fluid spaces.

Armstrong Associates was founded in 1986 by Kenneth Armstrong, and is based in London. Born in Paisley, Scotland, in 1954, he trained at the Mackintosh School in Glasgow and the Royal College of Art. He subsequently worked for Foster Associates on the Hong Kong and Shanghai Banking Corporation headquarters and at DEGW. Armstrong Associates have completed offices, shops and residential interiors. Their major projects include a consultancy with Foster Associates on the masterplan for Kings Cross, London; with Arup Associates on the Imperial War Museum; new offices and showrooms for Elementer Industrial Design.

Arquitectonica is a Florida-based practice founded in 1977 by Bernardo Fort-Brescia (born in Lima, Peru, in 1951) and Laurinda Spear. Both have Masters degrees in Architecture, from Harvard and Columbia Universities respectively. Their work in Miami has been extensive, including housing, offices, the Kitsos Medical Building, and the North Dade Justice Center. Elsewhere, they have designed houses in Illinois; a Center for Innovative Technology, Washington DC; and the Banco de Credito del Peru in Lima. Their Vice-President, architect Martin Wander joined the practice in 1982; Senior Architect Enrique Chuy oversees their Peruvian projects from his base in Lima. Fort-Brescia has received several Progressive Architecture and AIA Honor Awards.

Alfredo Arribas was born in Barcelona in 1954, and studied at the Escuela Tecnica Superior Architectura there from 1972–77 (he is currently professor of projects). An early collaboration with architects Basilio Tobias and Manuel de Llano lasted until 1982, when he became President of the Spanish interior design organization INFAD. Major projects include housing, a sports club, casino and public park. In 1986 he collaborated with Eduard Samso on the Network Cafe and the Francisco Valiente store. In 1987 Miguel Morte joined Arribas' practice, and they designed Velvet Bar and the discotheque Louis Vega. The restaurant Gambrinus was designed in 1988 in conjunction with Javier Mariscal, with whom Arribas is also working on an extension of the Science Museum in Barcelona.

Bach and Mora is a Barcelona-based architectural practice formed in 1976 by Jaume Bach Nunez (born in 1943), and Gabriel Mora Gramunt (born in 1941). Both architects studied at Barcelona School of Architecture in the late 1960s, and are currently design tutors there. Bach worked for Dols, Millet and Paez, and Mora for Hello Pinon and Albert Viapiana before their collaboration on projects such as the State School of Barcelona (1984–1988); a media center (1987), and offices for Raventos I Blanc.

Jeffrey Beers studied architecture at the Rhode Island School of Design until 1979. After a year in Brazil on a Fulbright Fellowship, he worked for I. M. Pei & Partners in New York for 6 years on projects such as Raffles City and The Gateway, large multi-use structures in Singapore before setting up Jeffrey G. Beers Architects in 1986. Projects completed include offices, housing, restaurants and commercial buildings, mostly in New York. Bar Lui and China Grill both reflect Beer's interest in applying craft techniques, particularly in glass, to architecture.

Behnisch and Partners is a Stuttgart-based practice established in 1958. Gunter Behnisch, Winfried Buxel, Manfred Sabatke and Erhard Trankner have designed a great variety of projects, many resulting from competitions. The bias is towards large-scale public buildings, amongst them educational, medical, office and sports centers. Their major projects are the award-winning development designed for the Olympic Games in Munich; the Solar Institute at the University of Stuttgart; government buildings in Bonn; and the library of the University of Eichstatt (which won the BDA-Preis Bayern in 1987).

Branson Coates Architecture was formed in 1985 by Nigel Coates and Doug Branson. Nigel Coates was born in Malvern, UK, in 1949, and studied at Nottingham University and the Architectural Association (AA), where he has taught since 1975, becoming Unit Master in 1979. In 1983 he founded NATO (Narrative Architecture Today) with eight unit members, publishing a magazine and exhibiting work. Doug Branson graduated from the AA in 1975, worked for DEGW and in practice as the Branson Helsel Partnership (until 1984). Branson Coates' first built project was a house for Jasper Conran in 1985. Major projects include the Metropole restaurant, Tokyo (1985), the Jasper Conran shop (1986), the Bohemia jazz club (1986), Caffe Bongo, Tokyo (1987), Silver jewellery shop, London (1987), Noah's Ark restaurant, Sapporo (1988), and the Katharine Hamnett shop, London (1988). Current projects include the Nishi-Azabu building, Tokyo, and the Hotel Maritimo, Otaru, Japan. Coates has also designed his own range of furniture (marketed by Rockstone in Japan, and Sheridan Coakley in the UK/Europe).

Building is a Los Angeles-based practice established in 1985 by Michele Saee, who was born in Iran in 1956. He studied architecture at the University of Florence, urban planning at Milan Polytechnic, and in 1981 worked for Adolfo Natalini at Superstudio, Florence, for two years. After moving to Los Angeles in 1983 he worked for Morphosis on local projects such as the Venice III House; Angeli Cafe (1984), and Kate Mantelini (1985), which won AIA and Progressive Architecture Awards. Building's subsequent work on residences, Trattoria Angeli (1988), and the store Ecru (1988) led to a Young Architects Award in 1987.

Santiago Calatrava Valls was born in 1951 in Benimamet, Valencia. He studied architecture in Valencia, and gained a doctorate in civil engineering from the ETH Zurich in 1981. In 1981 he set up his own office in Zurich, mostly working on Swiss projects but increasingly in his native country as his reputation has grown. In 1987 he won the August Perret Prize from the French UIA, and in 1988 further prizes in both Switzerland and Spain for his work on bridges – the core of his work since 1979. Apart from remodelling Tabourettli Cabaret in Basel, Calatrava has also designed a gallery and heritage square in Toronto, Canada, and an underground station in Bilbao, Spain. In 1989 he designed the Montjuic light for Artemide.

Canal was founded in Paris in 1981 by Daniel and Patrick Rubin. An office of 10 architects and interior designers, together with numerous outside consultants, Canal's major projects include the Mediatheque Tolbaic in Paris; newspaper offices for Libération; premises for Club Mediterranée; the entrance hall to the Ministry of Culture and Communication, Palais Royal, Paris; an extension to the Centre National des Lettres, Paris; and a showroom for Toyota in Kyoto, Japan. They are currently restoring an old hospital building for the advertising agency McCann Erickson, and a manor house for Claude Montana.

Tchaik Chassay was born in 1943 in Johannesburg, and studied at the Architectural Association from 1961–68. He worked for, and became a partner of Edward Cullinan Architects, London, working on housing schemes, schools and offices. Tchaik Chassay Architects was established in 1982, combining restaurant and housing design with high tech, light industrial and sports developments. In 1984 he formed a partnership with Gareth Wright until 1988, working on projects such as Coates Cafe, London for clients Corney & Barrow (1987); Fred's Club, London (1987); Bridge Wharf apartments, London (1988); and a mews conversion in Hampstead with Peter Wilson (1988). Chassay Architects are currently designing apartments in Little Venice, London.

David Chipperfield was born in 1953 in London, and trained at Kingston Polytechnic and the Architectural Association (1974–77). He worked with major practices including Richard Rogers and Partners and Foster Associates before founding David Chipperfield and Partners in 1984. A series of award-winning store interiors and residential commissions guided the transition to larger scale work in France, England and Japan. The practice has recently been involved with urban planning projects in London with Skidmore, Owings and Merrill, Stanley Tigerman and Frank Gehry; the master plan of sites at Canary Wharf; and with the King's Cross redevelopment with Foster Associates. Recent work includes the Arnolfini Gallery, Bristol; shops for Issey Miyake; the Wilson Gough showroom, London; Equipment shop, Paris; a discotheque in Tokyo. A private museum is currently under construction in Tokyo.

Antonio Citterio was born in Meda, Italy, in 1950. He studied architecture at Milan Polytechnic, and worked with Paolo Nava on industrial and furniture design projects. In 1981 Citterio set up his own studio, working with manufacturers such as B & B Italia. In 1983 he began to work on architectural projects, among them showrooms for Santini & Dominici; headquarters for Esprit in Milan, Amsterdam and Antwerp. He has collaborated with Gregotti Associati on the renovation of the Pinacoteca di Brera (1983). Architect Terry Dwan (born in Santa Monica, California, in 1957) joined the practice as partner in 1987 after studying at Yale, and with Citterio has designed houses, stores and offices in Italy, Japan, France and Holland.

Chris Connell is an interior designer based in Melbourne, Australia. He was born in 1955 and studied at the Royal Melbourne Institute of Technology. For a time owner of the shop Astrodesign, selling retro furniture, he began to take on commercial interior design commissions such as the shop Théâtre Végétal (1987). Current projects include bar-restaurants, an apartment and furniture prototypes.

Conran Design Group is a multi-disciplinary design consultancy based in London, with offices in Paris and Hong Kong. It was founded by Sir Terence Conran in 1956. Conran moved into retailing in 1964 when he founded Habitat, and in 1986 Storehouse plc was created by the merger of British Home Stores and Habitat Mothercare. The Group works for both Storehouse and external companies. Recent clients include Gatwick North Terminal, the Michelin Building, London, the Prudential and Boots. Rob Pickering, the Managing Director of the Architecture & Interiors Division, is an architect who trained at Bath University, and later worked with the American practice John Portman Associates in their Singapore office.

Coop Himmelblau was founded in Vienna in 1968 by architects Wolf Prix and Helmut Swiczinsky. Their work until a couple of years ago was mostly installations, speculative projects and conversions in Vienna such as the Baumann Studio (1985), the Iso-Holding offices (1986) and Passage Wahliss (1986). In 1987 they won two major competitions: the Ronacher Theatre, Vienna, and the Melun Senart city planning project in France. In 1988 another first prize was awarded for their scheme for the Hotel Altmannsdort, Vienna. Both partners have lectured internationally.

David Davies Associates was founded in London by David Davies, who began working on freelance interior design projects in 1981. DDA is now 100-strong, offering design services including graphics, packaging, interiors, furniture, architecture, and video. Earlier projects include the development of Next (over 4 years); W H Smith Do-It-All; St Anne's Shopping Centre, and the V & A Bookshop. In 1988 they launched Davies, their first retail venture selling furniture, clothes and accessories designed by DDA. Recent projects include the Design Centre, London; the Valentino headquarters, Rome; Valentino's Oliver shops in London and Rome; the Valentino flagship store in Paris. DDA's architecture and interior design directors are Peter Kent (born 1956], and Peter Moore (born 1955).

Din Associates was founded in 1986 by Rasshied Ali Din (born 1956). Din trained in interior design at Birmingham Polytechnic before working for Fitch & Co. and Studio Giardi, Rome; Peter Glynn Smith Associates; and Allied International Designers. During this time he worked on major projects including the State Bank of India; Gatwick Airport; Top Shop; and for AID, a number of House of Fraser refurbishments. Din Associates' own major projects include the Next Department Store, Kensington High Street, and Next childrens stores (1987), Next Jewellery, and Department X for Next (1988), French Connection showrooms (1988). Current work includes showrooms and offices for Nicole Farhi, a designer room for Fenwicks, Bond Street, and department stores in Sweden for KF.

Evans and Shalev was founded in 1965 by Eldred Evans and David Shalev. Evans qualified as an architect at the Architectural Association (1961) and took up a Scholarship at Yale. She has been an External Examinar and Assessor for the RIBA since 1980. Shalev trained at the Technion School of Architecture in Israel, graduating in 1960, and he is a Visiting Critic at many architectural schools in the UK and in Europe. The practice has designed schools, private residences and civic centers. From 1985–88 they worked on the Truro Courts of Justice in Cornwall, and current projects include an industrial development and rural master plan in Kent, and offices and residences in North London.

Fitch-RS is a major design consultancy with offices in the UK and the US. Its London-based company Fitch & Co. has divisions active in interior design, graphic communications, product design and architecture. The interior design team's major projects include Debenhams, Oxford Street, and other branches for the Burton Group; ASDA; Boots Childrens World; Midland Bank; and Hediard, the French food retailer. In 1984 the Special Project Unit was set up within Fitch & Co., run by Carlos Virgile, who trained as an architect in Argentina and ran his own business in Buenos Aires before joining Fitch & Co. in 1979, and Nigel Stone. Stone trained as a graphic designer in London, and worked as Design Director of Paperchase from 1980–84, joining Fitch & Co. in 1984. The Virgile/Stone collaboration has produced notable interior projects in London such as Braganza restaurant; a store for Janet Fitch; Jamdami restaurant; and Mitchell & O'Brien bar-restaurant. The duo have also completed a major development for the Dutch department store De Bijenkorf.

Norman Foster was born in Manchester in 1935, and studied architecture and city planning at the University of Manchester and at Yale University. He established Team 4 in 1963 with his wife Wendy, and Su and Richard Rogers. In 1976 Foster Associates was established. Foster has a world-wide reputation for his refined, high-tech approach exemplified by projects such as the Willis Faber and Dumas office, Ipswich (1975), the Sainsbury Centre for the Visual Arts at the University of East Anglia (1978), the Renault centre, Swindon (1983), and the Hong Kong and Shanghai Banking Corporation headquarters, Hong Kong (1979–86). Foster is currently working on proposals for King's Cross; Stansted Airport, East Anglia; a Mediatheque in Nimes; and an office tower in Tokyo. The practice has also designed a range of office furniture for Tecno as well as fashion stores for Katharine Hamnett and Esprit.

Kazuko Fujie was born in Toyama, Japan, in 1947. She graduated from Musashino Fine Art University in 1968, and worked until 1977 for the Miyawaki Architectural Office and Endo Planning. After ten years as a freelance interior designer she established Kazuko Fujie Atelier. In 1987 she designed the interiors for the Kirin Plaza, Osaka, for which Shin Takamatsu was architect.

Geyer Design is a major, Melbourne-based practice run by four directors: Peter and Sandra Geyer, Mark Bedford and Michael Greer. They established their name in the 1970s for their work on offices, retail centers, hotels, restaurants and banks. Their major projects include the Bank of New Zealand; Credit Suisse; Telecom Australia's State Network Centre, and branch offices for National Mutual, an award-winning project. They are currently working on interiors for the Australian Embassy in Beijing, China, with architects Denton Corker Marshall.

Naoki Iijima was born in Kawagoe City, Saitama Prefecture, Japan, in 1949. After graduating from the Design School of Musashino Art University in 1972 she worked for Superpotato until 1985 when he set up the Naoki Iijima Design Studio. Her major projects include the Arai bar/restaurant (1986), Ex Jun boutiques in New York and Kobe, and Sonia Rykiel boutiques in Aoyama and Roppongi, Tokyo (1987 & 1988).

Massimo Iosa Ghini was born in 1959 in Borgo Tossignano, and studied architecture at Florence University, where he began drawing comic strips for magazines such as Heavy Metal, and originated the concept of Bolidismo, the starting point of much of his furniture. In 1981 he joined the group Zak-Ark, and from 1984 has collaborated with the firm AGO. Since 1982 he has worked on television sets and graphics for RAI, and clubs such as Bolido, New York (1988). He designed a collection of furniture for Memphis in 1987, and in 1989 sofas for Moroso and glass for FIAM.

Franklin D. Israel was born in 1945 in New York City, and studied architecture at Yale University and Columbia University. From 1971–73 he worked for Giovanni Pasanella in New York City, before winning the Prix de Rome and becoming a Fellow in Architecture at the American Academy in Rome. In 1977 he became Associate Professor of Architecture at the University of California, and set up his own practice in Los Angeles. Work in New York and London gave him experience of working on schools and government buildings. His practice is now known for its private residences and offices in California, some exhibited in 'Architecture Tomorrow', Walker Arts Center, 1988–89. These include the Altman condominium (1987); the Lamy studio (1988); and offices for Propaganda Films (1988). The practice is currently refurbishing the headquarters of Mid-Atlantic Toyota.

Eva Jiricna was born in 1938 in Prague, Czechoslovakia. She qualified as an engineer and architect at the University of Prague in 1963, and gained an MA from the Academy of Fine Arts in the same year. After arriving in London in 1968 she worked in the Schools Division of the GLC before joining the Louis de Soissons Partnership as an associate in 1969. Eva set up in partnership with David Hodges in 1980, and then formed Jiricna Kerr Associates in 1985, becoming Eva Jiricna Architects in 1987. Her major projects include Le Caprice restaurant, London (1981), Joe's Cafe, London (1985), Legends nightclub, London (1985), interiors of Lloyd's headquarters (with Richard Rogers,

1985–86), and many stores for Joseph, including Kenzo (1982), Pour La Maison (1985) and Joseph, Brompton Cross (1988). In 1987–88 the practice designed a chain of shoe stores for Joan & David; boutiques in Florence and Riccione, and new headquarters for Swiss furniture manufacturer Vitra.

Kiyonori Kikutake was born in 1928 and is one of the founders of Metabolism. He has also been active as a writer and government adviser. Currently Lecturer at Tokyo University and Waseda University, Tokyo, Kikutake has also spoken at many international conferences. In 1959 he designed Marine City, the world's first floating city, a year after creating Japan's first skyscraper. A number of 'seaborn housing experiments' were floated in Tokyo Bay (1976–77). His recent projects include Fukuoka City Hall (1988), Ginza Theatre building, Tokyo (1987), and the Kawasaki City Museum (1988).

Sanzin Kim was born in Kyoto, Japan, in 1956. He graduated from the Department of Interior design of Tokyo University of Architecture in 1978. Following a stint at Ishimaru Co. he established the Kim Design Office in 1981. He has designed showrooms in Tokyo for Kumagai and Daikanyama; boutique I.S. in the Ueno Marui department store, and stores for Kenzo Homme within the Mitsukoshi store, and together with Biglidue at the OXY Building, Tokyo (1987).

Setsuo Kitaoka was born in Kouchi Shikoku, Japan, in 1946. In 1974 he graduated from the Department of Living Design at the Kuwazawa Design Institute and joined Yamaguchi Co. Ltd. He established the Kitaoka Design Office in Tokyo in 1977, designing many shops in Japan such as branches of Y's and Melrose in Yokohama and Tokyo; Barney's in New York (1986), AT and TKX in Tokyo (1986 and 1987), and Bar Akasaka in Fukuoka, and the Body and Bath shop in Tokyo (both 1988). Kitaoka is also an active furniture and lighting designer.

Kenji Komoriya was born in Gunma, Japan, in 1955. He graduated in architecture from the Meiji University, and for six years worked as an interior designer for Hanae Mori. In 1984 he set up his own company, Vinci Design, which has since been commissioned to design numerous boutiques, restaurants and bars in Japan, including Artigiano mens' boutique (1985), Heaven restaurant (1987), Hysterique Glamour (1988), Renoma Monsieur (1989) and the Edic Studio (1989).

Yasuo Kondo was born in Tokyo in 1950. He graduated from the Interior Architecture Department of Tokyo University of Art and Design in 1972, joining the Masahiro Miwa Design Office for four years. He moved to the Kuramata Design Office in 1976, and in 1981 founded his own practice. Kondo's many retail projects include stores for Renoma, Lanerossi, Plantation, and in 1988 boutiques for Commes des Garcons SHIRT in New York and Paris. In 1988 he designed Shima, a beauty salon, and a butcher's shop, both in Tokyo.

Shiro Kuramata was born in Tokyo in 1934, trained in woodwork at Tokyo College of Art and graduated from the Kuwasawa Design Institute in 1956. Since establishing his own practice in 1965 he has steadily become internationally renowned for his interior and furniture design projects. He has designed interiors for Issey Kiyake, Esprit, and Tokio Kumagai. Many exhibitions featuring his work, and projects with IDEE, Vitra and the Memphis group have been held, including 'Bodyworks'. In 1981 he was awarded the Japan Cultural Design Prize.

Kisho Kurokawa was born in Nagoya in 1934. He studied architecture at Kyoto University. In 1960, while studying for a doctorate at Tokyo University, he formed the Metabolist group, whose philosophy, closely linked with Buddhism, viewed urban architectural forms as organisms capable of growth and change. Kurokawa's philosophy of symbiosis has been the main theme of his numerous architectural and urban planning works including the National Bunraku Theatre, Osaka (1983), the Wacoal Kojimachi Building, Tokyo (1984), the Roppongi Prince Hotel, Tokyo (1984), and major national museums of modern art in Nagoya (1987) and Hiroshima (1988).

Christoph Langhof was born in Linz, Austria. He studied at the Technische Hochschule, Vienna, and the Düsseldorf Art Academy. After postgraduate studies at the Hochschule der Bildenden Kunste in Berlin, he set up Christoph Langhof Architekten with Thomas Hanni and Herbert Meerstein. In 1982 he was a founding member of the Wilde Akademie in Berlin, and in 1987 became Unit master at the Architectural Association, London. Major projects include a pavilion; housing and a day care center at the International Building Exhibition, Berlin; swimming baths, and a major fitness center, also in Berlin, where other public building projects are in preparation.

Thomas Leeser was born in West Germany and trained at the Technische Hochschule in Darmstadt. He joined Eisenman/Robertson Associates in 1980 and worked on the IBA Housing project in West Berlin; the Wexner Center for the Visual Arts at Ohio State University; La Villette, Paris; and projects for the Tokyo Opera House competition and the 1985 Venice Biennale. He began teaching, often with Peter Eisenman, in 1986. In 1988 he became Senior Associate of Eisenman Associates, currently designing the Carnegie Mellon Research Institute, offices in Tokyo and Pittsburgh, and the Convention Center Competition, Columbus, Ohio. Leeser's own projects include the Red Bar, New York (1981), lofts, a showroom, and the Gold Bar, New York (1987).

Mitchell/Giurgola & Thorp is one of Australia's largest architectural practices, established in 1980 by Romaldo Giurgola (born in 1920 in Rome) and Richard Thorp (born in 1944). Giurgola trained at the University of Rome and Columbia University, and initially established Mitchell/Giurgola Architects in 1958. He was design consultant to the Philadelphia City Planning Commission from 1962–66. Richard Thorp trained at the University of Melbourne. The third partner, Harold Guida, was born in 1941 and studied at the University of California. He has worked with the practice since 1968. Partner Pamille Berg was born in 1949 and has a doctorate in ancient art and archaeology. MGT's recent projects include the Parliament House in Canberra; Darling Harbour hotel casino development, Harrington Court offices, and a diverse range of other urban projects and developments.

Toshiko Mori was born in Kobe, Japan, in 1951 and studied art history in France and Italy before taking a degree in architecture at the Cooper Union School in New York. Since 1979 she has designed retail projects for Charivari, Comme des Garcons, Kashiyama (Jean Paul Gaultier showroom, New York), and many New York City-based offices and banks for Japanese firms. She is a visiting critic at Harvard Graduate School of Design, and in 1988 received a Citation for Distinguished Architecture (Interiors) from the New York Chapter of the AIA.

Morphosis is a Los Angeles-based architectural practice founded by Thom Mayne and Michael Rotundi in 1975. Mayne studied at the University of Southern California and Harvard University's Graduate School of Design. Rotundi studied at the Southern California Institute of Architecture, where he is now Director. Their projects include numerous residences, offices and restaurants in California, including 72 Market Street (1984), Sonia Rykiel (1985), the Kate Mantilini restaurant, Los Angeles (1986), and the Cedars-Sinai Comprehensive Cancer Centre (with Gruen Associates). Many of the practice's projects have been included in exhibitions, and have won a number of AIA and Progressive Architecture awards.

Murphy/Jahn is an architectural practice with offices in Chicago, New York and Frankfurt. Under the leadership of Helmut Jahn, who was born in 1940 in Nuremberg, West Germany, it has evolved from the original firm which was founded over 50 years ago. Jahn trained at the Technische Hochschule, Munich, and Illinois Institute of Technology. He became President of Murphy/Jahn in 1982. Completed buildings include court buildings in Illinois and Virginia; corporate headquarters and a convention center in Illinois. Murphy/Jahn works with private, corporate, institutional and governmental clients on many award-winning projects such as the United Airlines terminal 1 complex of O'Hare International Airport, Chicago.

Barton Myers was born in Norfolk, Virginia, and trained at the University of Pennsylvania. He went on to work with Louis Kahn, and in 1968 joined Diamond & Myers, Toronto, until 1975. In 1974 he formed Barton Myers Associates in Toronto, and in 1980 opened a Los Angeles office which is now the practice headquarters. Myers, who is a Professor at the University of California, continues to work with Canadian architects on projects such as the Seagram Museum, Waterloo, Ontario, and the Stratford Festival Theatre, Ontario. Pioneers in the development of high-density urban projects combining new and old structures, the practice renovated the Stratford Festival Theatre, Ontario, and in 1987 designed the Portland Center for the Performing Arts. Their current projects include the expansion of the Faculty of Fine Arts, York University, Toronto; a theater, offices and residences in California.

Claudio Nardi received his doctorate in architecture from the University of Florence in 1978. He has designed many stores, clubs and houses in Italy including Silvana, Florence (1985); the club Paramatta, Florence (1987), and Sbaiz (1988). He has also designed lighting and other products.

Office for Metropolitan Architecture (OMA) was founded in 1975 by Rem Koolhaas, Elia and Zoe Zenghelis and Madelon Vriesendorp. Rem Koolhaas was born in Rotterdam in 1944 and studied at the Architectural Association in London from 1968–72. A Harkness Fellowship enabled him to study at Cornell University (1972–73), and the Institute of Architecture and Urban Studies in New York, where he was a Visiting Fellow until 1979. The co-design with Laurinda Spear of a house in Miami in 1974 won a Progressive Architecture award. The result of many New York based theoretical projects was 'Delirious New York', a study of the effects of mass culture on architecture and the city, published in 1978. OMA's major projects include a prison in Arnhem (1980–88), the City Hall, The Hague (1987), and the Netherlands Dance Theater in The Hague (1987). OMA has also designed housing in Paris and Berlin, and an extension of the city of Lille is underway. Koolhaas' work was included in the exhibition 'Deconstructivism', held at MOMA, New York, in 1988.

Koji Okamoto was born in Hamamatsu-shi, Shizuoka, Japan, in 1953. He graduated in 1975 from Chiba University in Engineering Design, and worked for Shoukou-Bijutu Co. for four years. After working with Super Potato Co. he established his own practice in 1987 designing restaurants, stores and bars, including Libre Space with Takashi Sugimoto.

Pawson Silvestrin was established in 1982 by John Pawson and Claudio Silvestrin. John Pawson was born in Halifax, Yorkshire, in 1949. He studied at Nagoya University of Commerce and the Architectural Association. Claudio Silvestrin, born in 1954, trained at Milan Polytechnic, University of Bologna and the Architectural Association. They have designed many domestic and commercial interiors including the Waddington Galleries, London (1983), Wakaba restaurant, London (1987), Starkman offices, London (1987), Runkel Hue Williams Gallery (1988), and Cannelle Patisserie (1988).

Andree Putman was born in Paris. She studied the piano at the Paris Conservatoire with Francois Poulenc. After a few years as a journalist she moved into industrial design, and in the 1970s co-founded Createurs et Industriels, teaming up designers such as Issey Miyake or Castlebajac. In the mid-1970s her interest in Eileen Gray led to the reproduction of twentieth century furniture which came to be regarded as innovative classics. In 1978 she founded Ecart International, specializing in re-editions, and began to design her own interior projects. These include Bordeaux Museum of Contemporary Art (1984); Palladium nightclub (with Arata Isozaki in 1984); St James's Club Hotel, New York (1987); headquarters, boutiques, and a public relations center in Switzerland for Ebel (1987); Carita beauty salon, Paris (1989). Projects in progress include hotels in Cologne and Tokyo; a new image for Balenciaga, and work on the headquarters of the Foundation for the Rights of Man, La Defense, Paris.

Richard Rogers was born in Florence in 1933. After moving to London in 1938 he studied at the Architectural Association, and at Yale University on a Fulbright Scholarship. In 1963 he established Team 4 with his wife Sue Rogers, and Norman and Wendy Foster. In 1970 Piano and Rogers was founded with Italian architect Renzo Piano, and the practice designed the competition-winning project for the Centre Pompidou, Paris (1971–77). In 1977 Richard Rogers Partnership was founded with John Young and Marco Goldschmied, and in 1978 won a limited competition to design the now world-famous Lloyd's of London headquarters (1978–86). Other recent projects include the Inmos microprocessor factory, Newport, South Wales (1982); PA Technology, Princeton, New Jersey (1984); Thames Wharf (1984); and Magasin d'Usine, Nantes, France (1986). The practice is currently designing the new Court of Human Rights building in Strasbourg.

Eduard Samso was born in Barcelona in 1956, and studied at the Escuela Tecnica Superior de Arquitectura in Barcelona. He has designed interiors for stores and bars, such as the Nick Havanna bar (1986), Network cafe restaurant (1987, with Alfredo Arribas) and the Francisco Valiente showroom (1988), all of which have won design awards. His furniture designs for Akaba (1986) and rugs for Nani Marquina (1988) have won the Delta prize for industrial design.

Solberg & Lowe is a Santa Monica-based practice established in 1984 by Richard Solberg and Douglas Lowe. Solberg trained at Arizona State University in 1984, ran his own firm in Phoenix, and was a principal of Johannes Van Tilburg & Partners. Lowe studied at Cal-Poly San Luis Obispo, and worked both for Van Tilburg and Vito Cetta. Their major projects have been the Santa Monica Airport Administration building and the Supermarine of Santa Monica, comprising a restaurant, museum and offices. Projects in progress include the Samuel Goldwyn Child Care Center and theme attractions for Universal Studios.

Stanton Williams was established in 1986 by Alan Stanton (born in 1944 in Nottingham) and Paul Williams (born in 1949 in Birmingham). Stanton trained at the Architectural Association and the University of California. He worked with Piano and Rogers on the Centre Pompidou, Paris, and with Mike Dowd designed a major exhibition space at the Museum of Science and Industry, La Villette, Paris. Paul Williams trained at Birmingham College of Art and at the Yale Arts Centre. The practice is renowned for their work on temporary exhibitions for clients such as the Hayward Gallery (English Romanesque Art; Matisse); Royal Academy of Arts (The Age of Chivalry); and other notable projects such as a menswear shop for Issey Miyake (1987); the Japanese Gallery at the V & A (1986); and exhibition galleries for the Design Museum, Butler's Wharf. Current projects include the extension of Birmingham City Museum and Art Gallery; a new gallery at the RIBA; and a new wing for the twentieth century collection of the National Portrait Gallery.

Philippe Starck was born in Paris in 1949 and works as a product, furniture and interior designer. In Paris he was commissioned by President Mitterand to work on apartments at the Elysee Palace (1982–83), and designed Cafe Costes (1984), together with a number of fashion shops. In New York he remodelled the interior of the Royalton Hotel (1988), in Tokyo designed the Manin restaurant (1986), Cafe Mystique (1988), headquarters for Asahi (1988), and is currently working on a number of other buildings. His furniture design includes projects for Disform, Driade, Baleri and Idee. His industrial design projects include work for Vittel, Beneteau, Vuitton and Alessi.

James Stirling, Michael Wilford & Associates was established in 1971. James Stirling was born in Glasgow in 1926, and moved to Liverpool in 1927. He studied architecture at the University of Liverpool, and town planning in London. He has been in private practice since 1956 (with James Gowan until 1963). Michael Wilford was born in 1938 in Surbiton, Surrey, and studied at the Northern Polytechnic School of Architecture and Regent Street Polytechnic Planning School. In 1977 Stirling and Wilford won a limited competition for the State Gallery and Chamber Theater, Stuttgart, West Germany (1977–84), and in 1979 another for the Wissenschaftszentrum, Berlin (1979–87). Other major projects include the Clore Gallery extension to the Tate Gallery, London (1980–86); the Tate

Gallery, Albert Dock, Liverpool (1984–88). In 1988 the practice won limited competitions for the Los Angeles Philharmonic Concert Hall, a residential development at Canary Wharf in London's Docklands, a ballet/opera house in Toronto, Ontario; and in 1989 Music and Theater Academies in Stuttgart.

STUDIOS Architecture is an international practice with offices in San Francisco, Washington D.C. and London, founded in 1985 by Darryl Robinson, Erik Sueberkrop, Martin Yardley, Philip Olsen and Gene Rae. Principal Erik Sueberkrop graduated from the University of Cincinnati in 1972. He has directed many projects for Apple Computer, Silicon Graphics, and a headquarters in California for 3Com Corporation. Current projects include headquarters for Morgan Stanley International in London, the Pacific Stock Exchange in San Francisco and many US legal firms. STUDIOS has received many national and regional design awards in the US.

Takashi Sugimoto was born in Tokyo in 1945. He graduated from Tokyo University of Art in 1968 and founded the Super Potato Studio in 1971. He is a consultant to Seibu department store, Matsushita Inc. and Daiko Lighting, and has won a number of awards for his interior design work. Apart from numerous interiors for branches of Seibu, Sugimoto has designed projects such as Radio bar (1982 & 1987), Brasserie Ex (1984), Ex Jun boutique (1985), No Brand Shop (1987), and Libre Space (1988).

Shin Takamatsu was born in 1948 in the Shimane Prefecture of Japan. In 1971 he graduated from the Architectural Faculty of Kyoto University, and gained his doctorate from there in 1980. He established his own office in Kyoto in the same year. He is currently assistant professor at Seika University and lecturer at Kyoto University. His work has won many awards including the Japan Association of Architects' Prize for Young Architects. To date projects include houses, stores and clinics, mostly in Kyoto, such as the Origin I, II & III projects, but also the Kirin Plaza in Osaka. His ideas are explained in 'The Kyoto Origins of Non-Conceptual Form', published in English in 1988.

Nicholas Tedford was born in Hong Kong in 1959 and studied at Kingston Polytechnic. From 1982–84 he worked in Hong Kong for both Foster Associates and Leigh and Orange. Since 1984 he has been based in Florence, working on various competitions such as the urban redefinition at Castel di Sangro (1988), and small interior projects, mainly retail, such as Sbaiz (1988), often with Italian architect Claudio Nardi.

Katsuhiro Togashi was born in Hokkaido, Japan, in 1947. He graduated from Kuwazawa Design School in 1972 and worked for Shigeru Uchida's office. In 1984 he established his own practice, and became a lecturer at the Kuwazawa School. In 1988 he designed Cinderella 12 in Tokushima-shi.

Shigeru Uchida was born in Yokohama in 1943. He graduated from the Kuwazawa Design School in Interior Design in 1966, and set up the Uchida Design Office in 1970. In 1981 he founded Studio 80 with Ikuyo Mitsuhashi and Toru Nishioka. The practice has undertaken many interior design projects for Yohji Yamamoto and other innovative Japanese companies, as well as large scale commercial planning projects, and numerous private residences in and around Tokyo; Uchida set up his own furniture showroom, Chairs, at the AXIS Centre in Tokyo in 1981. Regular exhibitions have helped to build Uchida's notable reputation as a furniture designer.

Masanori Umeda graduated from the Kuwasawa Design Institute in 1962. From 1966–69 she worked in the Castiglione studios in Milan. Umeda won the Braun Prize in Germany in 1968, and was design consultant for Olivetti between 1970 and 1979. She founded her own practice in Tokyo in 1979. Umeda has also worked with the Memphis Group.

Peter Wilson was born in 1950 in Melbourne, Australia, and studied at the University of Melbourne and at the Architectural Association (AA), London (1972–74). He became a Senior Lecturer at the AA in 1979, and set up his own partnership in 1980. In 1988 this became Architekturbüro Bolles-Wilson, based in Munster, West Germany, with Julia Bolles-Wilson. Recent projects include urban planning of the Domplatz, Hamburg (1983, awarded first prize), Bridgebuilding designs in Paris, Venice, Amsterdam and Tokyo (the subject of an exhibition held at the AA in 1984); urban planning in Rotterdam (1988), and a house and office in London (with Chassay Wright Architects, 1989). In 1987 the practice won first prize to design the City Library in Munster (to be built in the early 1990s). Also in progress: a villa in Krakow, Poland; a commercial building in Tokyo, and pavilion at the Osaka Garden Expo 1990 (masterplan by Isozaki Associates).

ACKNOWLEDGEMENTS

1.1 Banco de Credito, Lima, Peru *12*
Architects: Arquitectonica International Corporation, Florida, USA *Principals:* Bernardo Fort-Brescia, Laurinda Spear *Project architects:* Martin J Wander, Enrique Chuy *Client:* Banco de Credito del Peru *Main contractor:* La Immobiliaria, SA *Structural engineer:* Gallegos, Rios. Casabonne & Ucelli, Arango *Electrical engineer:* Friba Ingenieros *Mechanical engineer:* Lagomasino Vital & Associates *Landscape architects:* Mercedes Beale de Porcari *Lighting consultant:* Philips Export BV *Windows:* Ford Motor Company (glass), 300 Renaissance Center *Furniture:* Arquitectonica, made by Linea SA (seating), Estudio 501 (systems furniture; desks), Canziani SA (tables), Guillermo Pena; Union (storage system) *Textiles:* Art Decor SA (wallcovering and upholstery fabrics) *Doors:* Vaisa, La Immobiliaria SA *Flooring:* Milliken & Co. (carpet), Clisa (handmade carpet) *Office hardware:* Schlage.

1.2 Edic Studio, Tokyo, Japan *16*
Designer: Kenji Komoriya, Vinci Inc. *Client:* Endo Lighting Co. Ltd. *Main contractor:* Nisshin SPP Co. Ltd. *Furniture:* Kenji Komoriya *Furniture contractor:* Aidic Co. Ltd. *Lighting:* Endo Lighting Co. Ltd. *Flooring:* Tajima.

1.3 Propaganda Films, Los Angeles, USA *18*
Architects: Franklin D Israel Design Associates *Principal architect:* Franklin D Israel *Client:* Propaganda Films *Main contractor:* Iverson Construction *Structural consultants:* Davis-Fejes Design *Mechanical consultants:* Hartich Mechanical *Electrical consultants:* Silver Engineering *Lighting consultants:* Sol Goldin & Associates.

1.4 PN Clubhouse, Tokyo, Japan *22*
Designer: Masanori Umeda, U-MetaDesign, Inc. *Client:* PAOS Inc. *Main contractor:* Sakura Construction Co. Ltd. *Lighting:* Yamagiwa Lighting Co. Ltd. *Furniture:* Haller Japan Ltd. (chairs), Mario Bellini for Vitra (chairs), Masanori Umeda (sofa), B & B Japan Co. (small tables) *A/V consultant:* Nomura Display Co. Ltd. *A/V system:* Sony Inc. (lighting control), Kenwood Corp. (stereo system and telecommunications), Matsushita Electric Co. (video tape recorder), Mitsubishi Electric Co. (37-inch monitor) *Flooring:* Awaji Kawara-Boh (tiles), Kawashima Textile Manufacturers Ltd. (carpet) *Ceiling:* International Communication Ltd.

1.5 Blackburn Office/Gallery/Flat, London, UK *24*
Architects: Peter Wilson, The Wilson Partnership, Tchaik Chassay and Gareth Wright, Chassay Wright Architects, with Tas Ahmed, Richard Buck, Nick Dowling and Lesley Hooper *Client:* David and Janice Blackburn *Main contractor:* Walter Llewelyn Ltd. *Quantity surveyors:* Monk Dunstone Associates *Structural engineers:* Trigram Design Partnership *Steel framing:* H L Smith Construction Ltd. *Metalwork:* Herman Metastruct *Ironmongery:* Elementer *Flooring:* Marriott & Price (terrazzo), Burlington Slate (slate), Interoc (UK) Ltd. (white artic oak) *Radiators:* Steetley Engineering Ltd. *Furniture:* Jasper Morrison, Ron Arad, Floris van den Broecke, Peter Wilson, Fred Baier, Jon Mills, Scott Burton *Ceramics:* Bruce McLean, Yvonne Preston, Jane Willingdale, Carol McNichol

1.6 Apple Worldwide Manufacturing & Operations HQ, California, USA *28*
Design firm: STUDIOS Architecture, San Francisco, USA *Project designers:* Erik Sueberkrop (Principal), David Sabalvaro, Doug Dworsky, Deborah Pfeiffer, Robert Bradsby *Client:* Apple Computer *Main contractor:* Walsh Building Contractors *Ceramic tiles (vending room):*

Dal-Tile *Terrazzo:* American Terrazzo Co. *Pre-fabricated hardwood floor:* Tarkett Inc. *Corrugated metal (rest rooms):* Acousta-lite Supply Co. *Polished flake board (sweeping arc wall):* Limited Production Inc. *Lighting:* Capri Lighting *Furniture:* Equa chair in saddle leather – Herman Miller (conference room chairs); STUDIOS, built by Limited Production Inc., terrazzo tables – American Terrazzo Co., lounge/dining chairs – Mandarin chair, from Knoll International, club chairs – Bonaventure Harvard, coffee tables – Metropolitan Furniture Corp. *Carpets:* Bentley Carpet Mills.

1.7 Shibuya Higashi T Building, Tokyo, Japan *30*
Architect: Kisho Kurokawa, Tokyo *Client:* Itoman Total Housing Co. *Main contractor:* Tobishima Construction Co. *Walls:* Nihon Terazzo Kogyo Co. *Flooring and Ceiling:* Shinwa Co. Ltd.

1.8 Esprit Italia, Milan, Italy *32*
Architects: Studio Citterio Dwan *Designers:* Antonio Citterio, Patricia Viel, Elisabetta Mainardi and Terry Dwan *Client:* Esprit Italia *Main contractor:* Sice Previt *Mechanical consultants:* Amman Progetti, Milan *Consultant engineer:* Antonio Brambilla *Steelwork:* Veronese *Flooring:* Junckers (beechwood) *Lighting:* Guzzini, Altalite, Sirio (custom-made lamp) *Furniture:* Antonio Citterio, Fritz Hansen by Cappellini; Caruso *Windows:* Silent Gliss *Kitchen equipment:* Teckner Ivrea.

1.9 Libération, Paris, France *36*
Architects: Canal Atelier D'Architecture, Paris *Project architects:* Daniel Rubin, Patrick Rubin *Client:* S.N.C.P. Libération *Main contractor:* S.N.C.E. *Woodwork:* Sermag, Maurice Andre *Walls:* Tolartois (metal) *Flooring:* Pinton (carpets), Briatte (inlaid flooring), La Thiezaquoise, Emaux de Briare (tiles) *Automatic doors:* Sorelec *Furniture:* Burotext *Lighting:* Jumo, Moles Richardson.

1.10 Rooftop Remodelling, Vienna, Austria *38*
Architects: Coop Himmelblau *Principal architects:* Wolf D. Prix and Helmut Swiczinsky *Project architect:* Franz Sam *Project team:* Max Pauly, Stefan Kruger, Karin Sam, Robert Hahn, Mathis Barz, Valerie Simpson *Clients:* Dr Walter Schuppich, Dr Werner Sporn, Dr Michael Winischhofer, Dr Martin Schuppich *Structural engineer:* Oskar Graf *Electrical consultants:* Diana, Kogler-Jung *Steel construction:* Metalbau Treiber *Concrete construction:* Uniprojekt *Glazing:* Baumann Glas *Wood construction/tiling:* Larisch Inc. *Furniture:* Sevcik.

1.11 Fafalios Ltd. Offices, London, UK *42*
Designers: Eva Jiricna Architects, London *Project architects:* Tim Bushe, Caroline Aivars *Client:* Fafalios Ltd. *Main contractor:* Dove Bros. Ltd. *Furniture:* Vosseler UK, Tecno (desks), Hille (chairs), Eva Jiricna Architects (boardroom table) *Lighting:* Siemens Lighting *Floor:* Polyresine *Acoustics:* Jerome Vicat Blanc SA.

1.12 Silicon Graphics Computer Systems Headquarters *44*
Design firm: STUDIOS Architecture, San Francisco, USA *Project designers:* Erik Sueberkrop (Principal), David Sabalvaro, Charles Dilworth, Robert Bradsby, Deborah Pfeiffer, Jimmy Talim *Client:* Silicon Graphics Computer Systems *Main contractor:* Devcon Construction *Furniture:* All-Steel Inc. *Lighting:* Halo Lighting *Carpets:* Bentley Carpet Mills *Ceiling tiles:* Armstrong (Ceiling Division) *Paint:* Fuller O'Brien Paint

1.13 Geyer Design Offices, Melbourne, Australia *48*
Designers: Geyer Design Pty Ltd. *Principal designers:* Peter Geyer, Sian Wright, John Bactiar *Client:* Geyer Design Pty Ltd. *Furniture:* B. W. Scott (meeting tables and joinery), Tecno (workstation desking), chairs: Tecno, Dee Dee Cee, Herman Miller *Lighting:* Massons, Rham/Famco *Fittings:* Westbury Joinery.

1.14 Wissenschaftszentrum (Science Center), Berlin *50*
Architects: James Stirling, Michael Wilford and Associates *Assistants:* Peter Ray, Peter Schaad, John Tuomey, Volker Eich, Robert Niess, Hannelore Deubzer *Associates:* Walter Nageli, Siegfried Wernik *Client:* Science Center for Social Studies, Federal Republic of Germany, Land of Berlin *Construction management:* Bauamt Nord, Berlin *Structural consultants:* Firma Raulf Bau *Stonework:* Firma Hofmann *Steelwork/canopies:* Acero *Structural engineers:* Prof Polonyi and Fink *Services engineers:* Schmidt Reuter *Building physics:* Dr Manfred Flohrer *Lighting/electrical consultants:* Firma Eltec KG. *Lighting:* Siebert, Grauwinkel *Furniture/fittings:* Lotter (library shelving) *Windows:* Firma Benecke, Firma Beutler *Doors:* Benecke *Floors:* Freudenberg *Acoustics:* Labor *Conservation:* Frank Augustin.

1.15 Elementer Headquarters, Berkshire, UK *54*
Architects: Armstrong Associates *Principal architect:* Kenneth Armstrong *Job architect:* Jenifer Smith *Client:* Elementer Industrial Design Ltd. *Main contractor:* Parallel Contracts Ltd. *Structural engineer:* Whitby & Bird *Colour consultancy:* Sally Greaves-Lord *Staircase:* Armstrong Associates, made by Eurostairs Ltd. *Handrail:* Carl F. Peterson (D-line) *Mild steel fabricator:* Fabricon Ltd. *Furniture:* Kjaerholm PK22 chairs & tables – Paul Kjaerholm, supplied by Dancontract A/S; P-O office furniture – designed by Knud Holscher, supplied by Dancontract; Jacobsen chairs & table – designed by Arne Jacobsen, supplied by Dancontract *Fittings:* D-line ironmongery, Toni t-line taps – Knud Holscher, supplied by Elementer Industrial Design *Textile wall hanging:* Sally Greaves-Lord *Lighting:* Triangel Data-lights – supplied by Scan-Q-Ltd., Erco Lighting (downlights).

1.16 Ebel-Villa Turque, La Chaux de Fonds, Switzerland *56*
Interior designer: Ecart *Principal designers:* Andree Putmann and Thierry Conquet *Assistant:* Laurent Buttazzoni *Client:* Ebel SA *General coordination:* R & P Studer Architects, Neuchatel, Switzerland *Furniture:* Maneau (chairs), Ecart International (chairs), Soutomier (armchairs), Ecart (armchairs), Dennery (wood and glass furniture) *Lighting:* Dennery *Floor:* Jules Flipo (carpets), Tisca (rugs), Vetricolour (mosaic tiles) *Blinds and curtains:* Soutumier.

1.17 Valentino, Rome, Italy *60*
Design firm: David Davies Associates *Project designers:* Peter Moore, Peter Kent *Client:* Valentino Garavani Spa *Main contractor:* L. Cenacchi Spa *Project management and engineering:* Studio Ziffer *Furniture and lighting:* David Davies Associates, L. Cenacchi Spa *Flooring:* Kirk Stone Ltd. (green slate), Junckers (maple wood).

2.1 Cafe Mystique, Tokyo, Japan *68*
Designer: Philippe Starck *Client:* Belle Tricot *Main contractor:* Casatec Ltd. *Furniture:* Philippe Starck; produced by Cassina, Japan *Lighting:* Philipe Starck.

2.2 Trattoria Angeli, Los Angeles, USA *72*
Architects: Building, Los Angeles, USA *Principal:* Michele Saee *Project architects:* Richard Lundquist, Max Massie, David Lindberg *Client:* Evan Kleiman and John Strobel *Main contractor:* Marty Herling *Structural consultant:* Miguel Castillo *Lighting consultant:* Saul Goldin *Mechanical engineer:* Dehbibi & Associates. *Furniture/lighting:* Building *Billboard:* Cor-ten steel.

2.3 Review, London *74*
Design firm: Conran Design Group *Client:* South Bank Centre *Main contractors:* Morgan Lovell Ltd. *Structural, mechanical and electrical engineers:* Ove Arup & Partners *Lighting:* Concord Lighting, Design Architectural Lighting Co., L.B. Lighting Ltd. (chandeliers) *Windows:* Hunter-Douglas Ltd. *Furniture:* Habitat (chairs), Conran Design Group (tables and service units), Mailer Webber Joinery (service units), Knightsbridge Furniture Productions Ltd. *Canopies:* Conran Design Group *Crockery:* Graham Meeson, Conran Design Group.

2.4 Noah's Ark, Sapporo, Japan *76*
Architects: Nigel Coates and Doug Branson, Branson Coates Architecture *Producer:* Shi Yu Chen, Creative Intelligence Associates Inc. *Corresponding architect:* Dan Architecture *Client:* Jasmac Co. Ltd. *Commissioned works from:* Jasper Morrison (rug), Tom Dixon (chandeliers), Annabelle Grey (hand-painted fabrics), Stuart Helm (murals), Adam Lowe (murals), Oriel Harwood (Animal cornucopia), Mark Quinn (Noah and his wife).

2.5 Mitchell & O'Brien, London, UK *80*
Design firm: Fitch & Co. (Special Projects Unit) *Project designers:* Carlos Virgile and Nigel Stone *Client:* Diners Ltd. *Main contractor:* Atelanda Shopfitters *Lighting:* L.A.S.S. Ltd. (at bar) *Flooring:* Focus Ceramics (mosaic tiles), DLW (Britain) Ltd. (lino) *Furniture:* Classic Furniture (tables), Laura Gottwald (US supply coordinator, aluminum dining chairs), W. M. Koniak Inc. (bar stools), Sit with Ease & Co. Ltd. (banquette seating), Advanced Commercial Equipment (waiter stations) *Fittings:* Barlow Shopfitters (deli metal shelving), The Inn Furnisher (bar foot rail), Great American Salvage Co. (Gimbels directories – menu frames) *Revolving door/zinc moulding:* Urban Archaology *Shopfront construction:* Basset & Findlay Ltd., Piazza (plaster coating façade) *Signs:* Rye Signs.

2.6 Kirin Plaza, Osaka, Japan *82*
Architect: Shin Takamatsu, Shin Takamatsu Associates *Designer (interiors):* Kazuko Fujie *Client:* Kirin Brewing Co. (Hotel and Insurance branch) *Main contractor:* Taisei Kensetsu Co. Ltd. *Materials (exterior):* Nippon Sheet Glass; Yabashi (marble) *Lighting:* Maxray Co. Ltd. (bracket), Matsushita Denko (computer-controlled lighting tower system) *Flooring and walls:* Daitoh Concrete Co. Ltd., Ost Co. (carpet) *Partitions:* Yamamoto Steel Co. *Furniture:* Daitoh Concrete Co. Ltd. (large table), Kintetsu Co. Ltd. (department store) *Sound system:* Jujiya Co. Ltd.

2.7 Royalton Hotel, New York, USA *84*
Designer: Philippe Starck *Architectural consultant:* Anda Andrei *Client:* Ian Schrager and Steve Rubell *Main contractor:* Maville *Mahogany work and stainless steel details:* Maville *Cast aluminum work:* Dacheville *Plasterwork:* S.O.E. *Furniture:* Maville, Dacheville, Yves Halard, Vinchenard (sofas), Lelieure (velvet) *Flooring:* Brigitte Starck (carpets).

2.8 Libre Space, Tokyo, Japan *90*
Designers: Takashi Sugimoto, Super Potato Co. Ltd., Koji Okamoto *Client:* Asahi Beer Co. *Main contractor:* Build Co. *Flooring:* Koyano Stone Co. (marble) *Walls:* Sakura Manufacture Co. (walnut), Metal Co. (steel) *Furniture:* Tagashi Sugimoto; made by Build Co. *Lighting:* Ushiospex Co. *Collage works:* Aijiro Wakita.

2.9 Gold Bar, The, New York, USA *92*
Architect: Thomas Leeser, Eisenman Architects *Client:* Von ALM Corporation *Furniture/lighting:* Thomas Leeser.

2.10 Bingo Bango Bongo, Tokyo, Japan *94*
Architect: David Chipperfield and Partners *Client:* Casatec Ltd. *Main contractor:* Cosmos Co. Ltd. *Furniture:* David Chipperfield and Partners, produced by Cassina Japan *Banners and wallpainting:* Bruce McLean *Staff uniforms:* Georgina Godley *Graphics:* Peter Saville.

2.11 Fred's, London, UK *98*
Architects: Tchaik Chassay, Lesley Hooper, Andrew Jamieson and Andrew Stone, Chassay Wright Architects *Client:* Fred Taylor *Main contractor:* Island Developments *Structural engineers:* Whitly & Bird *Mechanical engineers:* Bridcut & Co. *Electrical consultants:* P D Slack *Lighting:* Melanie Sainsbury *Metalwork:* Henry Taylor & Co. *Furniture:* Jasper Morrison (bar stools), Matthew Marchbank (bar top), Tyssen Construction Ltd. *Flooring:* Phoenix Floors Ltd. *Walls:* Glass & Glazing Services (curved glass screen).

2.12 Bar Akasaka, Fukuoka, Japan *100*
Designer: Setsuo Kitaoka, Kitaoka Design Office, Tokyo *Client:* Shin Planning Office Inc. *Main contractor:* Studio OB, Via Bo Rink Co. Ltd., NTC Co. Ltd. *Lighting:* Haruki Kaitou *Walls:* Plus-T Textile Studio (optical fiber cloth).

2.13 DC3, Santa Monica, USA *102*
Architects: Solberg & Lowe Architects *Project architects:* Jack Highwart, Michael McBurnette *Interior Design:* Chuck Arnoldi *Client:* Bruce Marder *Main contractor:* Cal-Pac Construction *Structural engineer:* Brian Cochran & Associates *Electrical engineer:* G & W Electrical Engineers *Mechanical engineering:* Interstate Mechanical Systems *Lighting:* CSL, Marco *Furniture:* Chairs: Thonet (dining), Vecta (banquette), Images (bar); Banquettes: Standard Cabinet Works Inc.; Tables: West Coast Industries; Falcon *Bronze sculpture:* Robert Graham *Paintings:* Chuck Arnoldi, Billy Al Bengston, Ed Ruscha *Upholstery/fabrics:* Mark Tursi *Wallcoverings:* Creative Walls Inc., Randi Smith, Elite Construction (plasterwork) *Floor:* US Axminster (carpets), Lees & Desso (carpets), La Vigne & Muffy (wood floor) *Ceiling:* La Vigne & Muffy *Windows:* Carvist & APG (glass), Levolor Lorensen (window covering).

2.14 Comblé, Shizuoka-Shi, Japan *106*
Designer: Shiro Kuramata *Main contractor:* Kuramata Design Office and Folm Co. Ltd. *Flooring/walls/ceiling:* OSB, from Katsumata-Meiki Co. *Lighting:* Ya-Ya-Ho by Ingo Maurer GmbH; Yamagiwa Co. Ltd. *Lighting (ceiling):* Tomahara Seisakujo Co. *Furniture:* designed by Kuramata, Nichinan Co. Ltd. (table), Seiko Plastic Co. Ltd. (stools), Terada Iron Co.

2.15 Kiyotomo Sushi Restaurant, Japan *110*
Designer: Shiro Kuramata *Main contractor:* Ishimaru Co. Ltd. *Flooring/ceiling (white granite):* Michikawa Sekizai Kogyosho *Walls (Japanese cedar):* Katsumatameiki Co. *Lighting:* Ya-Ya-Ho by Ingo Maurer, Yamagiwa Co. Ltd. *Furniture:* designed by Kuramata Terado Iron Co.: Ishimaru Co. Ltd. (table).

2.16 China Grill, New York, USA *112*
Architects: Jeffrey G. Beers Architects *Principal architect:* Jeffrey G. Beers *Job architect:* Peter Shinoda, with Timothy Schollaert and Beth Wells *Client:* Jeffrey Chodorow, China Grill Inc. *Main contractor:* Dolner construction *Design consultants:* Jeffrey Cain and Nancy Robinson *Graphic design consultant:* M & Co. *Lighting design consultant:* Jerry Kugler Associates *Lighting:* FTL Associates *Furniture/fittings:* Jeffrey G. Beers Architects; chairs and bar stools made by Creations Drucker *Ornamental metalwork:* Aileron Design *Glass/mirrors:* Abbott *Finishes/textures:* (decorative wall painting): Jane Thurn, Nancy Kearing, Billy Quinn.

2.17 Itchoh, Aoyama, Tokyo, Japan *114*
Designer: Shigeru Uchida, Studio 80 *Client:* Takeshi Yasuda *Main contractor:* Build Co. Ltd. *Lighting:* Ushiospax *Furniture, flooring, partitions:* Shigeru Uchida.

2.18 Itchoh, Roppongi, Tokyo, Japan *116*
Designer: Shigeru Uchida, Studio 80 *Client:* K.K. General Foods *Main contractor:* Nichiden Shoji K.K. *Lighting:* Minori Murayama/Ushiospax *Furniture, flooring, partitions:* Shigeru Uchida.

2.19 Bolido, New York, USA *118*
Designer: Massimo Iosa Ghini *Client:* Co.Ge.Com, Milan *Main contractor:* City Builders *Furniture/fittings:* Massimo Iosa Ghini.

2.20 Velvet, Barcelona, Spain *122*
Architects: Alfredo Arribas and Miguel Morte, Alfredo Arribas Arquitectos Asociados *Graphics:* Juli Capella and Quim Larrea *Client:* Gumersindo Adan *Masonry:* Construcciones Siglo XX *Electrical consultants:* Mage Industrial *Lighting:* Jordi Espinosa *Furniture:* J Santos/ A Solsona (upholstery) *Fittings/materials:* Vda Puig (marble), Reina (ornamental ironwork), Alabastros Sarreal (alabaster).

3.1 Marcel, Barcelona, Spain *128*
Architect: Eduard Samso *Client:* Marcel Montlleo *Main contractor:* Construcciones Barmo SA *Lighting:* Concord *Flooring:* Unifloor Formica *Furniture:* Driade.

3.2 Comme des Garçons, SHIRT, New York, USA *132*
Concept: Rei Kawakubo *Designer:* Yasuo Kondo *Architect (New York):* Toshiko Mori *Client:* Comme des Garçons Ltd. *Main contractor:* NYCON Building Corp. *Fittings:* Yasuo Kondo and Toshiko Mori; metal fabrication by Gregory Morrell.

3.3 Esprit, Antwerp, Belgium *134*
Architects: Studio Citterio Dwan *Designers:* Antonio Citterio, Terry Dwan, Silvio Caputo *Consultant Architect:* Atelier De Bondt, Antwerp *Client:* Esprit Benelux BV *Main contractor:* Bouwbedrijf Flore NV *Consultant engineers:* STB Pvba *Lighting/sound consultants:* Hans Wolff & Partners *Lighting:* Erco, Thomas *Steelwork:* CSM NV *Electrical services:* Technical Electrical Services *Furniture:* Antonio Citterio, and produced by Carlo Zago & Co., SRL, Arp, Mevo, Unifor, Fritz Hansen *Flooring:* Junckers (beechwood).

3.4 Esprit, Amsterdam, Netherlands *136*
Architects: Studio Citterio Dwan *Designers:* Antonio Citterio, Terry Dwan, Silvio Caputo *Consultant architect:* De Vries, Sas Bloem Bouma, Amsterdam *Client:* Esprit Benelux BV *Main contractor:* Hillen & Rosen Bouw BV *Consulting engineers:* Buro Strackee *Lighting and sound:* Hans Wolff & Partners *Lighting:* Erco Leuchten GmbH, Thomas *Steelwork:* Oskomera BV *Electrical services:* Nolte BV *Wall surfaces:* Viterzo *Flooring:* Conijn Parket *Furniture:* Antonio Citterio, and produced by Carlo Zago & Co., Arp, Fritz Hansen.

3.5 Esprit, London, UK *140*
Architects: Norman Foster, Ken Shuttleworth, Foster Associates *Client:* Esprit (UK) Ltd. *Management contractor:* Woolf Construction Management Ltd. *Mechanical and electrical consultants:* Antony Ross Ltd. *Structural engineer:* Ove Arup & Partners *Ceiling/ decoration/shopfitters:* Quickwood *Merchandising system:* Brent Architectural Metalwork Ltd. *Staircase metalwork:* Ray Theodore Welding Ltd. *Glasswork:* T & W Ide *Concrete columns and floor:* Underpin & Makegood *Furniture:* Tecno (UK) (tables) *Lighting:* Isometrix, Erco.

3.6 Ecru, Los Angeles, USA *142*
Architects: Building, Los Angeles, USA *Principal:* Michele Saee *Project architect:* Richard Lundquist *Client:* Ken Fasola and Elaine Kim *Main contractor:* Rotundi Construction *Engineer:* Miguel Castillo *Steel fabricator:* John McCoy *Lighting consultant:* Saul Goldin *Furniture/windows:* Building.

3.7 Department X, London, UK *146*
Designer: Rasshied Din, Din Associates *Consultant architects:* Crampin & Pring *Client:* Next Retail plc *Main contractor:* John Lelliot *Structural engineers:* Price & Myers *Electrical consultants:* Shepherd Engineering *Mechanical consultants:* Air Control *Moving equipment systems:* PSB Engineering (carousel) *Paternoster:* Kardex *Lighting:* Erco Lighting *Furniture/fittings:* Din Associates.

3.8 Conversation, Tokyo, Japan *148*
Designer: Shigeru Uchida, Studio 80, Tokyo *Client:* K.K. Marutaka Iryo *Main contractor:* Build Co. Ltd. *Lighting:* Harumi Fujimoto, MGS *Flooring:* Advan (marble tiles) *Furniture:* Shigeru Uchida; made by Build Co. Ltd.

3.9 Sbaiz, Lignano Sabbiadoro, Italy *150*
Architects: Claudio Nardi and Nicholas Tedford *Client:* Sbaiz *Main contractor:* Ometto Arredamento, Padova, Italy *Furniture:* Claudio Nardi and Nicholas Tedford, Zeus (stools).

3.10 Cannelle, London, UK *154*
Designers: John Pawson and Claudio Silvestrin, Pawson Silvestrin *Client:* Raja Cortas, Parfait Ltd. *Main contractor:* Design Workshop Ltd. *Structural engineer:* S. B. Tietz *Lighting:* Guzzini.

3.11 Sonia Rykiel, Tokyo, Japan *156*
Designer: Naoki Iijima *Client:* Kyoko Umeda *Main contractor:* Sparks Co. Ltd. *Lighting:* Ushiospex Co. Ltd. *Wall and ceiling surfaces:* Nextel *Furniture:* Naoki Iijima; made by Sparks Co. Ltd. *Flooring:* Minelba Co.

3.12 Joseph, London, UK *158*
Architects: Eva Jiricna Architects *Client:* Joseph Ltd. Shopfitters: Quickwood Ltd. *Structural engineers:* Whitby & Bird *Electrical consultants:* Artel Electrical *Lighting:* Isometrix *Flooring:* Frayley & Son Ltd. (marble), Waldorf Carpets *Staircase:* Springboard Design Ltd. *Balustrade:* John Grilli Contracts *Metalwork:* Brent Metal Ltd. *Shopfront:* Acton Aluminium Co. Ltd. *Display systems:* Click Systems Ltd. *Mirrors and glass:* Marcus Summers *Furniture:* Eileen Gray, from Joseph or Aram Designs, Ron Arad, from One Off.

3.13 Oliver, Rome, Italy *162*
Design firm: David Davies Associates *Project designers:* Peter Kent, Steve St Clair, Louise Hosker *Client:* Valentino Garavani Spa *Main contractor:* L. Cenacchi Spa *Project manager:* Studio Ziffer *Furniture and Lighting:* David Davies Associates.

3.14 Kenzo Homme, Tokyo, Japan *164*
Designer: Sanzin Kim, Kim Design Offices Co. Ltd. *Client:* Raika Co. Ltd. *Main contractor (exterior):* Makoto Construction Co. Ltd. *Main contractor (interior):* Ishimaru Co. Ltd. *Flooring, ceiling, walls:* Aoki-Kogei Co. Ltd. *Lighting:* Maxray Inc. *Furniture:* Sanzin Kim; made by Aoki-Kogei Co.

3.15 Joan and David, Los Angeles, USA *166*
Architects: Eva Jiricna Architects *Project architect:* Jon Tollit *Consultant architects:* Chatterton Jezek Partnership *Client:* Joan & David Helpern Ltd. *Main contractor:* Anderson Builders Inc. *Consultant engineer:* Whitby & Bird *Staircase/balustrade:* Marshall Howard *Furniture:* Matthew Marchbank with Steelchrome Ltd. *Shelving system:* Springboard Design Ltd. *Column claddings:* Special Acoustic Services Ltd. *Hanging rail/accessories:* T. W. Neville.

3.16 Galleria Akka, Osaka, Japan *168*
Architect: Tadao Ando *Client:* Section 2 Hitsuziya *Main contractor (exterior):* Fujiki Construction Co. Ltd. *Main contractor (interior):* Tsumura Kogei Co. Ltd. *Furniture:* Fritz Hansen *Lighting/flooring/ceiling and walls:* Tsumura Kogei Co. Ltd.

3.17 Théâtre Végétal, Melbourne, Australia *170*
Designer: Christopher Connell *Client:* Michele Doherty and Ian (Ducca) Cook *Lighting:* Studio Italia *Furniture/counter/sign:* Mark Douglas, Whitehall Enterprises.

3.18 Cinderella, Tokushima-ken, Japan *174*
Designer: Katsuhiko Togashi, Togashi Design Studio Ltd. *Client:* Nakamura Shoes Ltd. *Main contractor:* Build Co. Ltd. *Walls and ceiling:* Fukko Co. Ltd. *Furniture:* Katsuhiro Togashi; made by Build Co.

3.19 Issey Miyake, London, UK *176*
Architects: Alan Stanton and Paul Williams, Stanton-Williams *Client:* Issey Miyake UK Ltd. *Main contractor:* Howard & Constable Partnership *Structural consultants:* Ove Arup & Partners *Quantity surveyors:* Hanscomb Partnership *Lighting:* Ace McLaren *Handrails/clothes hangers:* Alan Evans *Plasterwork:* Mauro Perucchetti *Stonework:* Universal Stone *Balustrade glass:* Tektonic Ltd. *Lighting consultant:* John Johnson, Concord Lighting *Electrical services:* George Buxton/Omlex *Banners:* Architen Ltd. *Blinds:* Sky Craft.

3.20 Magasin d'Usine, Nantes, France *178*
Architects: Richard Rogers Partnership Ltd. *Project team:* Kieran Breen, Philippa Browning, Mike Davies, Pierre Ebbo, Florian Fischotter, Marco Goldschmied, Lennart Grut, Werner Lang, Stig Larsen, Richard Rogers, John Young *Interior design:* Richard Rogers Partnership with B & FL, Paris, France (C. Brullman) *Client:* Groupement Rhodanien de Construction (GRC) *Main contractor:* Groupe de Recherche et de Construction *Engineers (steel structure):* Ove Arup & Partners Ltd., RFR, Paris *Engineers (concrete):* OTH, Rhone-Alpes, Lyons, Rhone-Alpes Acier *Interior design:* B & FL, Paris *Metalwork:* Goyer & Fils, Duchemin *Floor finish/decoration:* Bury Industries *Contractors (steel structure):* Viry, B. P. *Lifts:* Otis *Escalators:* Kone *Doors:* Bestwick *Ironmongery:* G & S Allgood.

3.21 The Body & Bath Shop, Tokyo, Japan *180*
Designer: Setsuo Kitaoka *Client:* Uchino Co. Ltd. *Main contractor:* Build Co. Ltd. *Lighting:* Light Works – Haruki Kaitou *Furniture:* Minerva Co. Ltd. (chairs, mirrors and showcases) *Materials:* Mihoya Glass Shop Co. Ltd. (glass), Plus-T Textile Studio *Graphic design:* Ryohei Kojima Design Office.

4.1 Dance Theater, The Hague, Netherlands *186*
Architects: OMA (Office for Metropolitan Architecture) *Partner in charge:* Rem Koolhaas *Project team:* Jeroen Thomas, Willem-Jan Neuterlings, Frank Roodbeen, Jaap van Heest, Ron Steiner, Dirk Hendriks, Frans Vogelaar, Wim Kloosterboer, Hans Werlemann, Petra Blaisse *Client:* Stichting Nederlands Dans Theater *Main contractor/Engineering consultants:* Polonyi und Finck *Consultants:* Van Toorenburg Staakebrand *Acoustics:* Technisch Physische Dienst *Billboard:* Madelon Vriesendorp *Bars/seating:* BOA Contractors, Kamphoner (seats) *Lighting:* Philips bv.

4.2 United Airlines Terminal, O'Hare International Airport, Chicago, USA *192*
Architect: Murphy Jahn *Project team:* Helmut Jahn (Principal), Martin Wolf (Project architect), Sanford Gorshow, Tom Chambers, Nada Andric, Brian O'Connor, Jon Pohl *Client:* City of Chicago *Main contractor:* Turner Construction Co. *Structural consultants:* Lev Zetlin Associates, A. Epstein & Sons *Mechanical consultants:* A. Epstein & Sons *Lighting consultants:* Sylvan R. Schemitz & Associates *Art consultant:* Thinking Lightly *Interiors:* Murphy Jahn *Furniture:* Krueger (seating) *Fittings:* Jensen (ticket counters), American Woodcraft, Barsanti Woodwork, Carlson *Information displays:* Phillips & Brooks *Lifts/moving walkways:* Otis Elevator Co. *Stairs:* MTH Industries *Lighting:* (interior – halide and fluorescent), Morris Kurtzon, Sterner *Doors:* Firedoor *Floors:* Caretti/Metropolitan (terrazzo), Capitol/Marblette *Ceiling:* Alcan.

4.3 Australian Parliament Building, Canberra, Australia *196*
Architect: Mitchell/Giurgola & Thorp Architects, Canberra *Design architect:* Romaldo Giurgola *Project architect:* Richard G. Thorp *Design coordinator:* Harold S. Guida *Furniture and interiors coordination:* Rollin La France *Art/Craft coordinator:* Pamille Berg *Site architect:* Tim Halden Brown *Main contractor:* Concrete-Holland Joint Venture *Structural engineers:* Irwin Johnston & Partners *Consulting engineers:* Joseph R. Loring & Associates, W. E. Bassett & Partners Pty Ltd., Ledingham Hensby Oxley & Partners *Landscape architect:* Peter G. Rolland & Associates *Interiors:* Mitchell/Giurgola & Thorp Architects *Lighting:* George Sexton Associates *Roofing:* ARMM Consultants Inc. *Fountains:* Robert Woodward Pty Ltd. *Acoustics:* Louis A. Challis & Associates *Signs and graphics:* Emery Vincent Associates.

4.4 Splash, Sheringham, Norfolk, UK *200*
Architects: Alsop & Lyall Architects *Partners in charge:* Will Alsop, John Lyall *Project architect:* Peter Clash *Assistant architect:* Mike Waddington *Client:* Clifford Barnett Group Ltd. on behalf of North Norfolk District Council *Quantity surveyor:* Peter Drysdale de Leeuw & Partners *Electrical/mechanical engineer:* IEI Northern *Structural engineer:* Anthony Hunt Associates *Main contractor:* Clugston Construction *Groundworks/external works:* John Martin Construction *Frame:* Kingston Craftsmen (1981) *Filtration:* Thermelek Engineering Services *Roof:* Belmont Roofing (aluminum roof/rainwater system), Everlite Plastics (conservatory glazing), Sheffield Glazing (orangery glazing, screens) *Metal and steelwork:* R. J. Howlett Engineering *Doors:* Henderson Doors (glazed internal) *Floors:* Ross & Rossi (tiling), Town & Country Flooring (soft) *Flume slide:* Stuart Leisure, Denton Island, Newhaven, Sussex, UK *Walls/partitions:* Norwich Drylining W. S. Joinery Contracts (changing cubicles) *Shopfitting/bars/servery:* Second City Shopfitting *Signs:* Drakard & Humble *Entrance canopy:* East Anglian Blinds.

4.5 Museum of Modern Art, Nagoya, Japan *202*
Architect: Kisho Kurokawa *Client:* Nagoya City *Main contractors:* Kohnoike Gumi Co. Ltd., Toda Kensetsu Co. Ltd. *Walls and ceilings:* Yabashi Marble Co. Ltd. *Lighting:* Toshiba Electric Co. Ltd. *Carpets:* Sumitomo Shoji Co. Ltd. *Furniture:* Kosuga Co. Ltd.

4.6 Josep ma Jujol School, Barcelona, Spain *206*
Architects: Jaume Bach and Gabriel Mora *Collaborating architect:* Roberto Brufau *Client:* Town Council of Barcelona, Obra Social de la Caixa de Pensions per a la Vellesa i d'Estalvis *Main contractor:* Forcat SA.

4.7 Cedars-Sinai Comprehensive Cancer Center, Los Angeles, USA *210*
Architects: Morphosis/Gruen Associates, Los Angeles, California *Partner in charge:* Thom Mayne *Project architect:* Steve Johnson (Morphosis) *Partner in charge:* Ki Suh Park *Project architect:* Robert S. Barnett *Client:* Dr Bernard Salick, Salick Health Care *Main contractor:* Cal-Pac Construction Co. *Structural consultants:* Kurily & Szymanski *Mechanical consultants:* The Sullivan Partnership *Electrical consultants:* Engineering Design: *Civil engineering:* Engineering Technology, Inc. *Medical consultants:* Medical Planning Associates, James Staublin

Planning & Design *Landscape design:* Emmet L. Wemple & Associates *Interior consultants:* KMA Designs *Graphics:* Berry Sampler Graphic Design *Audio visual:* Andrew Barkin Sound Design *Art consultant:* Merry Norris.

4.8 La Cigale, Paris, France *214*
Designer: Philippe Starck *Client:* Program 33 (Fabrice Coat and Jacques Renault) *Furniture:* Philippe Starck; made by Cineconfort, Consce Saunier, France.

4.9 Kawasaki City Museum, Kawasaki City, Japan *218*
Architect: Kiyonori Kikutake, Keikaku-Rengo *Client:* Kawasaki City *Main contractor:* Shimizu Corporation, Tokyu Construction Co. Ltd. *Structural consultants:* Gengo Matsui & ORS Design Office, Teruaki Tanaka Design Office *Mechanical consultants:* P. T. Morimura & Associates, Sakurai Building Systems Consultants Co. Ltd. *Exterior walls:* Japan Ceramic Co. Ltd. *Roof:* Sumitomo Metal Industries Ltd. *Furniture:* Takashimaya Co. Ltd. Knoll Japan, Okamura Seisakujo Co. Ltd., Chitose Co. Ltd., Itoki Co. Ltd., Modern Furniture Sales Co. Ltd..

4.10 University Library, Eichstatt, West Germany *222*
Architects: Behnisch and Partners *Project team:* Manfred Sabatke, Christian Kandzia and Joachim, with Helmut Dasch, Jutta Schurmann, Cornelia Theilig, Birgit Weigel, Thomas Zimmermann, Sabine Behnisch-Staib *Project manager:* Martin Huhn *Client:* Stiftung der Katholischen Universität Eichstatt *Main contractor:* Mobil-Bau GmbH *Electrical consultant:* Emil Niethammer Elektrobau *Heating/ventilation consultant:* Kraftanlagen Heidelberg *Steel stairs:* Hans Hochreuther *Steel/glass partitions:* Rupert App GmbH & Co. *Flooring:* Sailer-Ernst Feuerlein GmbH & Co. (parquet), Donau-Tufting GmbH (carpet) *Furniture:* Schulz Bibliothekstechnik GmbH (library shelving), Kohler Objekteinrichtungen, Niederlassung Munchen, Fleiner Mobel, Rainer Tellmann, E. & H. Meyer.

4.11 Truro Crown Court, Truro, UK *226*
Architects: Eldred Evans and David Shalev, Evans and Shalev *Client:* Property Services Agency/LCD *Main contractor:* Dudley Coles *Mechanical and electrical engineers:* Max Fordham & Partners *Structural engineers:* Anthony Hunt Associates *Landscape consultant:* Janet Jack *Flooring:* Ritelay Floors Ltd. (carpets and vinyl) *Furniture:* Dudley Coles (manufacturers of courtroom fittings), Hille Ergonom (rotunda, courtroom seating, dining tables/seats), The Crown Suppliers.

4.12 Public Swimming Baths, Kreuzberg, Berlin, West Germany *230*
Architects: Christoph Langhof, Thomas Hanni, Herbert Meerstein, Christoph Langhof Architekten *Client:* Kreuzberg Local Authority *Main contractor:* Zublin AG *Heating, ventilation:* Dr Starck & Co. *Acoustics, ceilings:* SPR-Bau GmbH *Tiled partition walls:* Kerapid-Fertigung-Kruger & Co. *Doors, lockers, frames:* A. Schoenwerk GmbH & Co. *Tiles:* Juttner GmbH *Light domes:* Borner GmbH & Co.

4.13 Center for the Performing Arts, Portland, USA *234*
Architects: Barton Myers Associates, Toronto and Los Angeles, Broome, Oringdulph, O'Toole, Rudolf Assocs, Portland, ELS Design Group, Berkeley, California *Project architects:* Barton Myers, Chris Couse, Thomas Payne (BMA), Robert E. Oringdulph, Dennis O'Toole, Stanley Bowles (BOOR/A), Donn Logan, Kurt Schindler, Guillermo Rossello (ELS) *Client:* City of Portland *Main contractor:* Hoffman Construction Co. *Mechanical engineers:* C. W. Timmer Assocs *Electrical engineers:* Interface Engineering *Structural engineers:* CH2M-Hill *Acoustics:* R. Lawrence Kirkegaard & Associates, Chicago *Theater consultants:* Theater Projects Ltd. *Lighting consultant:* Richard Peters *Colour consultant:* Tina Beebe *Glass dome:* James Carpenter, New York.

4.14 Cabaret Tabourettli, Basel, Switzerland *240*
Architect: Santiago Calatrava, Santiago Calatrava Valls, SA *Clients:* Building Commission of the City of Basel and Neues Tabourettli Theater *Surveyors:* Meinrad Hert Architects *Furniture:* Santiago Calatrava, De Sede *Steel contractors:* Preewerk & Esser (steel staircase).

The publishers would like to thank Peter Olsen and Junko Popham for their help in the research of American and Japanese projects respectively; the designers and architects involved for their cooperation; and the photographers whose work is reproduced here. All photographs in this book are copyright, and none should be reproduced without the prior permission of the publishers. The following credits are given (page numbers are given in brackets):

Roger Allyn Lee (*46*) Tadao Ando (*168 not middle*) Gabriele Basilico (*134–136; 138; 139 top*) Hélène Binet (*27 below*) Roland Bishop (*72*) Tom Bonner (*210 top; 212 below*) Richard Bryant/ARCAID (*50; 52–54; 84–89; 140–141; 158–160; 226; 228–229*) © James Carpenter 1984–87 (*234; 239 top*) Mario Ciampi (*150; 152–153*) Peter Cook (*60–66; 73; 98; 118–121; 142; 144 except top; 161–163; 166; 176; 178–179; 186–191*) Grey Crawford (*103; 105 top; 144 top; 145*) Richard Davies (*24; 26; 27 except top*) Gilles de Chabaneix (*36–37*) Ian Dobbie (*154*) Shi Yu Chen/Creative Intelligence Associates, Inc (*76; 78–79*) Dennis Gilbert (*98–99*) © Jeff Goldberg/ESTO (*92*) John Gollings (*196–199*) Heinrich Helfenstein (*240; 242*) John Hewitt/*Architects' Journal* (*200*) Hiroyuki Hirai (*17; 94; 96–97; 168 middle*) Alastair Hunter (*42–43; 74*) Timothy Hursley (*12–15; 192–195; 235–238; 239 below*) Christian Kandzia/Behnisch and Partners (*222–225*) Kawasumi Architectural Photography Office (*218; 220–221*) Wilmar Koenig (*230–233*) Ian Lambot/ARCAID (*200–201*) Bérangère Lomont (*184; 214; 216–217*) Trevor Mein (*48; 170; 172–173*) Ian McKinnell (*80 middle*) Grant Mudford (*10; 18–21; 102; 104; 105 below; 210 below; 211–212 top; 213*) T. Nacása & Partners (*106; 108–110; 114–116; 148*) John O'Brien (*146–147*) Francesco Radino (*32–35*) Sharon Rasdorph (*137; 139 below*) Jordi Sarra (*122–125; 128; 130–131*) Yoshio Shiratori (*22; 82; 90; 100–101; 182–183*) © Paul Warchol (*28 top; 44; 47; 56–59; 112–113; 126; 132–133*) Gerald Zugmann (*38–41*)

ERRATUM

In the first volumes of *International Interiors* and *International Contract Design*, projects Caffè Bongo, Tokyo, and Metropole restaurant, Tokyo, were incorrectly described as designed by Nigel Coates with Shi Yu Chen. The designers of the projects are Nigel Coates and Doug Branson of Branson Coates Architecture (featured in this volume on page 76). Shi Yu Chen and his company Creative Intelligence Associates (C.I.A.) act as B.C.A.'s agents in Japan, or, as C.I.A. term their role, 'producer' or 'driving force' of the designers' many projects there. The publishers regret this error and any distress/inconvenience caused.

ADDRESSES OF PRODUCT SUPPLIERS & SUBCONTRACTORS

Acero, Bessemerstrasse 3, 2120 Luneberg, West Germany.
Acousta-lite Supply Co., 1020 Hansen Way, Redwood City, CA 94063, USA.
Acton Aluminium Co. Ltd., Unit 2, Acton Industrial Estate, Rosemont Road, London, W3, UK.
Advan, Advan Building, 4–32–12 Jingumae, Shibuya-ku, Tokyo 150, Japan.
Advanced Commercial Equipment, 441 Abbey Road, Belvedere, Kent, UK.
Aidic Co. Ltd., 4–16–13 Nishi-Azabu, Minato-ku, Tokyo, Japan.
Aileron Design, 16 Powers Street, Brooklyn, NY 11211, USA.
All-Steel Inc., All-Steel Drive, Aurora, Illinois 60507, USA.
Altalite, Via Pratese 164, Florence, Italy.
American Terrazzo Company, 36 Wood Street, San Francisco, CA 94118, USA.
Amman Progetti, Via Cremona 27, Milan, Italy.
Anderson Builders Inc., 10572 Barbette Avenue, Garden Grove, CA 92643, USA.
Aoki-Kogei Co. Ltd., 727 Kohirao, Mihara-machi, Kouchi-gun, Osaka-shi, Japan.
Rupert App GmbH & Co., 7970 Leutkirch im Allgäu 1, West Germany.
Ron Arad, One Off, 62 Chalk Farm Road, London NW1, UK.
Aram Designs, 3 Kean Street, London WC2, UK.
Architen Ltd., Arnos Castle Estate, Junction Road, Brislington, Bristol, UK.
Armstrong (Ceiling Division), P.O. Box 3000, Lancaster, PA 17604, USA.
Chuck Arnoldi, 721 Hampton Drive, Venice, CA 90291, USA.

Artel Electrical, 114 Windermere Avenue, Wembley, Middlesex, UK.
Ove Arup & Partners, 1st Floor, Adam House, 13 Fitzroy Street, London W1, UK.
Atelanda Shopfitters, 17/21 Sunbeam Road, Park Royal, London NW10, UK.
Awaji Kawara-Boh, 1787 Tsui, Nishiawa-machi, Mihara-gun, Hyogo-ken, Japan.
Fred Baier, c/o Crucial, 204 Kensington Park Road, London W11, UK.
Barlow Shopfitters, Birley Vale Avenue, Newport, Shropshire, UK.
Basset & Findlay Ltd., Talbot Road North, Wellingborough, Northants, UK.
B & B Japan Co., 2–9–8, Higashi, Shibuya-ku, Tokyo, Japan.
Bentley Carpet Mills, 1464 East Don Julian Road, City of Industry, CA 91746, USA.
Bonaventure Harvard, 849 Bloomfield Avenue, Montreal, Quebec, Canada.
Bouwbedrijf Flore NV, Bredabaan 938, B-2060 Merksem, Belgium.
Antonio Brambilla, Via della Passione 4, Milan, Italy.
Brent Architectural Metalwork Ltd., Fourth Way, Wembley, Middlesex, UK.
Bridcut & Co., 1 Station Chambers, Woodcote Road, Wallington, Surrey, UK.
Build Co. Ltd., 4–2–11 Jingumae, Shibuya-ku, Tokyo, Japan.
Cal-Pac Construction, 12121 Wilshire Boulevard, Los Angeles, CA 90025, UK.
Canziana SA, Avenue Venezuela 2305, Lima, Peru.
Capri Lighting, 7020 East Sauslon Avenue, Los Angeles, CA 90020, USA.
James Carpenter, Design Associates Inc. 485 Broome Street, New York, NY 10013, USA.
Cassina SPA, PO Box 102, 20036 Meda, Milan, Italy.
Cassina Japan Inc., 2–9–6 Higashi, Shibuya-ku, Tokyo, Japan.
Miguel Castillo, 154352 Firmona Avenue, Laudale, CA 90260, USA.
L. Cenacchi Spa, Via Speranza 36, 40068 San Lazzano di Saverna, Bologna, Italy.
Chitose Co. Ltd., 1–6–11 Nishi-shinbashi, Minato-ku, Tokyo, Japan.
Classic Furniture, Audley Avenue, Newport, Shropshire, UK.
Click Systems Ltd., 40 Blundells Road, Milton Keynes, UK.
Clisa, General Suarez 580, Miraflores, Lima, Peru.
Clugston Construction, St Vincent House, Normanby Road, Scunthorpe, Humberside, UK.
Brian Cochran & Associates, 2205 Stoner Avenue, Los Angeles, CA 90064, USA.
Concord Lighting, Griffin House, 161 Hammersmith Road, London W6, UK.
Concord, Mejia Lequerica 30, 08028 Barcelona, Spain.
Concrete-Holland Joint Venture, PO Box E437, Queen Victoria Terrace, Parkes, ACT 2600, Australia.
Construcciones Barmo SA, Plana de Canbertran 31, 08191 Rubi, Spain.
Cosmos Co. Ltd., Kibuka Building, 4–4–1 Ebisu, Shibuya-ku, Tokyo, Japan.
Creative Walls Inc., 4098 Glencoe Avenue, Marina del Rey, CA 90202, USA.
The Crown Suppliers, 13–15 Ridge Park Road, Plympton, Plymouth, Devon, UK.
CSL, 11150 Olympic Bld, Los Angeles, CA 90064, USA.
Dacheville, 36 Avenue Leon Crete-Mere, 78490 Montfort L'Amaury, France.
Daitoh Concrete Co. Ltd., 327 Sashogi, Omiya-shi, Saitama-ken, Japan.
Dal-Tile, 310 Littlefield Avenue, South San Francisco, CA, USA.
Dancontract A/S, Vinkelvej 3, dk-8240 Risskov, Denmark.
Davis-Fejes Design, 2265 Westwood Boulevard, Los Angeles, CA 90064, USA.
DeSede AG, Oberes Zegli, 5313 Klingnau, Switzerland.
Design Architectural Lighting Co., 10 Bowling Green Lane, London EC1, UK.
Design Workshop Ltd., 150 Penistone Road, Shelley, Huddersfield, West Yorkshire, UK.
Devcon Construction Inc., 555 Los Coches Street, Milpitas, CA 95035, USA.
Tom Dixon, 28 All Saints Road, London W11, UK.
DLW (Britain) Ltd., 38C Milton Park, near Abingdon, Oxfordshire, UK.
Dolner Construction, 320 West 13th Street, New York, NY 10014, USA.
Mark Douglas, Whitehall Enterprises, Whitehall Road, Footscray, Melbourne, Australia.
Dove Bros. Ltd., Cloudesley Pl., London N1, UK.
Driade SPA, Via Padana Inferiore 12, 29012 Fossadello di Caorso, Piacenza, Italy.
Driade, Villarroel 191-M, 08036 Barcelona, Spain.
Duchemin, rue des Fontaines, 49330 Chateauneuf-sur-Sarthe, France.
Ecart International, 111 rue Saint Antoine, 75004 Paris, France.
Elementer Industrial Design Ltd., Progress House, Whittle Parkway, Slough, Berkshire, UK.
Elite Construction, 2743 Dollar Street, Lakewood, CA 90712, USA.
Firma Eltec KG, Bismarckstr. 97, 1000 Berlin 12.
Endo Lighting Co. Ltd., 3–20–27 Ohimazato, Higashinari-ku, Osaka-shi, Japan.
Erco Leuchten GmbH, Postfach 2460, D-5880 Ludenscheid, The Netherlands.
Erco Lighting, 38 Dover Street, London W1, UK.
Jordi Espinosa, Berlin 30–32, 08028 Barcelona, Spain.
Estudio 501, Avenue Central 703, San Isidro, Lima, Peru.
Alan Evans, Makins, Whiteway, Stroud, Gloucestershire, UK.
Falcon, 1707 Pacific Coast Highway, Hermosa Beach, CA 90254, USA.
Focus Ceramics, Unit 4 & 5, Hamm Moor Lane, Weybridge, Surrey, UK.
Folm Co. Ltd., 126 Nakahara, Sizuoka-shi, Shizuoka-ken, Japan.
Forcat SA, c/o L'Avenir, 1 Baixos Interior, 08006 Barcelona, Spain.
Ford Motor Company, Glass Division, 300 Renaissance Center, PO Box 43343, Detroit, Michigan 48243, USA.
Frayley & Son Ltd., Continental Wharf, Gas Street, Birmingham, UK.
Friba Ingenieros, Avenue Central 671 of. 801 7, 3 Piso, San Isidro, Lima, Peru.
FTL Associates, 157 Chambers Street, New York, NY 10007, USA.
Fujiki Construction Co. Ltd., 1–3–9 Tokiwa-cho, Chuo-ku, Osaka, Japan.
Harumi Fujimoto, MGS, 2F Daini Yazawa Building, 3–2–11 Nishazabu, Minato-ku, Tokyo 106, Japan.
Gallegos, Rios, Casabonne & Ucelli, Arango Ingenieros Civiles, Avenue Central 671 of. 801, Lima 27, Peru.
G & W Electrical Engineers, 1729 W. Washington Bld, Marina del Rey, CA 90291, USA.
Glass & Glazing Services, 232 Norwood Road, West Norwood, London SE27, UK.
Sol Goldin & Associates, 1818 South Robertson Boulevard, Los Angeles, CA 90035, USA.
Laura Gottwald, 24 West 30th Street, New York, NY 10001, USA.
Goyer & Fils, Fougeres-sur-Bievre, rue H Goyer, 41120 Les Montils, France.
Grauwinkel, Prinzenstrasse 45, 1000 Berlin 45.
Great American Salvage Co., 34 Cooper Street, New York, NY 10003, USA.
Sally Greaves-Lord, 23 Camden Road, London N7, UK.
Annabelle Grey, 102 Reform Street, London SW11, UK.
John Grilli Contracts, Unit 27 Lake Business Centre, Tariff Road, London N17, UK.
Groupe de Recherche et de Construction, 1 quai Jules-Courmont, 69002 Lyon, France.
Guzzini, SS 77 KM 102, Reganati, Florence, Italy.
Habitat, The Heals Building, 196 Tottenham Court Road, London W1, UK.
Yves Halard, 252 Bis boulevard St Germain, 75–7, Paris, France.
Haller Japan Ltd., Phoenix Building, 1–4–3 Azabudai, Minato-ku, Tokyo, Japan.
Halo Lighting, 400 Busse Road, Elk Grove, Illinois 60007, USA.
Fritz Hansen, Depotvej 1, DK-3450 Allerod, Denmark.
Hartich Mechanical, 4523 Van Nuys Boulevard, Sherman Oaks, CA 94103, USA.
Haruki Kaitou, 302 2–30–22 Jingumae, Shibuya-ku, Tokyo, Japan.
Oriel Harwood, 149 Camberwell Road, London SE5, UK.
Stuart Helm, 29 Blenheim Grove, London SE15, UK.
Hille International, 365 Euston Road, London NW1, UK.
Hillen & Rosen Bouw BV, Prinsengracht 1123, 1017 JK Amsterdam, The Netherlands.
Howard & Constable Partnership, 2–4 Orsman Road, London N1, UK.
Anthony Hunt Associates, West End House, 37 Chapel Street, London NW1, UK.
Hunter-Douglas Ltd., Wellington House, New Zealand Avenue, Walton-on-Thames, Surrey, UK.
T & W Ide, Glasshouse Fields, London E1, UK.
Images, 829 Blair St., Thomasville, NC 273670, USA.
La Inmobiliaria, S.A., Canino Real 348, Torre del Pilar, piso 13, San Isidro, Lima, Peru.
The Inn Furnisher, 38 Bishwell Road, Gowertton, Swansea, Wales, UK.
International Communications Ltd., 306, 3–13–22 Sendagaya, Shibuya-ku, Tokyo, Japan.
Interstate Mechanical Systems, 11627 Cantara St, North Hollywood, CA 91605, USA.
Ishimaru Co. Ltd., Maison Akashi 101–202, 7–3–24 Roppongi, Minato-ku, Tokyo, Japan.
Island Developments, 1–3 Tyssen Road, Stoke Newington, London N16, UK.
Isometrix, 2–4 Frederic Mews, Kinnerton Street, London SW1, UK.
Itoki Co. Ltd., 3–5–8 Ginza, Chuo-ku, Tokyo, Japan.
Iverson Construction, 3162 Anderson Drive, Simi Valley, CA 93065, USA.
Japan Ceramic Co. Ltd., 43–9 Hakozaki-cho, Nihonbashi, Chuo-ku, Tokyo, Japan.

Jujiya Co. Ltd., Takatsujikado, Omiya-dori, Shimogyo-ku, Kyoto-shi, Japan.
Junckers, Industrier AS, Koge 4600, Vaerstsvet, Denmark.
Katsumata-Meiki Co., 354–1 Mukoda, Minami Ashigara-shi, Kanagawa-ken, Japan.
Kawashima Textile Manufacturers Ltd., 432 Tatetomita-cho, Ichi-jo, Agaru, Higashi Horikawa-dori, Kamigyo-ku, Tokyo, Japan.
Nancy Kearing, 80 Forsyth Street, New York, NY 10002, USA.
Kenwood Corp., 2–17–5 Shibuya, Shibuya-ku, Tokyo, Japan.
Kintetsu Co. Ltd., 2–1–43 Abenosugi, Abeno-ku, Osaka-shi, Japan.
Kirk Stone Ltd., Skelwith Bridge, Ambleside, Cumbria, UK.
Knoll International, 655 Madison Avenue, New York, NY 10021, USA.
Knoll Japan, 1st Floor, Kokusai Building, 3–1–1 Marunouchi, Chiyoda-ku, Tokyo, Japan.
Kohler Objekteinrichtungen, St 7000 Stuttgart 70, West Germany.
Kohnoike Gumi Co. Ltd., 2–19–1 Nishiki, Naka-ku, Nagoya-shi, Japan.
W. M. Koniak Inc., 191 Bowery, New York, NY 10002, USA.
Kosuga Co. Ltd., 1–6–7 Shimachi, Tabata, Kita-ku, Tokyo, Japan.
Koyano Stone Co., 1–117 Sengawa-cho, Toshima-ku, Tokyo, Japan.
Lagomasino Vital & Associates, 814 Ponce de Leon, Suite 307, Coral Gables, Florida 33134, USA.
L.A.S.S. Ltd., St Michaels Church, Mark Street, London EC1, UK.
L.B. Lighting Ltd., Metro Centre, St Albans House, St Albans Road, St Albans, Herts, UK.
La Vigne & Muffy, 11621 Los Nietos Road, Santa Fe Springs, CA 90670, USA.
Lelieure, 15 rue du Mail, 75002 Paris, France.
Lightolier, 501 W. Walnut Street, Compton, CA 90220, USA.
Limited Productions Inc., 1290 Bodega Avenue, Petaluma, CA 94952, USA.
Linea SA (seating), Avenue Camino Real 479, San Isidro, Lima, Peru.
Levolor Lorensen, 12052 Industry Street, Garden Grove, CA 92645, USA.
Lotter, Starenstrasse 62, 8420 Kelheim, West Germany.
Adam Lowe, Reeds Wharf, Mill Street, London SE1, UK.
McCoy FMG Co., 2200 East 89th Street, Los Angeles, CA 90002, USA.
Mage Industrial, Socrates 59 bajos, 08030 Barcelona, Spain.
Marshall Howard, Andre Street, London E8, UK.
Matthew Marchbank, 34 Brandon Road, London N7, UK.
Marco, 733 East San Bernardino Road, Covina, CA 91723, USA.
Matsushita Electric Co., 1–15 Matsuucho, Kadoma-shi, Tokyo, Japan.
Ingo Maurer GmbH, 47 Kaiserstrasse, 8000 Munich 40, West Germany.
Ingo Maurer, Yamagiwa Co. Ltd., 4–1–1 Sotokanda, Chiyoda-ku, Tokyo, Japan.
Maville, 2.l Le Ponteix, 87220 Feytiat, Limoges, France.
Maxray Inc., 1–4–20 Nakameguro, Meguro-ku, Tokyo, Japan.
Mercedes Beale de Porcari, Malecon Cisneros 1094, Miraflores, Lima, Peru.
Metal Co., 2–27–6 Komai-cho, Komae-shi, Tokyo, Japan.
Metropolitan Furniture Corp., 245 East Harris Avenue, South San Francisco, CA 94080, USA.
Michikawa Sekizai Kogyosho, 2–896 Shinmaruko-Higashi, Nakahara-Kawasaki-shi, Japan.
Mihoya Glass Shop Co. Ltd., 1–8–4 Nishiazabu, Minato-ku, Tokyo, Japan.
Herman Miller Inc., 8500 Byron Road, Zeeland, Michigan 49464, USA.
Herman Miller, Maple House, Tottenham Court Road, London W1, UK.
Milliken & Co., PO Box 2956, La Grange, GA 30241, USA.
Jon Mills, c/o Crucial, 204 Kensington Park Road, London W11, UK.
Minelba Co., 1–10–7 Hiratsuka, Shinagawa-ku, Tokyo, Japan.
Minerva Co. Ltd., 1–10–7 Hirasuka, Shinagawa-ku, Tokyo, Japan.
Mitsubishi Electric Co., 1 Babazusho, Nagaokakyo-shi, Kyoto, Japan.
Mobil-Bau GmbH, Kuntzestrasse 72, 7334 Sussen, West Germany.
Modern Furniture Sales Co. Ltd., 2nd Floor, Sumitomo-Seimei-Aoyama Building, 3–1–30 Minami Aoyama, Minato-ku, Tokyo, Japan.
Monk Dunstone Associates, Portland House, Stag Place, London SW1, UK.
P. T. Morimura & Associates, 1–2–9 Yoyogi, Shibuya-ku, Tokyo, Japan.
Jasper Morrison, 16a Hilgrove Road, London NW6, UK.
Nextel, 2–33–1 Tamagawadai, Setagaya-ku, Tokyo, Japan.
Nichiden Shoji K.K., 5–19–2 Ueno, Taito-ku, Tokyo 110, Japan.
Nichinan Co. Ltd., 1599–10 Yoshioka, Ayase-shi, Kanagawa-ken, Japan.
Emil Niethammer Eletrobau, Hoppenlaustrasse 14, 7000 Stuttgart 80, West Germany.
Nihon Terazzo Kogyo Co., 3–35–5 Higashi-Ueno, Daito-ku, Tokyo, Japan.
Nisshin SPP Co. Ltd., 2–2–21 Minami-Azabu, Minato-ku, Tokyo, Japan.
Nomura Display Co. Ltd., 4–6–4 Shibaura, Minato-ku, Tokyo, Japan.
NTC Co. Ltd., Nakagawa Building, 4–23–13 Higashi-Ikebukuro, Toshima-ku, Tokyo, Japan.
Okamura Seisakujo Co. Ltd., Sanno-grand Building, Nagata-chuo, Chiyoda-ku, Tokyo, Japan.
Ost Co., 2–2–9 Kayaba-cho, Nihonbashi, Chuo-ku, Tokyo, Japan.
Otis, 141 rue de Saussure, 75017, Paris, France.
Mauro Perucchetti, 87 Cadogan Gardens, London SW3, UK.
Philips Export B.V., International Projects Division, P.O. Box 218, 5600 MD Eindhoven, The Netherlands.
Philips Lighting, City House, 420–430 London Road, Croydon, Surrey, UK.
Phoenix Floors Ltd., Arisdale Avenue, South Ockendon, Essex, UK.
Piazza, 18 Alamein Road, Swansea, Wales, UK.
Plus-T Textile Studio, 5–1–19 Shinjuku, Shinjuku-ku, Tokyo, Japan.
Polyresine, 2 rue Mederic, 92250 La Garenne Colombus, France.
Vda Puig, Motores 151–155, 08004 Barcelona, Spain.
Quickwood, Unit 10, McKay Trading Estate, Kensal Road, London W10, UK.
Mark Quinn, 56 Shakespeare Road, London SE24, UK.
Firma Raulf Bau, Eichborndamm 167, 1000 Berlin.
Reina, Riera d'Horta 38, 08027 Barcelona, Spain.
Rhone-Alpes Acier, 88 rue villon, 69008 Lyon, France.
Antony Ross Ltd., Delta House, Rose Walk, West Wickham, Kent, UK.
Rotundi Construction, 8944 Burton Way, Beverly Hills, CA 90211, USA.
Rye Signs, Unit 4, 11 Fieldings Road, Cheshunt, Herts, UK.
Ryohei Kojima Design Office, 5–15–9 Minami-aoyama, Minato-ku, Tokyo, Japan.
Melanie Sainsbury, 275 Kensal Road, London W10, UK.
Sakura Construction Co. Ltd., 1242 Misawa, Hino-shi, Tokyo, Japan.
Sakurai Building Systems Consultants Co. Ltd., 1–30–10 Shinjuku, Shinjuku-ku, Tokyo, Japan.
J. Santos/A. Solsona, Anglesona 42, 08014 Barcelona, Spain.
Scan-Q-Ltd., Norwester House, 12 Fairway Drive, Greenford, Middlesex, UK.
Schlage, 2401 Bayshore Boulevard, San Francisco, CA 94134, USA.
Seiko Plastic Co. Ltd., 3–25–8 Kameido, Koto-ku, Tokyo, Japan.
Shimizu Corporation, 2–16–1 Kyobashi, Chuo-ku, Tokyo, Japan.
Shinwa Co. Ltd., 6–31–1 Kitakoiwa, Edogawa-ku, Tokyo, Japan.
Sice Previt, Via Moscova 68, Milan, Italy.
Silent Gliss, Worbstrasse, 210–CH–3073, Gumlingen, Berne, Switzerland.
Construcciones Siglo XX, Urgell 32, 08011 Barcelona, Spain.
Sirio, Piazzale Macciachini 11, Milan, Italy.
Siebert, 3017 Pattensen bei Hanover, West Germany.
Siemens Lighting, PO Box 17, East Lane, Wembley, Middlesex, UK.
Silver Engineering, 21121 Osborne Street, Canoga Park, California 91304, USA.
Sit with Ease & Co. Ltd., Mill Street, Kingston upon Thames, Surrey, UK.
Sky Craft, 9 Heneage Street, London E1, UK.
H. L. Smith Construction Ltd., Station Court, Station Road, Bourne End, Bucks, UK.
S.O.E., 204 rue de la Croix Nivert, 75015, Paris, France.
Sparks Co. Ltd., 1–1–5 Arai, Nakano-ku, Tokyo, Japan.
Sony Inc., 6–7–36 Kita-shinagawa, Shinagawa-ku, Tokyo, Japan.
Special Acoustic Services Ltd., Unit 31, Suttons Park Avenue, London Road, Reading, Berkshire, UK.
Springboard Design Ltd., 7 Unity St., Bristol, UK.
Standard Cabinet Works Inc., 1800 East Washington Bld, Los Angeles, CA 90003, USA.
Steelchrome Ltd., 46 Bideford Avenue, Perivale, Middlesex, UK.
Stuart Leisure, Denton Island, Newhaven, East Sussex, UK.
Studio Italia, 180 Coventry Street, South Melbourne, Australia.
Studio OB, 682–2 Futsukaichi, Tsukushino City, Fukuoka, Japan.
Sumitomo Metal Industries Ltd., Ote Center Building, 1–1–3 Ote-Machi, Chiyoda-ku, Tokyo, Japan.
Sumitomo Shoji Co. Ltd., 3–24–1 Nishi-cho, Kanda, Chiyoda-ku, Tokyo, Japan.
Marcus Summers, Unit 2, Admiral Hyson Industrial Estate, Hyson Road, London SE16, UK.

Taisei Kensetsu Co. Ltd., 4–38 Kitahama, Higashi-ku, Osaka-shi, Japan.
Tajima, 3–11–13 Iwamoto-cho, Chiyoda-ku, Tokyo, Japan.
Takashimaya Co. Ltd., 2–4–1 Nihonbashi, Chuo-ku, Tokyo, Japan.
Tarkett Inc., 800 Unidex Plaza, Box 254, Parsippany, New Jersey 07054, USA.
Henry Taylor & Co., St Johns, Skelmersdale Road, Clacton-on-Sea, Essex, UK.
Tecno (UK), 19 New Bond St., London W1, UK.
Tecno SPA, Via Bigli 22, 20121 Milan, Italy.
Tektonic Ltd., Jenson House, Flitch Industrial Estate, Dunmow, Essex, UK.
Terada Iron Co., 8–11–5 Ueda, Adachi-ku, Tokyo, Japan.
Teruaki Tanaka Design Office, 1––7–2–401 Hiroo, Shibuya-ku, Tokyo, Japan.
Ray Theodore Welding Ltd., Millers Yard, St Michael's Road, Newbury, Berkshire, UK.
Thonet, 5027 Ludgate Dr., Agoura, CA 91301, USA.
Jane Thurn, 334 West 85th Street, New York, NY 10024, USA.
Tobishima Construction Co., 3–2 Sanban-cho, Chiyoda-ku, Tokyo 102, Japan.
Toda Kensetsu Co. Ltd., 1–22–22 Izumi, Higashi-ku, Nagoya-shi, Japan.
Tokyu Construction Co. Ltd., 1–16–14 Shibuya, Shibuya-ku, Tokyo, Japan.
Tomahara Seisakujo Co., 5953–3 Tana, Sagamihara-shi, Kanagawa-ken, Japan.
Toshiba Electric Co. Ltd., 2–5–1 Higashi, Naka-ku, Nagoya-shi, Aichi-ken, Nagoya, Japan.
Trigram Design Partnership, 134 Lots Road, London SW1, UK.
Tsumura Kogei Co. Ltd., 2–12–24 Kyomachbori, Nishi-ku, Osaka, Japan.
Tyssen Construction Ltd., 1–3 Tyssen Road, Stoke Newington, London N16, UK.
Mark Tursi, PO Box 691061, Los Angeles, CA 90069, USA.
Universal Stone, 132 Ormsite Street, London SE15, UK.
Urban Archaeology, 137 Spring Street, New York, NY 10017, USA.
Ushiospex Co. Ltd., Chisei Building, 1–4–2 Moto Akasaka, Minato-ku, Tokyo, Japan.
Unifloor Formica, Via Augusta 166, 08006 Barcelona, Spain.
Vaisa, La Immobiliaria SA, Au Javier Prado Deste 869, San Isidro, Lima, Peru.
Floris van den Broecke, 28 Canning Cross, London SE5, UK.
Via Bo Rink Co. Ltd., Berna Heights 2A2, 5–4–11 Hiro, Shibuya-ku, Tokyo, Japan.
Vecta, PDC, Suite G 385, 8687 Melrose Avenue, West Hollywood, CA 90069, USA.
Veronese, Via Vittorio Veneto 11, Cinisello, Milan, Italy.
Vinchenard, 33 rue Jean Jaures, 93220, Gagny, France.
Viry, B.P. no. 8, Zone industrielle de Golbey, 88191 Golbey, France.
Vitra International AG, 15 Henric Petri Strasse, Postfach 257, 4010 Basel, Switzerland.
Vosseler UK, Elevations Ltd., 1st Floor, 24–26 Fournier Street, London E1, UK.
Waldorf Carpets, 278–280 Brompton Road, London SW3, UK.
Walsh Building Contractors, 22 North Almaden Avenue, San Jose, CA 95110, USA.
Aijiro Wakita, Studio A Co., Mita Apt 101, 2–8–12, Mita, Minato-ku, Tokyo, Japan.
West Coast Industries, 707 East 7th Street, Los Angeles, CA 90021, USA.
Whitby & Bird, 53–54 Newman Street, London W1, UK.
Woolf Construction Management Ltd., 10–12 Maclise Road, London W14, UK.
Hans Wolff & Partners, Herengracht 162, NL-1016 BP, Amsterdam, The Netherlands.
Yabashi Marble Co. Ltd., 273 Akasaka-cho, Ogaki-shi, Gifu-ken, Nagoya, Japan.
Yamagiwa Co. Ltd., 4–1–1 Sotokanda, Chiyoda-ku, Tokyo 101, Japan.
Yamamoto Steel Co., 6–11–15 Tanimach, Minami-ku, Osaka-shi, Japan.
Studio Ziffer, Via Oslavia 14, Rome, Italy.
Zublin AG, Johannesbergerstrasse 26, 1000 Berlin 33.

Index of Designers and Projects

Alfredo Arribas Arquitectos Asociados *122*
Alsop & Lyall *200*
Ando, Tadao *168*
Apple Worldwide Manufacturing & Operations Headquarters California, USA *28*
Armstrong Associates *54*
Arquitectonica *12*
Australian Parliament Building, Canberra, Australia *196*

Bach & Mora *206*
Banco de Credito Headquarters Lima, Peru *12*
Bar Akasaka, Fukuoka, Japan *100*
Beers, Jeffrey G, Architects *112*
Behnisch & Partners *222*
Bing Bango Bongo, Tokyo, Japan *94*
Blackburn Office/Gallery/Flat London, UK *24*
Bolido, New York, USA *118*
Body & Bath Shop, Tokyo, Japan *180*
Branson Coates Architecture *76*
Building *142*

Cabaret Taborettli, Basel, Switzerland *240*
Cafe Mystique, Tokyo, Japan *68*
Canal *36*
Cannelle London, UK *154*
Cedars-Sinai Comprehensive Cancer Center, Los Angeles, USA *210*
Center for the Performing Arts, Portland, USA *234*
La Cigale, Paris, France *214*
Chassay Wright Associates *98*
China Grill, New York, USA *112*
Chipperfield, David & Partners *94*
Cinderella 12, Tokoshima-Ken, Japan *174*
Comblé, Shizuoka-Shi, Japan *106*
Commes des Garçons Shirt New York, USA *132*
Connell, Christopher *170*
Conran Design Group *74*
Conversation, Tokyo, Japan *148*
Coop Himmelblau *38*
Courts of Justice, Truro, UK *226*

Dance Theater, The Hague, The Netherlands *186*
David Davies Associates *60, 162*
DC3, Santa Monica, USA *102*
Department X, London, UK *146*
Din Associates *146*

Ebel-Villa Turque, Switzerland *56*
Ecart *56*
Ecru Los Angeles, USA *142*
Edic Studio Tokyo, Japan *16*
Elementer Headquarters, Maidenhead, UK *54*
Esprit, Amsterdam, Holland *136*
Esprit, Antwerp, Belgium *134*
Esprit, London, UK *140*
Esprit Italia, Milan, Italy, *32*
Evans & Shalev *226*

Fafalios, London, UK *42*
Fitch RS *80*
Foster Associates *140*
Franklin D. Israel Design Associates *18*
Freds, London, UK *98*

Galleria Akka, Osaka, Japan *168*
Geyer Design *48*
Geyer Design Offices Melbourne, Australia *48*
Gold Bar, The, New York, USA *92*
Ghini, Massimo Iosa *118*

Iijima, Naoki *156*
Itchoh, Aoyoma, Tokyo, Japan, *114*
Itchoh, Roppongi, Tokyo, Japan *116*

Jiricna, Eva, Architects *42, 158, 166*
Joan & David, Los Angeles, USA *166*
Joseph, London, UK *158*
Josep ma Jujol School, Barcelona, Spain *206*

Kawakubo, Rei *132*
Kawasaki City Museum, Kawasaki-City, Japan *218*
Kenzo Homme, Tokyo, Japan *164*
Kim, Sanzi, Tokyo, Japan *164*
Kirin Plaza Osaka, Osaka, Japan *82*
Kitaoka, Setsuo *180*
Kiyonori Kikutake Associates & Keikaku-Rengo *218*
Kiyotomo Sushi Restaurant, Tokyo, Japan *110*
Komoriya, Kenji *16*
Kuramata, Shiro *106, 110*
Kurokawa, Kisho *30, 202*

Langhof, Christoph, Architekten *230*
Leeser, Thomas *92*
Libération, Paris, France *36*
Libre Space, Tokyo, Japan *90*

Magasin d'Usine, Nantes, France *178*
Marcel, Barcelona, Spain *128*
Mitchell & O'Brien, London, UK *80*
Mitchell/Giurgola & Thorp Architects *196*
Miyake, Issey, London, UK *176*
Morphosis Gruen Associates *210*
Murphy/Jahn *192*
Museum of Modern Art, Nagoya, Japan *202*
Barton Myers Associates, BOOR/A & ELS Design Group, *234*

Nardi, Claudio *150*
Noah's Ark, Sapporo, Japan *76*

Oliver, Rome, Italy *162*
OMA *186*

Pawson Silvestrin *154*
PN Clubhouse Tokyo, Japan *22*
Propaganda Films, Los Angeles, USA *18*
Public Baths, Kreuzberg, Berlin, West Germany *230*

Review, London, UK *74*
Richard Rogers Partnership *178*
Rooftop Remodelling, Vienna, Austria *38*
Royalton Hotel, New York, USA *84*
Rykiel, Sonia, Tokyo, Japan *156*

Samso, Eduard *128*
Santiago Calatrava Valls *240*
Sbaiz, Liguano Sabbiadoro, Italy *150*
Shibuya Higashi T Building, Tokyo, Japan *30*
Silicon Graphics, Mountain View, California *44*
Solberg & Lowe Architects *102*
Splash, Sheringham, UK *200*
Stanton Williams *176*
Starck, Philippe *68, 84, 214*
Stirling, James, Michael Wilford & Associates *50*
Studio Citterio Dwan *32, 134, 136*
Studio 80 *148*
STUDIOS *28, 44*
Sugimoto Takashi, Kogi Okamoto *90*

Takamatsu, Shin *82*
Tedford, Nicholas *150*
Théâtre Végétal, Melbourne, Australia *170*
Togashi, Katushiko *174*
Trattoria Angeli, Los Angeles, USA *72*

Uchida, Shigeru *114, 116, 148*
Umeda Masanori, *22*
United Airlines Terminal, O'Hare International Airport *192*
Chicago, USA *192*
University Library, Eichstatt, West Germany *222*

Valentino, Rome, Italy *60*
Velvet Bar, Barcelona, Spain *122*

Wilson, Peter with Chassay Wright *24*
Wissenschaftszentrum, Berlin *50*